CYBERBULLYING PREVENT AND RESPONSE

Just as the previous generation was raised in front of televisions, adolescents at the turn of the 21st century are being raised in an internet-enabled world where blogs, social networking, and instant messaging are competing with face-to-face and telephone communication as the dominant means through which personal interaction takes place. Unfortunately, a small but growing proportion of our youth are being exposed online to interpersonal violence, aggression, and harassment via cyberbullying. The mission of this book is to explore the many critical issues surrounding this new phenomenon. Key features include the following.

Comprehensive – The book provides a comprehensive, up-to-date look at the major issues that teachers, school administrators, counselors, social workers, and parents need to be aware of with respect to cyberbullying identification, prevention, and response.

Practical – While the information is informed by research, it is written in an accessible way that all adults will be able to understand and apply.

Expertise – Justin W. Patchin and Sameer Hinduja are Co-directors of the Cyberbullying Research Center (www.cyberbullying.us). Chapter authors represent a carefully selected group of contributors who have demonstrated both topical expertise and an ability to write about the topic in clear, easily accessible language.

This book is appropriate for teachers, administrators, parents and others seeking research-based guidance on how to deal with the rising tide of cyberbullying issues. It is also appropriate for a variety of college-level courses dealing with school violence and educational administration.

CYBERBULLYING PREVENTION AND RESPONSE

Expert Perspectives

Edited by Justin W. Patchin and Sameer Hinduja

Routledge
Taylor & Francis Group

NEW YORK AND LONDON

First published 2012
by Routledge
711 Third Avenue, New York, NY 10017

Simultaneously published in the UK
by Routledge
2 Park Square, Milton Park, Abingdon, Oxon OX14 4RN

Routledge is an imprint of the Taylor & Francis Group, an informa business

Library of Congress Cataloging in Publication Data
Cyberbullying prevention and response : expert perspectives / edited by
Justin W. Patchin, Ph.D., Sameer Hinduja, Ph.D.
   p. cm.
   Includes bibliographical references and index.
   1. Cyberbullying. 2. Bullying in schools. 3. Computer crimes. 4.
   Internet and teenagers. I. Patchin, Justin W., 1977–II. Hinduja,
   Sameer, 1978–
   LB3013.3.C94 2011
   371.5′8–dc22

                                                            2011005152

ISBN: 978-0-415-89236-0 (hbk)
ISBN: 978-0-415-89237-7 (pbk)
ISBN: 978-0-203-81831-2 (ebk)

Typeset in Bembo
by Wearset Ltd, Boldon, Tyne and Wear

Printed and bound in the United States of America on acid-free paper
by Walsworth Publishing Company, Marceline, MO

SUSTAINABLE
FORESTRY
INITIATIVE

Certified Sourcing
www.sfiprogram.org
SFI-00555
The SFI label applies to the text stock.

CONTENTS

PREFACE

Justin W. Patchin and Sameer Hinduja

So much has changed over the last two decades with regard to the ways youth interact using technology. Many of us grew up experimenting with online communications through dial-up bulletin board services such as Prodigy, CompuServe, and America Online using the one desktop computer that our families could afford. And, we used the landline phone to talk to our friends from school – but couldn't talk for too long unless it was really late at night, to keep the line free in case there was a more important call that needed to come in. There was also the expense of long-distance calls – and no "free nights and weekends." Today, teens are texting, Facebooking, and instant messaging their friends all over the nation and world through their portable devices – from which they can often access the entire Internet and all it has to offer – day and night. Many also have personal laptops, tablets, and webcams, which provide for previously unheard-of opportunities to be as close as possible to someone else – irrespective of geographical distance.

The advances in technology have, without question, been an extremely positive development. Indeed, many educational and social benefits have resulted from our headfirst plunge into the Information Age, but sometimes we feel there should have been obligatory bungee cords tied around our ankles before we leapt. As adults, we often feel that we are constantly trying to keep up with technological changes and sometimes don't understand the immense appeal that our kids see in certain devices, environments, applications, or games. Nevertheless, we can acknowledge some of the value they add in allowing us to keep in closer contact with loved-ones, to be more efficient and organized with work responsibilities, and to access various sources of entertainment and information more readily.

Apart from the obvious benefits of encyclopedic amounts of content at one's fingertips, the welcome digital diversions which pass our time and keep us amused, and the speed with which we can correspond with others, online participation has tremendous utility in teaching youth various social and emotional skills that are essential to successfully navigating life. For example, cyberspace provides a venue to learn and refine the ability to exercise self-control, to relate with tolerance and respect to others' viewpoints, to express sentiments in a healthy and normative manner, and to engage in critical thinking and decision-making. These skills, however, cannot be effectively internalized if the online learning environment is unwelcoming or altogether hostile to the user.

If adolescents are uncomfortable or unwilling to explore technology and take advantage of all of its positive attributes, they will be sorely lacking in certain developmental qualities that others who do embrace electronic communications will naturally obtain. Over the last decade, the vast majority of youth have quickly acquired a propensity for digital devices and the Internet, and have tended to outpace their adult counterparts who were not raised in a wired world. Nonetheless, a respectable proportion of kids online are being exposed to interpersonal violence, aggression, mistreatment, and harassment through what has been termed *cyberbullying*.

In our previous work, we defined cyberbullying as "willful and repeated harm inflicted through the use of computers, cell phone, or other electronic devices" (Hinduja & Patchin, 2009:5). Using technology, a bully can send or post hurtful, humiliating, or even threatening messages and content to a victim, to third parties, or to a public forum or environment that many other online participants visit. Cyberbullying is the unfortunate byproduct of the union of adolescent aggression and electronic communication, and its growth gives us cause for concern. Moreover, there is no shortage of potential offenders or targets of cyberbullying because of the widespread availability of personal technological devices in the developed world.

Given the prominence of several high-profile incidents in recent months, cyberbullying has been all over the media. The tragic suicides of several teens who experienced cyberbullying have shined a bright light on a significant social problem that, if left unchecked, stands to detrimentally affect the current generation of youth. Wanting to intervene in some way, many parents, school personnel, and other professionals who work with adolescents are looking for information to educate themselves about this problem. Even though it may seem fairly new to them, a core group of researchers, educators, counselors, and others have been exploring this problem for years, and therefore have a unique, empirically-informed perspective to offer. This book represents a compendium of the lessons learned through their efforts.

We hope that *Cyberbullying Prevention and Response: Expert Perspectives* will serve as the definitive guide to assist you in addressing the ways teens misuse technology to cause harm to their peers. This book voices the views and experiences of the best and brightest youth online risk professionals in the United States – those widely recognized in our nation and abroad as experts in this area. The knowledge and resources shared in this book are guided by research, but presented in an accessible way that will be useful for all who work with teens. What is more, they can be considered some of the "best practices" currently known regarding preventing and responding to cyberbullying. We hope that you benefit greatly from what is shared throughout these chapters.

The Book

The book begins with an overview of the current state of knowledge concerning the ways in which youth are using and abusing online technologies. First, Anne Collier discusses "the living Internet," a place that is constantly evolving and reflecting the personalities of its varied user base. She argues that the (mis) behaviors of teens are generally the same as they have always been, except that in the 21st century they are occurring on a landscape unfamiliar to many adults. One solution, then, is to take traditional safety messages and augment them with instruction and modeling of digital citizenship and media literacy. In Chapter 2, we review and summarize the body of cyberbullying research to inform readers about the nature, extent, and consequences of online aggression. We present results from our own data collected in 2010 involving over 4,400 students, along with findings from several other published research projects on the topic. We explain how cyberbullying affects a meaningful number of youth on a regular basis and that those who experience cyberbullying also report having emotional and psychological issues, suicidal thoughts, low self-esteem, and academic and behavioral problems at school.

Next, Patricia Agatston, Robin Kowalski, and Susan Limber present the perspectives of students who have experienced cyberbullying as targets, bullies, or bystanders. From the students we learn that cyberbullying isn't often reported to adults, despite being a significant problem. Youth are more likely to report their experiences to adults when they know they will be taken seriously and *appropriate* actions will be taken.

Chapter 3 summarizes some of the important legal issues surrounding cyberbullying. Nancy Willard argues that schools, parents, law enforcement officers, and others need to work together to respond to on- and off-campus cyberbullying incidents, and that they are endowed with the responsibility and right to informally or formally intervene, depending on the situation.

Chapter 5 presents a framework for school counselors to use when addressing cyberbullying, and shows how they can play a significant role in meeting the needs of parents and youth in the midst of their victimization and struggles. Parents who are wrestling with what to do when faced with a cyberbullying incident should consider consulting with an informed school counselor as they can often provide knowledgeable guidance to pragmatically deal with a variety of adolescent relationship problems. Accordingly, Russell Sabella provides concrete solutions and strategies to aid counselors in their efforts.

In Chapter 6, Stan Davis and Charisse Nixon stress the role of bystanders in responding to cyberbullying. Very rarely does bullying or cyberbullying occur without witnesses. What observers do, then, is very important in terms of developing a culture where no form of harassment or mistreatment is tolerated.

Educator Mike Donlin presents components of promising school-based efforts to prevent cyberbullying in Chapter 7. Included in this chapter are a number of strategies, activities, and initiatives school professionals can use to educate their community about cyberbullying. An underlying theme of this chapter, though, is that it will take a comprehensive, coordinated, and concerted approach involving multiple stakeholders to address the problem.

Building on the groundwork laid in Chapter 7, in Chapter 8 Jenny Walker presents a detailed and categorized list of "tools" that all adults can use to help prevent cyberbullying in their communities. Numerous readily available resources are identified and reviewed for adults looking to equip themselves and the youth they care for.

In Chapter 9 Elizabeth Englander provides practical strategies for school administrators and parents to consider employing when responding to cyberbullying incidents. Inherent in her suggestions is the idea that all parties must carefully consider the most appropriate response for the particular situation. No two incidents are the same and therefore adults should use their discretion and knowledge of the youth involved to respond accordingly.

In the final chapter, we present information for school-based police officers who are charged with dealing with these problems. We argue that their role extends far beyond their formal duties to enforce the law, and that they too should be encouraged to use creativity in their efforts to reduce and respond to peer victimization and conflict. They must also serve as leaders in educating the school community about the harmful effects and possible legal consequences of all forms of harassment.

In summary, we present this book as an anthology of valuable approaches to meaningfully deal with cyberbullying – whether you are the parent, the teacher, the principal, the counselor, the law enforcement officer, or any number of other adults concerned about the well-being of youth in the digital age. Without your efforts, adolescents will be forced to navigate this largely uncharted and ever-changing territory alone. They need your support, understanding, insight, and guidance about how and why their responsible and appropriate use of technology is so important.

For More Information

For constantly updated information, a wealth of downloadable resources, and numerous interactive activities, please visit the Cyberbullying Research Center's website at www.cyberbullying.us. Please also spread the word about cyberbullying. With your help, we hope to continue making great headway in educating youth-serving adults and enlisting their active support. Finally, keep us informed (patchin@cyberbullying.us or hinduja@cyberbullying.us) with regard to your struggles and successes on the front lines of this issue. We will do all we can to help you, and keep you encouraged and equipped.

Reference

Hinduja, S., & Patchin, J. W. (2009). *Bullying beyond the schoolyard: Preventing and responding to cyberbullying*. Thousand Oaks, CA: Sage Publications (Corwin Press).

ACKNOWLEDGMENTS

We would like to thank our families and friends for their continued support as we pursue our passion of providing up-to-date information about cyberbullying to those who can take steps to prevent and respond to it. The heartbreaking and sometimes tragic stories we hear of distressing online experiences continually inspires us to do our part to inform and equip educators, parents, counselors, law enforcement officers, and adolescents in this sphere of life. We would also like to heartily thank our colleagues – those included in this volume and the many others who share in our commitment to identify and develop best practices to address cyberbullying. While there is still much to learn, your tireless efforts have shined a powerful light on this problem, and together we can continue to offer research-based, practical guidance so that all youth can benefit from new technologies. Finally, we would like to thank God for giving us the abilities and opportunities to try and make a meaningful difference in the lives of others.

Justin W. Patchin and Sameer Hinduja

1

A "LIVING INTERNET"

Some Context for the Cyberbullying Discussion

Anne Collier

It would be an understatement to say we all have a pretty good idea that the media environment our children are experiencing is not like the one in which we grew up. And yet, we see so many news stories, blog posts, books, school policies, and even research reports written from the perspective of that by-gone mass-media environment. It's as if we know there's something major going on, but we haven't yet fully grasped it, maybe aren't even quite sure we want to and – because we fear what we don't understand – we expect, believe, or dwell on the worst implications and cases.

That's what we're doing when we think about our children's "online safety," I find as I survey the technology news headlines each day, talk to parents at speaking engagements around the country, and serve on national Net-safety task forces. One of those task forces found in its review of youth online risk research through 2008, that cyberbullying is the most common online risk kids face (Palfrey, boyd, & Sacco, 2009). But the extreme cases we see in the news are exactly that: extreme and far from common, and extrapolating the experiences of all youth online from those headlines is not good for our children. They find today's social media very compelling and spend a lot of time communicating, playing, socializing, and producing with their friends, mentors, collaborators, relatives, and us in these new media.

Please note that I didn't use the verb "consuming" in that last sentence. They do that too, when they watch all sorts of videos on YouTube or Hulu, for example, whether produced by peers or professionals, as well as watching TV and reading "content" in books and on the Web and all sorts of devices. "Consuming" isn't top of the list, though, because young people's use of media is considerably more active and less passive than that of previous generations.

But let's back up for a moment and focus on just how different today's media environment – the context in which the subject of this book, cyberbullying, occurs – is. When we were growing up, people consumed media; they didn't participate the way our children do now. Media were produced by what most of us thought of as professionals and were distributed in one direction ("head-end," as Nicholas Negroponte, founder of MIT's Media Lab, wrote years ago, from the regulated media industry to the masses) through a relatively small number of "channels" (books, radio, broadcast TV, movies, etc.).

Now, all media – user-produced and professionally produced – are moving in all directions, in real time (instantly), and are all mashed up together on the same virtually unregulated, borderless platform: the Internet. In addition to that set of revolutionary conditions, there's one more very key difference: the social part. A large cross-section of today's media environment, the part our children find so compelling – whether it involves text, music, photos, or video on phones, the Web, game consoles, and handhelds of all sorts – is social, or behavioral. And it's all embedded in their everyday lives.

In effect, the Internet is a "living thing." That's what we, the Online Safety and Technology Working Group (OSTWG), called it in the title of the 150-page report we sent to Congress in June 2010: "Youth Safety on a Living Internet" (Nigam & Collier, 2010). We did so because we wanted to send a message to law-makers, as well as everyone who has an impact on children's lives, that this highly social medium our kids find so compelling can't really be handled the way media were in the past, whether by regulators in Washington, school officials, or parents in households throughout the country (or the world in a global media environment).

First, let me repeat for emphasis that this is not just technology, media, or "content" I'm talking about. And it's not just about young people's use of it. The Internet, as we all are using it now, is the product of a growing portion of humanity's creativity, learning, production, and sociality; it mirrors them as well as serves as a platform for them. The fixed – and increasingly mobile – Internet is another "place" where our socializing, gaming, productions (blogs, family photos, videos, etc.), research, communication, and many aspects of our lives – positive, negative, and neutral – play out in real time. But not separate from or in addition to "real life"; rather, all this activity is rooted in it and part of it.

What does all this mean where young people's online safety is concerned? A lot of things. Here is just a sampler:

1.   *The new meaning of "content."* We're talking about behavioral as well as informational content. Cyberbullying is just one very negative example of behavioral content. It might take the form of a conversation, carried out in text messages on two people's cell phones, that turns into an argument and ends up with a cruel message posted on a Facebook page. Or a friend becoming an ex-friend and using a password shared in confidence to post mean things about a third party that gets the password owner in trouble.

A person can be blocked from commenting on a Facebook wall or sending text messages, but it's impossible to block behavior happening in real time (e.g., to stop a mean comment when you don't know it's coming), the way filtering software blocks content: It's like trying to anticipate a particular behavior in a social interaction or to isolate a single child's part of a social circle's activity. A colleague of mine recently likened social networking sites to oil rigs – they're more like the infrastructure *around* the "product" and definitely not the producers of it. But even that metaphor breaks down when we consider how life-like the product is, that it's the expression of at least parts of people's lives, and it changes as they and their lives do. It's also not necessarily a single person's self-expression. Very often it expresses real-life relations between two or more people, the expression of which is hard for a single participant to control.

2. *It's constantly changing.* What we're talking about is a "moving target." That goes for the Internet, its "content," and its users. Its dynamic conditions, added to its diversity, mean that: (1) once-and-for-all, one-size-fits-all solutions do not exist; (2) it's tough to regulate or legislate adolescent behavior; and (3) we need a very large "toolbox" with a diverse array of "tools" for protecting kids at different developmental stages and in different situations, just like in real life (for some additional ideas, see especially Chapter 8). Those tools include education (including an ongoing parent–child conversation), a range of filtering and other technologies, families' values (such as the Golden Rule or "our family treats people with respect"), family and school rules and policies, sometimes mental healthcare, law enforcement, and privacy and safety features in websites and on devices. And ideally, each tool is calibrated to individual kids' changing maturity and trust levels. I'm sure you see where I'm going with this: Because the content (i.e., behavior) changes as the kid changes, so the "tools" need to be calibrated. As parenting has always been offline, so it goes with online kids.

3. *The Net is everywhere.* This is in terms of both location and devices. It may be filtered on computers at school and home, but much less on the cell phones that – according to early 2010 data from the Pew/Internet researchers – 75% of US 12–17-year-olds own and usually take with them to school (Lenhart, Purcell, Smith, & Zickuhr, 2010), where it's tough to enforce policies concerning devices that fit in pockets and under desks. It's difficult to regulate behavior in a medium produced from the grassroots up, whether the "regulator" is a technology, a parent, a school, or a government. What that means is that the onus is more and more on education rather than regulation – on creating cultures of *self*-regulation which include critical thinking about the content consumed or downloaded, as well as posted or uploaded, and respect for others at home and school. As my co-director of ConnectSafely.org, Larry Magid, put it back in the late 1990s, "the best filter is the one between kids' ears." That is even more true today, as the Internet has become so user-driven.

A February 2010 report released by Ofsted, the UK education watchdog, deemed "outstanding" in online-safety instruction and practices schools that were employing "managed" rather than "locked down" filtering. The "managed" filtering schools did not employ across-the-board strict filtering, but rather taught students to "take responsibility themselves" for using the Internet safely (Ofsted, 2010). They did so by helping students to assess the risk of accessing certain sites. For example, at the elementary level in one of the top five schools, students are taught to ask themselves these questions: "Who wrote the material on this site?"; "Is the information on it likely to be accurate or could it be altered by anybody?"; "If others click onto the site, can I be sure that they are who they say they are?"; and "What information about myself should I not give out on the site?"

The BBC cited Ofsted inspectors as saying that "pupils given a greater degree of freedom to surf the Internet at school are less vulnerable to online dangers in the long-term" (Sellgren, 2010). The Ofsted report points to the ever-growing importance of teaching children a new media literacy that develops on-the-spot critical thinking about what they're sharing and uploading (how they're behaving toward others) – on computers, cell phones, game consoles, handhelds, and so on – as well as what they're seeing, reading, and downloading.

4. *It's embedded in "real life."* I mentioned this before, but let's drill down because it's so important. The research shows that young people's social lives happen both online and offline, and on multiple devices, as well as in school and at home (Ito, Horst, Bittani, boyd, Herr-Stephenson, Lange et al., 2008). Adults often make a distinction between "virtual" and "real." To the detriment of informed parenting, we often think about youth's approach to media in a binary way – online vs. offline; entertaining vs. learning; public vs. private; bully vs. victim – where to them, as in life, it's many shades of gray, a fluid experience. They just socialize, produce, play, do their informal learning, etc., whenever and wherever, with online being just one "location" in the "where." What we see in Facebook, one of those hangouts, is the online expression of what's happening in everyday school life, relationships, and peer groups – and certainly not all of the online expression, which happens just as much on cellphones, in gaming communities, and other parts of a vast digital platform

So, when we think about that, how much can a single website realistically fix problems occurring in those settings, as some of us adults expect – for example, by getting Facebook to delete cruel comments, hate groups, or even the account of a socially aggressive child? A determined aggressor often finds alternative or multiple ways of acting out his or her aggression. Getting an account deleted from Facebook or Formspring – even if the aggressor doesn't just set up a new (free) account in minutes, as anyone can – is unlikely to end the behavior, unfortunately; in fact, getting an aggressor's account deleted could potentially make matters worse. Problems in relationships are usually resolved by the people involved and the supporters around them. The new media conditions do not change this age-old reality.

What is often being talked about when we hear the word "cyberbullying" – which will be much better defined for you later in this book – is digitally enabled, 24/7 school drama (Collier, 2010). We all need to get better at distinguishing between cyberbullying and spikes of bad behavior, annoyance, frustration, and anger in the "reality TV" of school life. This book will help us with that. But for now, know that, just as there's a whole spectrum of negative action and reaction in "real life," there is on cell phones, in game communities, and in social networking sites too. It's just that it's all much more on display now, which naturally increases our anxiety levels, but which we don't have to lump in with the more egregious phenomena of bullying and cyberbullying. Know, too, that some of what increases our collective concern levels and what is very different now, is the increased *exposure* of adolescent socializing, not the socializing itself – which is probably not that different from the socializing we did as teens.

5. *So the risk spectrum matches that of real life.* Because the Internet increasingly mirrors all aspects of human life, it mirrors the full spectrum of *offline* risks, not just the really frightening ones covered in popular TV shows or news reports about the most egregious cases, whether adult predation or peer harassment. Consider cyberbullying, the risk identified by the last task force I served on, the Berkman Center report of January 2009 (Palfrey et al., 2009), as the one that affects the most kids. Cyberbullying isn't a single identifiable behavior happening on any single device or platform. Its range of causes reflects the complexity of school life, students' own lives and teenage socializing; it requires a multidisciplinary, whole-school-community approach.

This very social medium is, by definition, a collective experience (affected by individuals' actions). Safety in social media is a collaboration and sometimes a negotiation – a shared experience and outcome. Think about a group photo in Facebook. Because it depicts a group, its posting affects everyone in the group. The outcome, the way each individual in the photo is perceived by others, is an effect of one individual posting that photo. If some people in the photo – e.g., a party photo depicting underage drinking or a sleepover photo showing some people in their underwear – appear in a way that could cause negative reactions or punishment from some viewers, its posting could be an act of cyberbullying (or revenge, harassment, etc.). Not only because mean behavior often gets a reaction in kind, but also because we need to model and teach good citizenship online as well as offline, we need to help our children share media responsibly and respectfully, not just for their peers' benefit, but for their own.

And, as if to illustrate how its complexity matches that of offline life, social media use is also very individual. As illustrated above, how positive or negative it turns out to be is determined by both the individual and by the tenor of his or her relations with others. An important risk factor reported in a 2007 article in *Archives of Pediatrics* is aggressive behavior itself; researchers found that aggressive behavior online at least doubles the aggressor's risk online (Ybarra, Mitchell, Finkelhor, & Wolak, 2007). This sounds a lot like "what goes around, comes around," doesn't it? So young people are stakeholders in their own well-being online as well as offline, and it behooves the people who work with them to help them understand that.

Another key finding in the Berkman task force's review of the youth online risk research through 2008 (Palfrey et al., 2009) was that not all youth are equally at risk online. We found that the young people who are most at risk online "often engage in risky behaviors and have difficulties in other parts of their lives," a strong indicator that – because the Internet and cell phone use are embedded in young people's everyday lives – the risk spectrum online increasingly matches that of "real life." It also indicates that young people who maintain positive, healthy relationships with peers may, generally speaking, be at lower risk of anti-social victimization online. But it may also help to keep in mind that, just as anything can happen in and around peer groups at school – from positive behaviors to conflict to bullying – so it can happen in virtual worlds, games, and social networking sites.

A child's psychosocial makeup and home and school environments are better predictors of online risk than any technology a child uses, the Berkman task force also found. We have long known that, if a child is treated unkindly or abusively at home, he or she sometimes acts out that hurt with harassing behavior toward peers at school. The same behaviors happen in the online environment and on cell phones, which to them are simply other "places" where they interact with friends and peers.

Risk vs. Harm

It's so important to remember, as we're inundated with negative reports of young people's social media use, that, "significantly, risk does not often result in harm," as reported in the international study of youth online risk, *EU Kids Online*, released in October 2010 (Livingstone, Haddon, Gorzig, & Olafsson, 2010). When we hear about youth online "risk," let's not reflexively sub in "harm." Risk and harm are not the same thing. Even in situations where kids are at risk of being harmed, there is no certainty that they will be. For example, a boy with a crush on a girl finds out that she's hanging out with another boy. The former may act out his jealousy in mean comments on the new boyfriend's Facebook wall, but that doesn't necessarily mean he'll physically threaten the recipient, that the recipient will feel psychologically vulnerable, or that the sender will make the kind of repeated malicious comments that turn into cyberbullying. The risk is there, but the harm isn't – necessarily. This is the kind of scenario we can discuss with our kids to help them strategize how to avoid such harm.

It may help to know that risk assessment is a necessary task of adolescent development, of growing up. The lead author of the *EU Kids Online* study, Sonia Livingstone, wrote recently that:

a world without risk is undesirable. Children must learn to take calculated risks and, insofar as is possible, cope with the consequences. Developmental psychologists are clear that facing and coping with risk is important.... Without experience of adversity, a child may be protected but has nothing to adapt to positively and so will not become resilient. A risk-averse society will, paradoxically, exacerbate rather than reduce the very vulnerabilities it seeks to protect by undermining the development of resilience.

Livingstone, 2010:12

So, instead of trying to remove all risk from our children's lives, it's actually better to let them work through issues with peers, letting them know we're their back-up and can help with strategizing if needed.

What's Different in Today's Media?

I've mentioned a number of ways in which young people's experiences in and with new media mirror their offline lives. But there are ways in which new media do change the equation: the Net effect, if you will. Social media researcher danah boyd (whose legal name is in lower-case) described these effects in her doctoral dissertation, *Taken Out of Context: American Teen Sociality in Networked Publics* (boyd, 2008). They include persistence and searchability (the Net as a permanent, searchable archive); replicability (the ability to copy and paste from anywhere on the Net, to anywhere online); scalability (high potential visibility well beyond the audience you had in mind); invisible audiences (never being sure about who's seeing, reading, or watching what you post); and the blurring of public and private (an extension of invisible audiences because boundaries aren't clear – private from whom?). Each of these factors can be present in online harassment and cyberbullying incidents. A fit of anger at someone expressed in a text message to a third party can be forwarded to the person who caused the anger (replicability). Something said in a private Facebook message one evening can be all over school the next day (scalability, invisible audiences, and the public/private blur). Somebody who has a compromising photo of herself on her cell phone leaves the phone on a school library table while she goes to find a book. While she's in the stacks, other students at the table go through her phone, find the photo, and send it to other students. You are probably not surprised to hear that these incidents actually happened.

Another very important factor we're all familiar with is online disinhibition, the effect of not having facial expressions, body language, and other visual cues from people with whom we interact online. Inhibitions break down, which can be good but also bad. It can have the effect of reducing empathy and civility – which makes it increasingly imperative to remind each other and teach our children that those are human beings with feelings behind the text messages, wall posts, and avatars in their social media experiences. There is no one-size-fits-all antidote to the behaviors that can arise from all these factors, but it can help to share this knowledge with our kids so they can use social media more mindfully.

A Spectrum of Online Safety, Too

So, we begin to see that the online kind of safety – just like safety in the offline world – is so much more about behavior and humanity than it is about technology. And just as the risk spectrum increasingly matches that of the offline world, there are many kinds of online safety too (http://os3.connectsafely.org). In addition to physical safety, or freedom from physical harm that may result from Internet use, there are psychological safety (freedom from cruelty, harassment, and exposure to potentially disturbing material), reputational and legal safety (freedom from negative personal, social, professional, and legal consequences that could affect us for a lifetime), and identity, property, and community safety (freedom from theft of or harm to identity and property and attacks against our networks and online communities at local, national, and international levels).

To me, these "freedoms" suggest the rights and freedoms of citizenship, which is one reason why, in the OSTWG report to Congress, we recommended instruction in *digital* citizenship, or citizenship in digital media, as well as the traditional kind of citizenship, pre-K–12, in all appropriate classes, including the core curriculum. We also recommended more use of social media in school as one of the environments where citizenship can be *practiced*, not just modeled and taught. It was our belief that school needs to do for social, or new, media what it has done with traditional media for generations of students: guide and enrich their experience of media.

BOX 1.1 WHAT IS DIGITAL CITIZENSHIP?

Etiquette: electronic standards of conduct or procedure
Communication: electronic exchange of information
Education: the process of teaching and learning about technology and the use of technology
Access: full electronic participation in society
Commerce: electronic buying and selling of goods
Responsibility: electronic responsibility for actions and deeds
Rights: those freedoms extended to everyone in a digital world
Safety: physical well-being in a digital technology world
Security (self-protection):   electronic precautions to guarantee safety

Source: Ribble, Bailey, & Ross (2004)

When University of Southern California media professor Henry Jenkins spoke to the Working Group in the fall of 2009, he said youth are engaged in four activities that are "central to the life of young people in participatory culture: circulating media, connecting with each other, creating media, and collaborating with each other." He told us that it's crucial for them to be engaging in these activities in school so that all youth have equal opportunity to participate in what is now more participatory culture than merely participatory media; and so that school can play a guiding role in their use of new media as much as that of traditional media. Dr. Jenkins said young people are "looking for guidance often [in their use of new media] but don't know where to turn" (Nigam & Collier, 2010:3). Because schools largely block social media and technologies, and online-safety education has perhaps unthinkingly taught parents to fear social media, we have left kids on their own in these media, rather than provided them with guidance in their best, safest, most enriching uses. It makes no more sense to leave children on their own to figure out how to navigate online spaces with no adult guidance than it does to leave them on their own in physical spaces such as skate parks, public pools, and shopping malls before they're ready.

New-Media Literacy and Citizenship

In September 2010 I had the privilege of co-moderating a panel on digital citizenship at the Internet Governance Forum in Lithuania. My co-moderator, Martin Cocker, who directs New Zealand's national online-safety organization, NetSafe, told us that in his country they've found that "online safety" (the way we've been teaching it since the mid-1990s in many parts of the world) doesn't work. NetSafe, which works closely with every sector of youth safety – young people, parents, educators, juvenile judges, researchers, mobile and Web companies, and policy-makers – focuses entirely on digital citizenship now. Many European countries seem to be coming to this too, seeing the need for a more positive approach to Net-safety education that, like digital citizenship and media literacy, blends technology literacy (effective use of technology), media literacy, and social literacy. Based on all we've learned in various US task forces and both the youth risk and social-media bodies of research to date, this seems to be the most realistic approach going forward – the approach that directly addresses online behavior, the source of both cyberbullying and its unfolding solutions.

But what is meant by "media literacy"? Certainly not only the traditional kind that addresses only how media are *consumed*. In today's information overload, of course children, and all of us, really, need to develop the critical thinking that traditional media literacy teaches. But more is demanded of media literacy now that media are social. I like to think of it as a two-way proposition: critical thinking about what is posted, produced, and uploaded as much as what is read, consumed, and downloaded. This is *social*, or behavioral media literacy.

It's partly media literacy and partly what my European colleagues call social literacy. How can it be both? Again – because media are social, or behavior, now – media literacy and digital citizenship are melting into each other.

That, I gathered, is why NetSafe focuses all its education efforts solely on digital citizenship. Though it was a US study (cited above) which found that aggressive behavior online increases online risk, NetSafe, too, has decided that civil, respectful behavior online reduces risk. Citizenship and literacy in new media – the kind of learning that develops children's cognitive filter that goes with them wherever they go – are *protective*. And they have never been needed more, which is why the OSTWG recommended to Congress that we make new media literacy and citizenship training at all grade levels, throughout the curriculum, a national priority.

Some parents, educators, and law enforcement people might say, "That's nice. Digital citizenship and literacy sound good and may be nice to teach in schools *if* teachers have time, but why universal? Can it protect *all* kids?" That's a good question. The answer is "no." It's baseline online-safety instruction for all kids. Because not all kids are equally at risk online, we need to implement a much more realistic (as in mapped to "real life"), *layered* approach to online-risk prevention and intervention, like the Levels of Prevention of the public health field. So-called at-risk kids – those with established patterns of risk behavior disrupting their lives – need prevention and intervention help from the offline experts who work with them: school counselors, risk-prevention specialists, social workers, and mental health practitioners. These experts need training in social media so they can use them in their prevention and intervention work with youth as much as they use phones and in-person communication.

Conclusion

The new media environment in which we all find ourselves is demanding a lot of us:

Thought change. It requires a shift of thought. Because "media" is behavioral now, we need, perhaps counter-intuitively, to focus on our humanity – who we are and how we treat one another, online or offline – more than ever. Technology is neither the problem nor the solution, really. Behavior is. A new kind of social contract is in place, and we're all signed onto it, in a "by using this, you consent" sort of way. We need to recognize and act on the fact that – because the new media environment around us is affecting child development, education, business, the economy, law-making, and every other aspect of life – young people will have better, safer experiences online when (1) they treat themselves, their peers, and their (online and offline) communities with respect; (2) we approach social media and children's participation in them with respect, or at least open-mindedness; and (3) we bring social media into the formal learning environment so that children are not left on their own in new media to the extent that they are now.

Modeling. A shift of thought is not hard once we've recognized the need for it. What's a little harder is shifting behavior – and not just that of our children. Our teaching of responsible behavior is much less effective if we're not ourselves modeling citizenship, civility, humanity – offline and on all connected devices – for our children. We need to show them by example that civil, ethical behavior is protective of our well-being and our relationships online *and* offline. On a broader scale, for example, in school communities, this takes the form of establishing social norms and whole-school cultures that demonstrate tolerance and respect.

Working inside-out. We've long been approaching online safety from the outside-in, extrapolating from worst-case scenarios one-size-fits-all education that is based more on our mass-media sensibilities and fear of the new-media unknown than on research. It's time to get more granular. We need at least to *balance* that outside-in approach with the inside-out one, the way loving parents and caring teachers have always approached our children: from the kid-out. When things come up between siblings or in school hallways, we talk with our children, get to the bottom of what happened, get other perspectives, and figure out solutions with them, hopefully turning them into "teachable moments" so they can learn from them and become more resilient for the next time a social challenge occurs. It's no different when the expression of a social challenge appears online. Because it usually involves the same peer group or set of friends, the conversation is no different and no less challenging. The good news is, it's in front of our eyes – *if* they've come to us about it – and the "evidence" can be captured. The bad news is, it may be more public or more widely distributed than anybody involved would like. But we still work with the kids immediately involved. That's what I mean by working from the kid-out. Technology has not changed that.

If all this makes you feel uneasy, that's okay. This is a radical media shift we're all experiencing, and you're not alone. Every generation of parents feels concerns about what their teens are "up to," and added to that today are flood-tides of media, produced by anybody, moving in all directions, 24/7. Even Socrates felt uneasy about a radical new medium of his time: the book. Author Jonah Lehrer wrote in the *New York Times* that Socrates lamented that the book would "create forgetfulness" in the soul. Instead of remembering for themselves, Socrates warned, new readers were blindly trusting in "external written characters" (Lehrer, 2010). So we're in good company, but let's include our intrepid young social media users in that company and be willing to learn a few things from them. This is essential because we need them to come to us when their online and offline socializing gets tough, and they won't if we overreact and handle the technology they find compelling with fear and misunderstanding. Until youth and adults – from parents to educators to social workers – are on the same page with social media, we need to make sure we're communicating with youth about their online experiences just as we would with offline ones.

Their technology literacy and our life literacy are both essential to the social media literacy and citizenship that will help protect all of us, help our children navigate media *and* growing up, and help us adults set sound policy at the household, school, state, and federal levels.

References

boyd, d. (2008). Taken out of context: American teen sociality in networked publics. Retrieved from www.danah.org/papers/TakenOutOfContext.pdf.

Collier, A. (2010). "Recombinant art," life?: Parenting & the digital drama overload. *Net Family News*. Retrieved from www.netfamilynews.org/?p=28767.

Ito, M., Horst, H., Bittani, M., boyd, d., Herr-Stephenson, B., Lange, P. G. et al. (2008). Living and learning with new media: Summary of findings from the Digital Youth Project. *The John D. and Catherine T. MacArthur Foundation Reports on Digital Media and Learning*. Retrieved from http://digitalyouth.ischool.berkeley.edu/files/report/digitalyouth-WhitePaper.pdf.

Lehrer, J. (2010). Our cluttered minds. *New York Times*. Retrieved from www.nytimes.com/2010/06/06/books/review/Lehrer-t.html?_r=1.

Lenhart, A., Purcell, K., Smith, A., & Zickuhr, K. (2010). Social media and young adults. *Pew Internet & American Life Project*. Retrieved from www.pewinternet.org/~/media//Files/Reports/2010/PIP_Social_Media_and_Young_Adults_Report.pdf.

Livingstone, S. (2010). *e-Youth: (future) policy implications: Reflections on online risk, harm and vulnerability*. Paper presented at e-Youth: balancing between opportunities and risks, Antwerp, Belgium.

Livingstone, S., Haddon, L., Gorzig, A., & Olafsson, K. (2010). Risks and safety on the Internet: The perspective of European children. *EU Kids Online*. Retrieved from www2.lse.ac.uk/media@lse/research/EUKidsOnline/EUKidsII%20(2009-11)/EUKidsOnlineIIReports/Initial_findings_report.pdf.

Nigam, H., & Collier, A. (2010). Youth safety on a living Internet. *National Telecommunications and Information Administration*. Retrieved from www.ntia.doc.gov/reports/2010/OSTWG_Final_Report_060410.pdf.

Ofsted. (2010). The safe use of new technologies. *Office for Standards in Education, Children's Services and Skills*. Retrieved from www.ofsted.gov.uk/content/download/10750/128225/file/The%20safe%20use%20of%20new%20technologies.pdf.

Palfrey, J. G., boyd, d., & Sacco, D. (2009). *Enhancing child safety and online technologies: Final report of the Internet Safety Technical Task Force*. Durham, NC: Carolina Academic Press.

Ribble, M. S., Bailey, G. D., & Ross, T. W. (2004). Digital citizenship: Addressing appropriate technology behavior. *Learning & Leading with Technology, 32*(1), 6–12.

Sellgren, K. (2010). Pupils "must manage online risks." *BBC News*. Retrieved from http://news.bbc.co.uk/2/hi/uk_news/education/8505914.stm.

Ybarra, M. L., Mitchell, J. K., Finkelhor, D., & Wolak, J. (2007). Internet prevention messages: Are we targeting the right online behaviors? *Archives of Pediatrics and Adolescent Medicine, 161*, 138–145.

2

CYBERBULLYING

An Update and Synthesis of the Research

Justin W. Patchin and Sameer Hinduja

> I was on AIM minding my own business, then all of a sudden a screen name I didn't recognize popped up. They started to talk to me and call me really horrible names. I felt like crying. I asked who it was a bunch of times and all they said was "none of your business." I blocked them but they always made a different screen name. I remember every word they said to me. I will never ever let it go because from that day on I was harassed badly and still never figured out who it was.
>
> *11-year-old from California*

This chapter will summarize the latest research on cyberbullying and online harassment. As will become evident, the findings vary widely by study because of the different ways cyberbullying is defined, and the different strategies employed to examine the problem. The goal of this chapter will be to synthesize the information in a way that provides a clear and relatively concise summary of what we currently know about the problem. This includes who exactly is being cyberbullied, in what venues and with what mediums, and how it is happening. We also will explain what contributing factors can be identified, as well as the negative consequences that seem to stem from cyberbullying and affect youth on an emotional, psychological, behavioral, and physical level. This should illustrate in vivid detail its frequency and scope, which can consequently serve as a necessary foundation before proceeding to appropriate prevention and response strategies.

To date, there have been at least 42 articles[1] published in peer-reviewed journals across a wide variety of academic disciplines. Although there are additional articles being published quite regularly and it is likely that we have missed some published works since the printing of this chapter, this review represents the most comprehensive summary of available research findings at the time of its writing. In addition to reviewing existing cyberbullying research, we also present details from our most recent study. This research, conducted in the spring of 2010, involved surveying a random sample of over 4,400 11–18-year-old middle- and high-school students from a large school district in the southern United States. Additional information about this project can be obtained by contacting the authors. By supplementing the existing body of research with our most recent study, we seek to present an extensive yet contemporary picture of the nature and extent of cyberbullying.

Defining Cyberbullying

If you ask five people to define cyberbullying for you, you will probably get five somewhat different answers. This is one of the biggest problems we have encountered, especially when attempting to obtain a 30,000-foot view of the research conducted on the topic. Some researchers use very broad definitions of cyberbullying that include every experience with any form of online harassment. Others focus only on specific types of harm – such as humiliation or threats to one's physical safety, without also including other forms like name-calling and insults. Some researchers cover any and all mediums and venues through which cyberbullying can occur, while others may leave out a few technologies (such as webcams) or places (such as in online gaming networks). These definitional inconsistencies then lead to different measurements of the nature and extent of harassment in cyberspace, which at best provides an incomplete picture and at worst leads to misinformation and confusion.

Conceptually, there are a few necessary elements that almost everyone can agree upon when specifying exactly what cyberbullying is. Most importantly, it involves using *technology* to bully another person. This technology could be a computer, cell phone, tablet, wifi digital camera, or another electronic device. Second, it involves harm. The victim or target of the behavior is negatively impacted (psychologically, emotionally, socially, etc.) by the incident. Also included in most definitions of cyberbullying is that the behavior is repeated. Like the bullying that occurs in traditional contexts (in the schoolyard or classroom hallway), one isolated incident is not typically considered "bullying." That said, the nature of technology almost ensures that the victimization is repeated since the devices employed usually make it very easy to duplicate and redistribute hurtful digital content (e.g., forwarding harassing comments, posting embarrassing pictures online, downloading and then modifying videos before re-uploading them again).

In our research, we confront these definitional inconsistencies by asking about experiences with cyberbullying in two different ways. We first ask youth about their experiences with (or participation in) several specific types of online harassment (see Box 2.1). We then ask them if they have been cyberbullied (or if they have cyberbullied others) after informing them: "Cyberbullying is when someone repeatedly harasses, mistreats, or makes fun of another person online or while using cell phones or other electronic devices." In this way we are able to invoke and reference cyberbullying and online harassment without limiting behaviors to particular forms or devices.

To be sure, our own definition has required expansion over the years (when we first started studying this problem in the early 2000s, we formally characterized cyberbullying as occurring through electronic text, which of course did not cover pictures or videos). As we have continued to immerse ourselves in the study of this problem, though, we have made modifications and improvements to help us better capture and measure the "what, when, where, why, and how" of adolescent electronic aggression. Now that we have a better understanding of what exactly cyberbullying is, we can examine the extent to which youth have experienced it.

How Many Youth Have Experienced Cyberbullying?

When we first started exploring cyberbullying, there was literally no research that existed. We had seen a popular poll about the issue in *People Magazine*, and a brief anecdotal account of its occurrence in another popular press outlet, but no scientific studies had, at that time, been done. Since 2002 we have conducted seven formal research projects that have included over 12,000 adolescents from over 80 schools using a variety of quantitative and qualitative methodologies. Based on our work (and that of other very capable scholars in the field), we know that a meaningful proportion of adolescents have been cyberbullied or have cyberbullied others at some point in their lifetime. As discussed earlier, though, the proportion of youth who experience cyberbullying varies significantly based on: the age and demographic makeup of those from whom the data were collected; the way cyberbullying was defined and measured; the time period over which youth were asked to reflect when recounting their experiences (previous month, previous year, lifetime, etc.); and the way the data were collected (through interviews, focus groups, paper-based surveys, Web-based surveys, etc.). Among 35 papers published in peer-reviewed journals of which we are aware (as of January 1, 2011) that include cyberbullying victimization rates, figures ranged from 5.5% to 72%, with an average of 24.4% (see Figure 2.1). For example, Michele Ybarra (2004) found that about 6.5% of youth had been harassed online in the previous year, while a more recent study by Jaana Juvonen and Elisheva Gross (2008) found that 72% of youth had been cyberbullied (also within the previous year). Most studies ($n = 22$) estimate that anywhere from 6% to 30% of teens have experienced some form of cyberbullying (Kowalski, Limber, & Agatston, 2008; Lenhart, 2007; Rivers & Noret, 2007; Smith, Mahdavi, Carvalho, & Tippett, 2006).

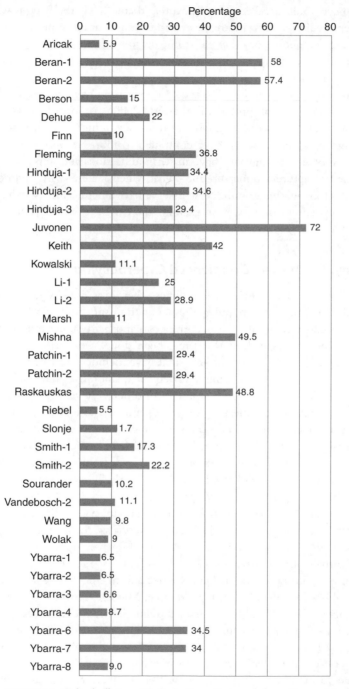

FIGURE 2.1 Cyberbullying Victimization Rates Across Peer–reviewed Journal Articles (n = 35).

These findings are consistent with our own research over the last nine years. As illustrated in Figure 2.2, the percentage of youth who responded to our surveys who have experienced cyberbullying at some point in their lifetime ranges from 18.8% to 40.6%, with an average of 27.3%. Our most recent study based on data collected in the spring of 2010 found that about 21% of youth had been the target of cyberbullying. To be clear, this generally means that one out of every five kids you know has been cyberbullied.

As noted above, in addition to the single question we use to ask respondents about their experiences with cyberbullying, we also ask them about a variety of behaviors that could be *considered* cyberbullying (see Box 2.1). When presented in this more nuanced and detailed way, 17% of respondents in our 2010 study reported that they had experienced one or more of the stated behaviors, two or more times in the 30 days prior to the survey. The most common type of online harassment reported was "someone posted mean or hurtful comments about me online," with 14% of youth indicating that experience. Only 3% of youth said someone posted a mean or hurtful video of them online. In addition, about 13% of respondents said someone spread rumors about them online and 7% reported that they had been threatened online.

BOX 2.1 TYPES OF CYBERBULLYING

- Been cyberbullied
- Someone posted mean or hurtful comments about me online
- Someone posted a mean or hurtful picture of me online
- Someone posted a mean or hurtful video of me online
- Someone created a mean or hurtful webpage about me
- Someone spread rumors about me online
- Someone threatened to hurt me through a cell phone text message
- Someone threatened to hurt me online
- Someone pretended to be me online and acted in a way that was mean or hurtful

---

Relatedly, the number of youth who admit to cyberbullying others at some point in their lives is a bit lower, though quite comparable. Among 27 papers published in peer-reviewed journals of which we are aware (as of January 1, 2011) that included cyberbullying offending rates, 3–44.1% of teens reported cyberbullying others (average of 18%, see Figure 2.3).

Across all of our studies (see Figure 2.4), the rates range from about 11% to as high as 20%, which occurred in our most recent study. The average percentage of youth who reported cyberbullying others in our studies was 16.8%. This, once again, means that generally speaking, slightly less than one out of every

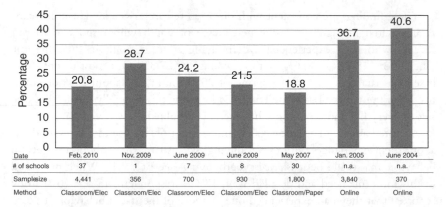

Date	Feb. 2010	Nov. 2009	June 2009	June 2009	May 2007	Jan. 2005	June 2004
# of schools	37	1	7	8	30	n.a.	n.a.
Sample size	4,441	356	700	930	1,800	3,840	370
Method	Classroom/Elec	Classroom/Elec	Classroom/Elec	Classroom/Elec	Classroom/Paper	Online	Online

FIGURE 2.2 Lifetime Cyberbullying Victimization Rates: Seven Different Studies, 2004–2010.

five adolescents has at some point cyberbullied someone else. These rates are also consistent with the weight of the available research conducted by others (Dehue, Bolman, & Vollink, 2008; Kowalski et al., 2008; Li, 2007; Ybarra, Espelage, & Mitchell, 2007b).

In our own studies, we also asked if youth have engaged in any of the nine types of online harassment listed in Box 2.1. Approximately 11% acknowledged that they had participated in one or more of these behaviors, two or more times in the previous 30 days. About 9% of youth admitted that they had posted mean or hurtful comments about someone online, and 5% said they had threatened to hurt someone online at least once in the past month.

Demographic Differences in Cyberbullying Experiences

One important research question is the extent to which cyberbullying experiences differ based on gender, race, or age. Several published articles have addressed this question and we summarize these findings next. It is important at the outset, however, to stress that these findings are generalizations and do not necessarily and consistently reflect the individual experiences of adolescents or the adults who work with them. Every child, community, and culture is different and we should take care not to apply group labels to specific individuals. That said, it is instructive to examine the nature and extent of cyberbullying by gender, race, and age.

Gender

A number of studies have attempted to determine the differences in cyberbullying experiences by gender. Most research has found that girls are just as likely, if not more likely, to be involved in cyberbullying (Lenhart, 2007; Wolak, Mitchell, &

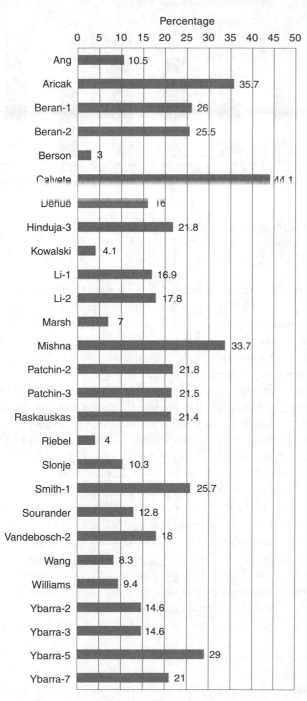

FIGURE 2.3 Cyberbullying Offending Rates Across Peer-reviewed Journal Articles ($n = 27$).

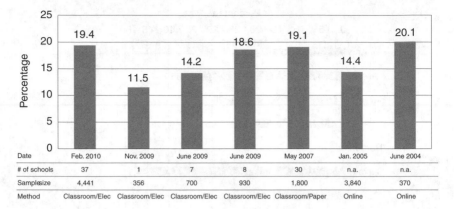

FIGURE 2.4 Lifetime Cyberbullying Offending Rates: Seven Different Studies, 2004–2010.

Finkelhor, 2006). This is particularly true when looking at victimization rates. For example, among 13 published papers that explicitly provide differences in cyberbullying victimization by gender, eight found that girls are more frequently victims, three found that boys are more often victims, and two reported no difference in prevalence rates by gender. Across these studies, 21.8% of girls and 19.5% of boys reported being victims of cyberbullying.

When looking at offending, boys appear more likely than girls to admit to engaging in cyberbullying behaviors. Among the 13 studies that report offending rates by gender, 11 found that girls were less likely to report involvement, while two found no difference. Across these studies, 14.1% of girls and 18.5% of boys admit to cyberbullying others.

These differences were also evident in our 2010 data. As illustrated in Figure 2.5, girls are more likely to report being the victim and offender when referring to lifetime experiences, but boys are more likely to report bullying others within the previous 30 days. This seems to suggest that girls have more historical experience with cyberbullying, but that boys are catching up and are perhaps more involved (especially as a bully) in recent times. The type of cyberbullying also tends to differ based on gender, with girls more likely to have mean or hurtful comments posted online about them and boys more likely to have a mean video posted online about them. Girls are more likely to spread rumors online, while boys are more likely to post a mean or hurtful picture online.

While a complete discussion of the reasons for these gender differences is beyond the scope of this chapter, it is important to highlight a couple of potential explanations. First, girls have long had more experience with relational and other indirect (non-physical) forms of aggression, and technology enables would-be bullies to act out in these ways somewhat anonymously and from a

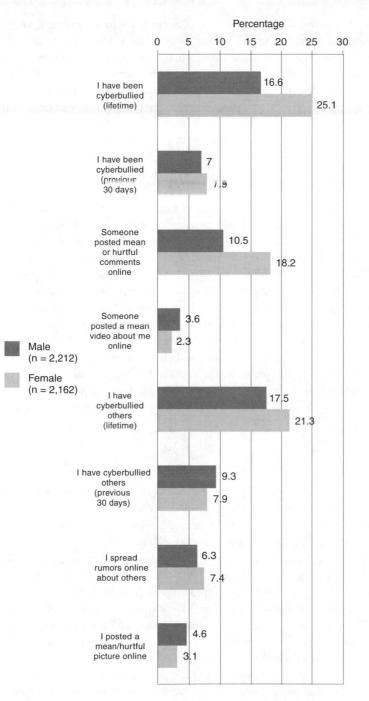

FIGURE 2.5 Cyberbullying by Gender: A Random Sample of 10–18-year-olds from a Large School District in the Southern US.

distance (Simmons, 2003). Second, adolescent girls have routinely employed weapons other than fists or direct threats of physical force; they often choose more covert methods such as discussions behind a target's back or by disrupting social relationships (Wiseman, 2002). Technology is tailor-made for this kind of clandestine hostility and girls have quickly gained skills in utilizing high-tech devices to inflict harm. To be sure, more research is necessary to better understand the gender dynamics at play in various forms of bullying.

Race

It is also enlightening to examine how cyberbullying experiences vary by race. Interestingly, most research does not find much of a difference with respect to this demographic characteristic and experience with cyberbullying (Hinduja & Patchin, 2008; Ybarra, Diener-West, & Leaf, 2007a). Consistent with previous findings, we did not find a significant difference in experience with cyberbullying by race in our 2010 data (see Figure 2.6), and in general it appears that youth from all races are subject to online victimization at comparable rates. It is possible that gender, race, and similar demographic characteristics are rendered less relevant in cyberspace since most communication is textual, rather than visual or aural. It is also possible that historically marginalized minority groups may be able to participate, interact, or behave online in ways that are not socially or culturally acceptable in the real world. These same groups may also be emboldened to do so if the perceived likelihood of repercussions is minimized (as tends to be the case in cyberspace due to anonymity, pseudonymity, and physical distance).

Grade

While it is true that people of all ages are potentially subject to online harassment, it appears to be most prominent among middle-school-aged youth. Several studies have found that cyberbullying peaks in middle-school and diminishes in high-school (Cassidy, Jackson, & Brown, 2009; Williams & Guerra, 2007). Other research has identified a steady increase in prevalence rates starting in the middle-school years and continuing through high-school (Wolak et al., 2006). In our most recent study, we found an initial peak in middle-school, followed by a steady increase later in high-school (see Figure 2.7). While there appears to be some leveling off during eighth through tenth grades, especially for offending behaviors, eleventh and twelfth graders report among the highest rates of experiences with cyberbullying (10–12% in the previous 30 days).

Of course, there are a number of other demographic variables that may be related to cyberbullying experiences that have not yet been thoroughly explored in empirical research. For example, it would be interesting to see whether socioeconomic status (SES) is related to cyberbullying since one would theorize

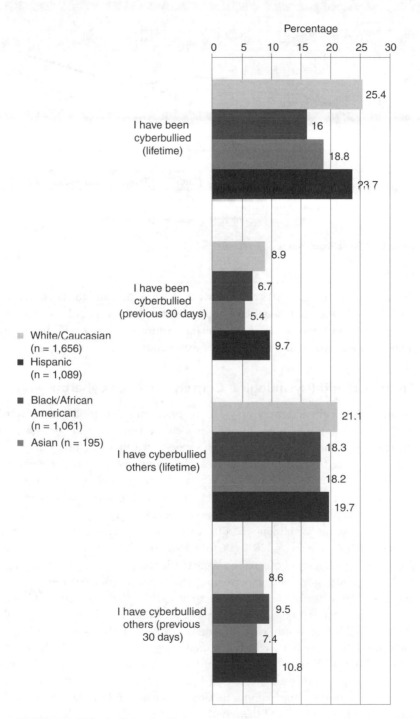

FIGURE 2.6 Cyberbullying by Race.

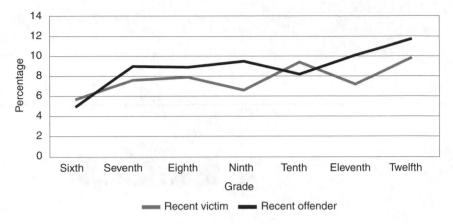

FIGURE 2.7 Cyberbullying by Grade ($n = 4{,}441$).

that families with higher SES would have access to more, and the latest, technology devices. Other individual-level characteristics (such as sexual orientation or personality traits) and social context characteristics (such as family makeup or neighborhood) would also be worthy of exploration.

Emotional and Psychological Consequences of Cyberbullying

While some might like to simply ignore or dismiss cyberbullying because it occurs online and therefore does not explicitly threaten the physical safety of the target, a significant body of research suggests that there are real, offline consequences linked to cyberbullying. It is clear from the available research that experience with cyberbullying (both as a target and as a bully) can have a significant effect on the emotional and psychological well-being of adolescents. For example, many victimized youth report feeling angry, frustrated, sad, and depressed (Patchin & Hinduja, 2006). In our most recent study, 45% of the recent victims were angry, 28% felt frustrated, and 27% were sad. Fewer than 30% said they were not bothered by the experience.

Along similar lines, and underscoring the weighty reality of these negative emotions, Janis Wolak and her colleagues at the Crimes against Children Research Center at the University of New Hampshire (2006:39) found that about one-third of youth who experienced online harassment described the incident as "distressing ... which left them feeling very or extremely upset or afraid." Michele Ybarra (2004:254) similarly found that "three times as many young people who report being harassed [online] also indicate major depressive-like symptomology compared to non-targets." Finally, Allison Dempsey and her colleagues (2009) also found that youth who were cyberbullied had an increase in social anxiety. These findings are particularly relevant because researchers have found that delinquency and interpersonal violence are likely responses that stem from such negative emotions among a population of adolescents who have not fully developed positive coping mechanisms and resiliency skills to deal with stress (such as peer conflict) in a healthy manner (Aseltine, Gore, & Gordon, 2000; Broidy & Agnew, 1997; Mazerolle, Burton, Cullen, Evans, & Payne, 2000; Mazerolle & Piquero, 1998).

In addition to the negative emotions associated with cyberbullying, our own research has also identified a link between cyberbullying and low self-esteem (Patchin & Hinduja, 2010). Students who reported being the victim of cyberbullying scored lower on a well-validated self-esteem measure (Rosenberg, 1965). This specific research endeavor, though, was unable to determine whether experience with cyberbullying *caused* a teenager to have lower self-esteem, or if those with lower self-esteem are more likely to be targeted for cyberbullying. Self-reported cyberbullies also scored lower on the self-esteem scale than those who did not cyberbully others. Perhaps individuals with lower self-esteem are drawn to technology to harass others as a way to make themselves feel better.

We have also found a relationship between cyberbullying and suicidal ideation (Hinduja & Patchin, 2010). Specifically, we found that those who experience bullying or cyberbullying – either as a victim or offender – are significantly more likely to report suicidal thoughts or attempts. This was particularly true for victims of cyberbullying, who were almost twice as likely as non-victims to have attempted suicide. This finding is unfortunately affirmed by several recent examples in the media, where teens have taken their own lives after being harassed online. That said, we are once again unable to conclude from this or any other research of which we are aware that cyberbullying *causes* teen suicide. Teens who have committed suicide have had a number of issues going on in their lives that likely compounded to cause the worst-case scenario. Some had been struggling socially and academically, others were wrestling with low self-confidence or clinical depression, and still others were on psychotropic medications.

It is important to repeat that cyberbullying by itself is unlikely to lead to suicide. Rather, it appears that cyberbullying intensifies the stress and personal torment experienced by youth in their real worlds, and contributes partially but meaningfully – along with other problems – to the tragic end result. Without question, though, we need to take all forms of bullying seriously so that victims do not feel that suicide is the best course of action to stop the pain. This specific research finding provides additional reasons to pay attention to even minor forms of peer conflict and harassment, as they can easily lead to long-term, real-world consequences for those involved.

Cyberbullying and Offline Behaviors

A relatively large body of research has emerged that sheds light on the relationship between cyberbullying and a variety of offline behaviors and problems. For example, studies have found that victims of cyberbullying are at a higher risk for school problems (e.g., suspensions, cheating on tests, skipping school, assaulting peers) and other deviant behaviors (e.g., alcohol consumption, marijuana use, running away from home) (Hinduja & Patchin, 2007, 2008; Ybarra et al., 2007a). Ybarra and Mitchell (2004b), for example, discovered that cyberbullies were more likely to report illicit substance use and participation in delinquent behaviors (see also Hinduja & Patchin, 2008). These researchers also found that cyberbullies were significantly more likely to be bullied offline (defined as "being hit or picked on by another child during the previous year") and to display other problematic behavior (e.g., purposefully damaging property, police contact, physically assaulting a non-family member, and taking something that did not belong to the respondent) within the previous year (Ybarra & Mitchell, 2004a:1310).

Relatedly, cyberbullies also reported lower commitment to school, and increased alcohol and tobacco use compared to youth who did not engage in online harassment. More recent studies by the same authors have identified that cyberbullies are more likely to act aggressively and engage in rule-breaking behavior (Ybarra & Mitchell, 2007), and that cyberbullying victims are eight times as likely as non-victims to report carrying a weapon at school in the last 30 days (Ybarra et al., 2007a). Our own research underscores how online harassment can meaningfully affect the lives of youth in the real world. We were able to identify a moderately strong link between cyberbullying victimization and adolescent problem behaviors, such as recent school difficulties, alcohol and drug use, shoplifting, property damage, physical assaults on peers or adults, and carrying a weapon (Hinduja & Patchin, 2007).

Traditional Bullying and Cyberbullying

A significant body of research also notes the close connection between experiences with online and offline bullying. While it is difficult to determine whether being a bully or being bullied in the real world *causes* similar experiences in cyberspace (or vice versa), a clear correlation between the two spheres of interaction exists. To illustrate, Ybarra and Mitchell (2004b) found that about half of cyberbullying victims and offenders report also experiencing traditional, offline bullying (see also Hinduja & Patchin, 2009). In one of our previous studies (Hinduja & Patchin, 2008), we found that traditional bullies were more than twice as likely to be both the victims and the perpetrators of electronic forms of bullying compared to those who do not engage in traditional bullying. Moreover, we determined that victims of offline bullying were 2.7 times as likely to be the victim of cyberbullying. Based on our data from 2010, 65% of the youth who reported being cyberbullied in the previous month said they were also bullied at school within that same time period. Similarly, 77% of those who admitted to cyberbullying others also admitted to bullying others at school in the previous 30 days. It appears that with this phenomenon, we are often dealing with a population of targets who are doubly susceptible to victimization – both online and in the real world – and a population of aggressors who do not discriminate when it comes to who they mistreat and where.

Victim–Offender Relationship

Internet technologies allow individuals to connect to many people of different backgrounds, cultures, traditions, worldviews, and opinions throughout the world. Nonetheless, we know that most people spend most of their time communicating and interacting with others whom they already know in real life – those in their regular circle of friends and acquaintances. This is particularly true among adolescents. It should come as no surprise, then, that the majority of cyberbullying incidents occur between individuals who have had some relationship with one another. In a recent study, we found that 84% of cyberbullying victims reported that they were bullied by someone they knew (e.g., friend, ex-friend, former romantic partner, someone from school) (Hinduja & Patchin, 2009). Less than 7% of youth in this same study reported being cyberbullied by a stranger. In their own research, Michele Ybarra and her colleagues (2007a) noted that fewer than 13% of youth did not know who the harasser was. Other research has likewise identified that adolescents are more likely to be victimized by people they know (Kowalski & Limber, 2007; Slonje & Smith, 2008), and that most victims know who their bully is (Kowalski & Limber, 2007; McQuade & Sampat, 2008; Slonje & Smith, 2008; Wolak, Mitchell, & Finkelhor, 2007; Ybarra & Mitchell, 2004a). It is also clear that when there is a known relationship between the bully and the target (e.g., classmates at school), the target is most likely to be distressed by the experience (Ybarra et al., 2007a).

Moreover, there is evidence to suggest that many victims of cyberbullying are also bullies themselves. For example, Kowalski and Limber (2007) found that over 30% of youth involved in cyberbullying were both victims and bullies. These "aggressor/targets" were also significantly more likely to report other offline problem behaviors such as delinquency, school violence, and others previously described.

Much of the overlap between victimization and offending may be due to the fact that technology allows those who are cyberbullied to retaliate instantaneously. Indeed, one of the most frequently cited reasons youth provided for engaging in cyberbullying was *revenge*. Sometimes, the revenge stems from peer disagreements online via instant messaging, chatting, or turn-by-turn commenting on Facebook, or relates to specific experiences with cyberbullying (e.g., "she got me very mad and was spreading rumors about me and I don't take things like that, I handle it"). Other times, the instigation originated offline ("they went behind my back and went with my boyfriend"). Either way, many who self-report cyberbullying behaviors believe they are justified in their actions. And because technology is a readily available, always-on tool that enables targets to retaliate with such immediacy, it is not surprising that we see significant overlap between victimization and offending.

Conclusion

As this chapter has illustrated, there have been major steps forward in recent years with regard to the state of knowledge about the nature and extent of cyberbullying. We know that it happens to a significant number of adolescent boys and girls from all racial backgrounds, and that it can have lasting emotional, psychological, and behavioral effects. We know that experiences with online harassment are associated with other problem behaviors offline – including violence against persons and property, substance use, and suicidal thoughts and actions.

Many people theorize that the bullying problem has gotten worse with technology. While kids have been bullying each other for generations, content posted on the Internet and sent around via cell phones and other handheld devices has provided us with a very vivid picture of its nature. This picture has shaken our sensitivities and inflamed our emotions because we are presented in shocking detail with cruel, humiliating, or threatening text, pictures, or video used by some to hurt others. Historically, perhaps many bullying experiences never came to the attention of adults. Or if they did, it would be a filtered, second-hand account of the events. New communications technologies, though, have made the problem more visible, for better *and* worse. This visibility likely contributes to the overall harm caused, but also allows parents, school administrators, and others to see it more precisely.

Moreover, the media attention surrounding high-profile incidents related to cyberbullying over the last few years has likely resulted in more students coming forward about their own experiences. Our research, along with the work of others from the last decade, shows that more teens are now telling adults about their experiences with cyberbullying, which is a step in the right direction. That said, it is difficult to determine when reviewing the available research whether the problems of bullying and cyberbullying have gotten *worse* overall. More research is necessary to better assess the growth trajectory of these types of behaviors.

Despite the strides that have been made in more fully understanding cyberbullying, additional work is necessary on a variety of fronts. We as researchers need to better coordinate our efforts so that our results can more easily be understood by the public, and more strategically integrated into our own prevention and response efforts (and that of others). This means settling on a uniform definition of cyberbullying – or at least clearly specifying how cyberbullying was measured in the work that researchers do (Sourander et al., 2010).

Scholars also need to utilize the most rigorous methods possible to attempt to answer all of the possible research questions, and describe exactly how the study was conducted to enable thorough analysis and replication. Longitudinal, nationally representative samples are not always feasible, but we should never sacrifice rigor for convenience.

In addition, we also need to move toward evaluating formal programs and curriculums that have been designed to address cyberbullying. A handful of initiatives have been developed and give attention to various cyberspace-based dangers with varying amounts of focus, creativity, duration, and intensity. Some of these are well-intentioned but lack research-based insight. Others are created by businesspeople instead of professionals with experience working with at-risk youth, and play into fear mongering and the moral panic perpetuated by the media. Still others are created by those on the front lines, with innovative strategies to implement in schools and communities. It bears mentioning that the Olweus Bullying Prevention Program has demonstrated effectiveness at reducing *traditional bullying* in a variety of school contexts, and has been formally reviewed and evaluated by a number of reputable researchers (Limber, 2009). Similar evaluations *must* be conducted to better understand the processes and outcomes of initiatives focused on addressing cyberbullying.

Even with these concerns, we are hopeful for the future of cyberbullying research. There are a number of studies under way that should illuminate more clearly the contributing factors and consequences, and others will surface as cyberbullying continues to receive national and international attention from the media, legislators, and other state and national leaders. That said, we all need to be mindful that media reports can sometimes misrepresent and slant research findings to serve a certain purpose. Please take the time to read the original research yourself so that you can be personally educated and well-informed about these issues.

Cyberbullying is not occurring at epidemic levels, but neither is it something that should be disregarded or trivialized. The high-profile tragic examples reported in the media certainly grab the headlines and turn heads, but most cases of cyberbullying do not result in suicide. Of course, this doesn't mean that the problem should be dismissed as a rite of passage or an otherwise normal, acceptable part of growing up. There currently exists a respectable and growing body of knowledge regarding the correlates and consequences of cyberbullying, which can supplement the volumes of information published about traditional bullying. How we use this information to direct future studies, prevention and intervention efforts, and policy is the real question. Rigorous research grounded in well-conceived multidisciplinary theory can help us to distill the fact from the fiction, and can help link good ideas to great action plans. As such, it can consequently serve as the strongest foundation of any policy and practice intended to promote healthy participation and interaction among youth online.

TABLE 2.1 A List of Cyberbullying Studies Included in the Systematic Review

Abbreviation	Source	Percent victim	Percent offender
Agatston-1	Agatston, P. W., Kowalski, R., & Limber, S. (2007). Students' perspectives on cyber bullying. *Journal of Adolescent Health, 41*, S59–S60.		
Ang	Ang, R. P., & Goh, H. D. H. (2010). Cyberbullying among adolescents: The role of affective and cognitive empathy and gender. *Child Psychiatry and Human Development, 41*, 387–397.		10.5
Aricak	Aricak, T., Siyahhan, S., Uzunhasanoglu, A., Saribeyoglu, S., Ciplak, S., Yilmaz, N., et al. (2008). Cyberbullying among Turkish adolescents. *CyberPsychology and Behavior, 11*, 253–261.	5.9	35.7
Beran-1	Beran, T., & Li, Q. (2005). Cyber-harassment: A study of a new method for an old behavior. *Journal of Educational Computing Research, 32*, 265–277.	58.0	26.0
Beran-2	Beran, T., & Li, Q. (2007). The relationship between cyberbullying and school bullying. *Journal of Student Wellbeing, 1*, 15–33.	57.4	25.5
Berson	Berson, I. R., Berson, M. J., & Ferron, J. M. (2002). Emerging risks of violence in the digital age: Lessons for educators from an online study of adolescent girls in the United States. *Journal of School Violence, 1*(2), 51–71.	15.0	3.0
Calvete	Calvete, E., Orue, I., Estevez, A., Villardon, L., & Padilla, P. (2010). Cyberbullying in adolescents: Modalities and aggressors' profile. *Computers in Human Behavior, 26*, 1128–1135.		44.1
Dehue	Dehue, F., Bolman, C., & Vollink, T. (2008). Cyberbullying: Youngsters' experiences and parental perception. *CyberPsychology and Behavior, 11*, 217–223.	22.0	16.0
Finn	Finn, J. (2004). A survey of online harassment at a university campus. *Journal of Interpersonal Violence, 19*, 468–483.	10.0	
Fleming	Fleming, M. J., Greentree, S., Cocotti-Muller, D., Elias, K. A., & Morrison, S. (2006). Safety in cyberspace: Adolescents' safety and exposure online. *Youth and Society, 38*(2), 135–154.	36.8	
Hinduja-1	Hinduja, S., & Patchin, J. W. (2007). Offline consequences of online victimization: School violence and delinquency. *Journal of School Violence, 6*(3), 89–112.	34.4	
Hinduja-2	Hinduja, S., & Patchin, J. W. (2008). Cyberbullying: An exploratory analysis of factors related to offending and victimization. *Deviant Behavior, 29*, 129–156.	34.6	

Hirduja-3	Hinduja, S. & Patchin, J. W. (2010). Bullying, cyberbullying, and suicide. *Archives of Suicide Research, 14*, 206–221.	29.4	21.8
Juvonen	Juvonen, J., & Gross, E. F. (2008). Extending the school grounds? Bullying Experiences in cyberspace. *Journal of School Health, 78*, 496–505.	72.0	
Keith	Keith, S., & Martin, M. E. (2005). Cyber-bullying: Creating a culture of respect in a cyber world. *Reclaiming Children and Youth, 13*(4), 224–228.	42.0	
Kowalski	Kowalski, R. M., & Limber, S. P. (2007). Electronic bullying among middle school students. *Journal of Adolescent Health, 41*, S22–S30.	11.1	4.1
Li-1	Li, Q. (2006). Cyberbullying in schools: A research of gender differences. *School Psychology International, 27*, 157–170.	25.0	16.9
Li-2	Li, Q. (2007). Bullying in the new playground: Research into cyberbullying and cybervictimisation. *Australasian Journal of Educational Technology, 23*(4), 435–454.	28.9	17.8
Marsh	Marsh, L., McGee, R., Nada-Raja, S., & Williams, S. (2010). Brief report: Text bullying and traditional bullying among New Zealand secondary school students. *Journal of Adolescence, 33*, 237–240.	11.0	7.0
Mishna	Mishna, F., Cook, C., Gadalla, T., Dacuik, J., & Solomon, S. (2010). Cyber bullying behavior among middle and high school students. *American Journal of Orthopsychiatry, 80*(3), 362–374.	49.5	33.7
Patchin-1	Patchin, J. W., & Hinduja, S. (2006). Bullies move beyond the schoolyard: A preliminary look at cyberbullying. *Youth Violence and Juvenile Justice, 4*(2), 148–169.	29.4	21.8
Patchin-2	Patchin, J. W., & Hinduja, S. (2010a). Cyberbullying and self-esteem. *Journal of School Health, 80*(12), 614–621.	29.4	21.8
Patchin-3	Patchin, J. W., & Hinduja, S. (2010b). Traditional and nontraditional bullying among youth: A test of general strain theory. *Youth & Society.* (forthcoming)		21.5
Raskauskas	Raskauskas, J., & Stoltz, A. D. (2007). Involvement in traditional and electronic bullying among adolescents. *Developmental Psychology, 43*, 564–575.	48.8	21.4
Riebel	Riebel, J., Jager, R. S., & Fischer, U. C. (2009). Cyberbullying in Germany: An exploration of prevalence, overlapping with real life bullying and coping strategies. *Psychology Science Quarterly, 51*(3), 298–314.	5.5	4.0

continued

TABLE 2.1 continued

Abbreviation	Source	Percent victim	Percent offender
Slonje	Slonje, R., & Smith, P. K. (2008). Cyberbullying: Another main type of bullying? *Scandinavian Journal of Psychology, 49,* 147–154.	11.7	10.3
Smith-1	Smith, P. K., Mahdavi, J., Carvahlo, M., Fisher, S., Russell, S., & Tippett, N. (2008a). Cyberbullying: Its nature and impact in secondary school pupils. *The Journal of Child Psychology and Psychiatry, 49,* 376–385.	17.3	25.7
Smith-2	Smith, P. K., Mahdavi, J., Carvahlo, M., Fisher, S., Russell, S., & Tippett, N. (2008b). Cyberbullying: Its nature and impact in secondary school pupils. *The Journal of Child Psychology and Psychiatry, 49,* 376–385.	22.2	
Sourander	Sourander, A., Klomek, B., Ikonen, M., Lindroos, J., Luntamo, T., Koskelainen, M., et al. (2010). Psychosocial risk factors associated with cyberbullying among adolescents. *Archives of General Psychiatry, 67*(7), 720–728.	10.2	12.8
Twyman	Twyman, K., Saylor, C., Taylor, L. A., & Comeaux, C. (2010). Comparing children and adolescents engaged in cyberbullying to matched peers. *Cyberpsychology, Behavior, and Social Networking, 13*(2), 195–199.		
Vandebosch-1	Vandebosch, H., & Van Cleemput, K. (2008). Defining cyberbullying: A qualitative research into the perceptions of youngsters. *CyberPsychology and Behavior, 11,* 499–503.		
Vandebosch-2	Vandebosch, H., & Van Cleemput, K. (2009). Cyberbullying among youngsters: Profiles of bullies and victims. *New Media & Society, 11*(8), 1349–1371.	11.1	18.0
Wang	Wang, J., Iannotti, R. J., & Nansel, T. R. (2009). School bullying among adolescents in the United States: Physical, verbal, relational, and cyber. *Journal of Adolescent Health, 45,* 368–375.	9.8	8.3
Williams	Williams, K. R., & Guerra, N. G. (2007). Prevalence and predictors of internet bullying. *Journal of Adolescent Health, 41,* S14–S21.		9.4

Wolak	Wolak, J., Mitchell, K., & Finkelhor, D. (2007). Does online harassment constitute bullying? An exploration of online harassment by known peers and online-only contacts. *Journal of Adolescent Health, 41*, S51–58.	9.0	
Ybarra-1	Ybarra, M. L. (2004). Linkages between depressive symptomatology and internet harassment among young regular internet users. *CyberPsychology and Behavior, 7*, 247–257.	6.5	
Ybarra-2	Ybarra, M. L., & Mitchell, K. J. (2004a). Youth engaging in online harassment: Associations with caregiver–child relationships, internet use, and personal characteristics. *Journal of Adolescence, 27*, 319–336.	6.5	14.6
Ybarra-3	Ybarra, M. L., & Mitchell, K. J. (2004b). Online aggressor/targets, aggressors, and targets: A comparison of associated youth characteristics. *Journal of Child Psychology and Psychiatry, 45(7)*, 1308–1316.	6.6	14.6
Ybarra-4	Ybarra, M. L., Mitchell, K. J., Wolak, J., & Finkelhor, D. (2006). Examining characteristics and associated distress related to internet harassment: Findings from the second youth internet safety survey. *Pediatrics, 118*, 1169–1177.	8.7	
Ybarra-5	Ybarra, M. L., & Mitchell, K. J. (2007). Prevalence and frequency of internet harassment instigation: Implications for adolescent health. *Journal of Adolescent Health, 41*, 189–195.		29.0
Ybarra-6	Ybarra, M. L., Diener-West, M., & Leaf, P. J. (2007). Examining the overlap in internet harassment and school bullying: Implications for school intervention. *Journal of Adolescent Health, 41*, S42–S50.	34.5	
Ybarra-7	Ybarra, M. L., Espelage, D. L., & Mitchell, K. J. (2007). The co-occurrence of internet harassment and unwanted sexual solicitation victimization and perpetration: Associations with psychosocial indicators. *Journal of Adolescent Health, 41*, S31–S41.	34.0	21.0
Ybarra-8	Ybarra, M. L., Mitchell, K. J., Finkelhor, D., & Wolak, J. (2007). Internet prevention messages: Are we targeting the right online behaviors? *Archives of Pediatrics and Adolescent Medicine, 161*, 138–145.	9.0	

Note

1 Note that some of the articles report findings from the same samples. This is especially true with the work of Michele Ybarra and her colleagues and Hinduja and Patchin. See the list of articles included in this analysis in the appendix to this chapter for more information.

References

Aseltine, R. H., Gore, S., & Gordon, J. (2000). Life stress, anger and anxiety, and delinquency: An empirical test of general strain theory. *Journal of Health and Social Behavior, 41*(3), 256–275.

Broidy, L. M., & Agnew, R. (1997). Gender and crime: A general strain theory perspective. *Journal of Research in Crime and Delinquency, 34*(3), 275–306.

Cassidy, W., Jackson, M., & Brown, K. N. (2009). Sticks and stones can break my bones, but how can pixels hurt me? *School Psychology International, 30*, 383–402.

Dehue, F., Bolman, C., & Vollink, T. (2008). Cyberbullying: Youngsters' experiences and parental perception. *CyberPsychology & Behavior, 11*(2), 217–223.

Dempsey, A. G., Sulkowski, M. L., Nichols, R., & Storch, E. A. (2009). Differences between peer victimization in cyber and physical settings and associated psychosocial adjustment in early adolescence. *Psychology in the Schools, 46*(10), 962–972.

Finkelhor, D., Mitchell, K. J., & Wolak, J. (2000). *Online victimization: A report on the nation's youth.* Retrieved June 30, 2000, from www.ncmec.org/en_US/publications/NC62.pdf.

Hinduja, S., & Patchin, J. W. (2007). Offline consequences of online victimization: School violence and delinquency. *Journal of School Violence, 6*(3), 89–112.

Hinduja, S., & Patchin, J. W. (2008). Cyberbullying: An exploratory analysis of factors related to offending and victimization. *Deviant Behavior, 29*(2), 1–29.

Hinduja, S., & Patchin, J. W. (2009). *Bullying beyond the schoolyard: Preventing and responding to cyberbullying.* Thousand Oaks, CA: Sage Publications (Corwin Press).

Hinduja, S., & Patchin, J. W. (2010). Bullying, cyberbullying, and suicide. *Archives of Suicide Research, 14*(3), 206–221.

Juvonen, J., & Gross, E. F. (2008). Extending the school grounds? Bullying experiences in cyberspace. *Journal of School Health, 78*, 496–505.

Kowalski, R. M., & Limber, S. P. (2007). Electronic bullying among middle school students. *Journal of Adolescent Health, 41*, S22–S30.

Kowalski, R. M., Limber, S. P., & Agatston, P. W. (2008). *Cyber bullying: Bullying in the digital age.* Malden, MA: Blackwell Publishing.

Lenhart, A. (2007). *Cyberbullying and online teens.* Retrieved June 27, 2007, from www.pewinternet.org/pdfs/PIP%20Cyberbullying%20Memo.pdf.

Li, Q. (2007). Bullying in the new playground: Research into cyberbullying and cyber victimisation. *Australasian Journal of Educational Technology, 23*(4), 435–454.

Limber, S. (2009). Research on the Olweus Bullying Prevention Program. *Olweus Bullying Prevention Program.* Retrieved from www.clemson.edu/olweus/Research_OBPP.pdf.

Mazerolle, P., Burton, V., Cullen, F. T., Evans, D., & Payne, G. L. (2000). Strain, anger, and delinquent adaptations: Specifying general strain theory. *Journal of Criminal Justice, 28*, 89–101.

Mazerolle, P., & Piquero, A. (1998). Linking exposure to strain with anger: An investigation of deviant adaptations. *Journal of Criminal Justice, 26*(3), 195–211.

McQuade, S. C., & Sampat, N. (2008). *Survey of Internet and at risk behaviors*. Retrieved January 9, 2011, from www.rit.edu/cast/cms/rrcsei/RIT%20Cyber%20Survey%20Final%20Report.pdf.

Patchin, J. W., & Hinduja, S. (2006). Bullies move beyond the schoolyard: A preliminary look at cyberbullying. *Youth Violence and Juvenile Justice, 4*(2), 148–169.

Patchin, J. W., & Hinduja, S. (2010). Cyberbullying and self-esteem. *Journal of School Health, 80*(12), 616–623.

Rivers, I., & Noret, N. (2007). *The prevalence and correlates of cyberbullying in adolescence: Results of a five-year cohort study*. American Psychological Association.

Rosenberg, M. (1965). *Society and the adolescent self-image*. Princeton, NJ: Princeton University Press.

Simmons, P. (2003). *Odd girl out*. New York: Harcourt.

Slonje, R., & Smith, P. K. (2008). Cyberbullying: another main type of bullying. *Scandinavian Journal of Psychology, 49*, 147–154.

Smith, P., Mahdavi, J., Carvalho, M., & Tippett, N. (2006). An investigation into cyber bullying, its forms, awareness and impact, and the relationship between age and gender in cyber bullying. A report to the Anti-Bullying Alliance. Retrieved January 9, 2011, from www.anti-bullyingalliance.org.uk/downloads/pdf/cyberbullyingreportfinal230106.pdf.

Sourander, A., Klomek, A. B., Ikonen, M., Lindroos, J., Luntamo, T., Koskelainen, M. et al. (2010). Psychosocial risk factors associated with cyberbullying among adolescents: A population-based study. *Archives of General Psychiatry, 67*(7), 720–728.

Williams, K., & Guerra, N. G. (2007). Prevalence and predictors of Internet bullying. *Journal of Adolescent Health, 41*, S14–S21.

Wiseman, R. (2002). *Queen bees and wannabes: Helping your daughter to survive cliques, gossip, boyfriends and other realities of adolescence*. New York: Crown Publishers.

Wolak, J., Mitchell, K., & Finkelhor, D. (2006). *Online victimization of youth: Five years later*. Retrieved October 26, 2007, from www.unh.edu/ccrc/pdf/CV138.pdf.

Wolak, J., Mitchell, K., & Finkelhor, D. (2007). Does online harassment constitute bullying? An exploration of online harassment by known peers and online-only contacts. *Journal of Adolescent Health, 41*, S51–S58.

Ybarra, M. L. (2004). Linkages between depressive symptomatology and Internet harassment among young regular Internet users. *CyberPsychology and Behavior, 7*(2), 247–257.

Ybarra, M. L., Diener-West, M., & Leaf, P. J. (2007a). Examining the overlap in Internet harassment and school bullying: Implications for school intervention. *Journal of Adolescent Health, 41*, S42–S50.

Ybarra, M. L., Espelage, D. L., & Mitchell, K. J. (2007b). The co-occurrence of Internet harassment and unwanted sexual solicitation victimization and perpetration: Associations with psychosocial indicators. *Journal of Adolescent Health, 41*, S31–S41.

Ybarra, M. L., & Mitchell, J. K. (2004a). Online aggressor/targets, aggressors and targets: A comparison of associated youth characteristics. *Journal of Child Psychology and Psychiatry, 45*, 1308–1316.

Ybarra, M. L., & Mitchell, J. K. (2004b). Youth engaging in online harassment: Associations with caregiver–child relationships, Internet use, and personal characteristics. *Journal of Adolescence, 27*(3), 319–336.

Ybarra, M. L., & Mitchell, K. J. (2007). Prevalence and frequency of Internet harassment instigation: Implications for adolescent health. *Journal of Adolescent Health, 41*, 189–195.

3

CYBERBULLYING AND THE LAW

Nancy Willard

When young people get entangled in a cyberbullying incident, school administrators, parents, and law officers will need to be mindful of the legal issues that
might arise. This chapter will address a range of legal issues that are associated
with cyberbullying that may be occurring between young people, in and out of
school. The issues that will be addressed include:

- search and seizure;
- free speech;
- district liability;
- other legal considerations.

Disclaimer. The following material will discuss areas of law where standards have
not been clearly established. This chapter should not be interpreted as providing
legal guidance. It is important for school administrators to consult with the district's legal counsel on these matters.

Search and Seizure

When can a school administrator search the records of students' Internet activity
when using the district's Internet system or a student's personal digital devices
when used at school? A student's personal digital device may be a cell phone or
a personal computer and may be used for personal purposes or in the context of
classroom instruction. Monitoring the records of student Internet use, and
records on student-owned digital devices such as cell phones used personally or
for instructional purposes must be addressed in the context of the legal standards
on "search and seizure." The Fourth Amendment of the US Constitution states:

The right of the people to be secure in their persons, houses, papers, and effects, against unreasonable searches and seizures, shall not be violated, and no Warrants shall issue, but upon probable cause, supported by Oath or affirmation, and particularly describing the place to be searched, and the persons or things to be seized.

This amendment has been interpreted extensively in the context of searches of student personal belongings in school, as well as school lockers and desks, by school administrators or law officers. However, there is limited case law related to electronic communications.

The initial analysis in such cases relates to the expectation of privacy. The question is whether the person has a reasonable expectation of privacy. The constitutional standards relate to expectations of privacy and have established a two-part test that has been enunciated by the US Supreme Court in the case of *Katz* v. *United States* (1967).[1] The first part of the test requires that "[t]he person must have had an actual or subjective expectation of privacy." The second part requires that this subjective "expectation be one that society is prepared to recognize as 'reasonable'." If these two tests are satisfied, then there is said to be a "reasonable expectation of privacy." Under this analysis there would be no expectation of privacy in what a young person has posted in a public area of his or her social networking profile, but there would be an expectation of privacy in what a young person has texted to another person.

For a law officer to conduct a search requires a finding of "probable cause." *Probable cause* means there are sufficient facts or evidence that a reasonable person would believe that a crime had been committed and evidence of the crime will be found in the context of the search. In order to conduct a search, the law officer must obtain a search warrant from a judge; however, there is an exception to this under exigent circumstances – circumstances that justify the need for a more rapid search.

In *New Jersey* v. *T.L.O.* (1985), the Supreme Court considered the application of these search standards in relation to searches conducted in school. This was a case that involved the search of a student who had been found smoking. A subsequent search of her purse revealed drug paraphernalia, marijuana, and documentation of drug sales. In this case, the Supreme Court enunciated the standards for school officials when they conduct a search of a student or student's belongings in the school setting. The standards enunciated were:

- Was the search "justified in its inception"? A search is justified when there are reasonable grounds for suspecting that the search would turn up evidence that the student has violated or is violating either the law or rules of the school.
- Was the search "reasonably related in scope to the circumstances which justified the interference in the first place"? A search is reasonable when "the

measures adopted are reasonably related to the objectives of the search and not excessively intrusive in light of the age and sex of the student and the nature of the infraction".

Thus, when there is an intent by either a school administrator or a law officer who has been called to a school to conduct an individualized search of electronic records or a personal cell phone or laptop of a student, the administrator and law officer must consider the student's expectation of privacy, the justification for the search, and the permissible scope of that search. If a law officer is involved, there will also need to be a determination of when the standard will shift from "reasonable suspicion" to "probable cause." Unfortunately, there is a lack of clarity on when the standard changes, due to a range of standards that have been applied by the courts in different states.

Monitoring and Search of Internet Records on the District's Internet System

Most districts will follow an approach to monitoring and searching student Internet use records using the district's Internet system that resembles the manner in which they handle desk and locker searches. The first consideration is what the expectation of privacy in these records is. Districts likely will take the perspective that students have no expectation of privacy or only a very limited expectation of privacy.

Routine supervision, monitoring, and maintenance utilizing both staff supervision and technical monitoring systems may lead to discovery that a user has violated district policy or the law. For example, as a teacher walks around the room when students are working at computers, the teacher certainly has the authority to look at what the student is doing and also look at the student's history file. Some schools also use remote access viewing systems.

A more individual search can be conducted if there is reasonable suspicion that a user has violated district policy or the law. For example, if there is a report that a student is posting hurtful material on Facebook and this is occurring during the school day, a principal may need to know if the student is bypassing the district's filter to access Facebook to do this. If not, the student may be using a cell phone. Generally, the administrator responsible for the student should authorize the search and the staff who will conduct an individualized search should be the district's technology director or his/her designee. Schools should provide notice to users of the use of technical monitoring because this can assist in deterring inappropriate use.

Districts must exercise care in the degree to which they perceive they have the right to use available technologies to track student use of the district system. A noteworthy case addressing this issue is the situation that emerged in Lower Merton School District in Pennsylvania. This district implemented an electronic monitoring program that used the webcams on computers to capture images of students when they were at home. Several law suits have been filed in this case (Nunnally, 2010).

Personal Use of Digital Devices at School

There is arguably a higher degree of expectation of privacy in students' records that are maintained on their personal digital devices, computers, or cell phones, as long as those records have not been publicly shared, even if the devices are used at school. The extent of privacy of these records is under some debate. However, there are federal and state laws that protect the privacy of electronic communications. The Electronic Communications Privacy Act (1986) provides protections at a federal level. States also have similar state statutes protecting the privacy of electronic communications. Further, considering this in terms of the Katz standards, most people would expect the records on their computer or cell phone to be highly private, which is an expectation that society would consider reasonable.

In 2006 a federal court in Pennsylvania applied the T.L.O. reasonableness standard in the context of a search of cell phone records in the case of *Klump* v. *Nazareth Area School District* (2006). In Klump, a teacher had confiscated a student's cell phone because it was visible in class, which was violation of a school policy that prohibited the display or use of cell phones during instructional time. An administrator then searched through the student's stored text messages, voicemail, and phone number directory. The student filed a suit, asserting that these actions constituted an unreasonable search.

The court determined that the district had reasonable suspicion that the display/use policy was violated, but did not have reasonable suspicion that any other law or policy had been violated. Thus, the confiscation of the cell phone was justified, but the search of the phone records violated the student's Fourth Amendment rights.

Litigation is emerging in other situations of a similar nature. It appears that sometimes when school administrators confiscate a student's cell phone simply because it was used during a time that was inappropriate, they think this gives them the right to look through all of the records. Clearly, this is not the case. Administrators only have the right to search through the records if the circumstances that led to the seizure provides reasonable suspicion that a search of the records will review evidence that the student had violated the law or a policy. That a cell phone was simply used when it should not be used provides no justification to search any records. Being used in class during a test would provide reasonable suspicion that would justify looking at the recent text messages to see if the student was cheating. A credible report that a student has been distributing a nude image would provide reasonable suspicion to justify looking at photos.

In September 2010, the American Civil Liberties Union of Pennsylvania announced that it had settled a lawsuit alleging that the Tunkhannock Area School District (Wyoming County) illegally searched a student's cell phone (ACLU, 2010). The situation in this case related to the concern of students who were charged with "sexting" – sending nude images via cell phones. The images of the students that were stored on cell phones were discovered by school officials, who then brought in local law enforcement. As of this writing, the ACLU-PA is working with the Pennsylvania School Boards Association to draft a policy that will cover searches of students' cell phones. This is an area in which school administrators must obtain guidance from their legal counsel.

However, there are several additional complicating factors. As noted above, one of these is the question of which standard applies when a law officer is called to the school in relation to an intention to search. This is most likely to occur in situations where the cyberbullying also involves the distribution of nude images. Does the reasonable suspicion standard apply, or must the officer establish probable cause and obtain a search warrant or obtain consent to search? Or can the officer search if there are exigent circumstances – an important need to search to protect the safety of someone whose image is being distributed? If a law officer does not have a search warrant, that officer must obtain consent. This consent must be knowing and voluntary – that is, the student must know that he or she has the ability to refuse consent. Can a school administrator search without consent? This is unclear. Should students and their parents be advised of their right to refuse consent to search by a law officer without a search warrant? The standards in this area are unclear, and vary based on interpretations in different states. Obviously, this is an issue that must be addressed with the district's legal counsel.

Because of the lack of clarity in this area, no school staff members, other than the school administrators, should make a decision about the appropriateness of a search. This is simply too complicated an area to seek to communicate these standards to other staff. Staff should only confiscate a device and then give it to the administrator.

Parents should advise their children that if their cell phone or personal computer is taken by a school staff member, they should immediately say, in the presence of witnesses, that they do not give consent for a review of the records on their device without a parent present. This will give parents the opportunity to determine whether the administrator has the justification to search, and make sure the search is within reasonable bounds. If the situation involves a possible criminal matter, such as nude images, parents should insist that the law officer obtain a search warrant. This will ensure that the law officer can establish probable cause.

Student Personal Digital Devices Used in School for Instructional Purposes

There is an emerging trend of schools allowing or even encouraging student use of personal digital devices for instructional activities. For example, students can use cell phones to conduct Internet searches, to read news articles and look up current events, to capture images of a class activity, or to respond to a class-based survey or poll. Concerns associated with such use can range from concerns that a student is not attending to the instructional task to more serious concerns such as student involvement in cyberbullying or other forms of digital abuse.

Thus, in this situation there are clearly legitimate reasons to support the argument that teachers or administrators must have the ability to review the records on these devices. For example, if a teacher is involving students in an instructional activity using cell phones, but suspects that a student is off-task, the teacher will need to be able to look at the records to verify this. But under what circumstances, with what justification, and to what extent should a search be permitted? The standards in this area are particularly unclear.

Likely, it should be justifiable, under routine monitoring, for a teacher to view recent history records on these devices to ensure the student has been on-task during the class session. A more extensive search of records would need to be justified based on a reasonable suspicion. There also may be situations where there is a suspicion that a student is engaging in cyberbullying. A review based on this concern should only be done by an administrator.

Given the non-existence of specific case law in this area, it is recommended that districts formulate a policy that is grounded in the T.L.O. standards and is clearly communicated to all teaching staff, administrators, parents, and students. Possibly, it would be safest to have parents and students sign the document that sets forth the expectations.

Free Speech Standards

US federal courts have recognized that students have rights to free speech and free expression that must be balanced against schools' interest in maintaining an appropriate learning environment and protecting the rights of other students. There have been four Supreme Court cases addressing students' First Amendment speech rights. The cases are: *Tinker* v. *Des Moines Independent Community School District* (1969), *Bethel School District* v. *Fraser* (1986), *Hazelwood School District* v. *Kuhlmeier* (1988), and *Morse* v. *Frederick* (2007).

The landmark case involving student free speech rights is the case of *Tinker* v. *Des Moines Independent Community School District*. Tinker involved a group of high-school students who decided to wear black armbands to school to protest the Vietnam War. The Court began its opinion by stating that students do not "shed their constitutional rights to freedom of speech or expression at the schoolhouse gate." However, the Court acknowledged "the special characteristics of the school environment" by permitting school officials to prohibit student speech if that speech "would substantially interfere with the work of the school or impinge upon the rights of other students," including the right "to be secure." The Court upheld the rights of the students to protest because their protest had not created a substantial disruption or interference. However, this standard has been applied at the lower court level supporting the authority of school officials to respond if student speech has, or there are good reasons to believe it could, cause a substantial disruption or interference.

In Fraser, the Supreme Court found in favor of school officials who disciplined a student whose speech before a school assembly included sexual references. The Court distinguished between the purely political speech in Tinker and the student's vulgarity, and held that school officials had the authority "to prohibit the use of vulgar and offensive terms in public discourse." Justice Brennan's statement in his concurrence in Fraser is particularly relevant to the present discussion. Brennan noted that "if [the] respondent had given the same speech outside of the school environment, he could not have been penalized simply because government officials considered his language to be inappropriate." This last statement is very important from the perspective of school officials in terms of response to student off-campus speech merely on the basis that they find such speech to be vulgar and offensive.

The issue involved in Hazelwood was a principal's decision to remove several articles from publication in the school newspaper. The Court found that the school newspaper was not a public forum because the school did not intend to open the paper to indiscriminate use by the students. Therefore, the Court indicated it was appropriate for school officials to impose educationally related restrictions on student speech. This standard would apply to any material that students might post on a publicly accessible school website, because this material would be presented as if coming from the school.

Morse involved a cryptic, pro-drug use statement, "Bong hits 4 Jesus," on a banner raised by a student across the street from a school during a time when students had been released to watch a parade for the Olympic torch, which was considered to be a school activity. The Court ruled that public school officials may restrict student speech at a school activity when the speech is reasonably viewed as promoting illegal drug use. The Court specifically rejected the arguments of the school district and school leadership organizations that the First Amendment permits school officials to censor any speech that could be considered offensive. Instead, the focus of the Court was on the importance of allowing school officials to respond if the speech is related to student safety concerns.

The importance of the focus on student safety was strengthened by the comments made by Justice Alito in his concurring opinion:

[A]ny argument for altering the usual free speech rules in the public schools cannot rest on a theory of delegation but must instead be based on some special characteristic of the school setting. The special characteristic that is relevant in this case is the threat to the physical safety of students. . . . But due to the special features of the school environment, school officials must have greater authority to intervene before speech leads to violence. And, in most cases, Tinker's "substantial disruption" standard permits school officials to step in before actual violence erupts.

Applying the above standards, it would appear that Hazelwood, Frasier, Tinker, and Morse would all apply to student speech conducted through the district Internet system or transmitted by students using their personal digital devices while on campus. However, when student speech originates off-campus, it appears that only Tinker and Morse would apply.

Numerous cases have held that the Tinker substantial disruption standard applies to student speech that originated off-campus.[2] These cases have involved off-campus student newspapers, as well as cases related to student online speech. Further, intervention by school officials has been upheld in situations where there were reasons to predict the potential of school violence or significant disruption of the delivery of instruction or school operations. For example, schools can prevent students from wearing confederate symbols if there has been a history of racial violence (Mahling, 1996); or they can respond to student off-campus speech that provides directions for how to hack the school's computer (*Boucher* v. *School Board of the School District of Greenfield*, 1998).

All but one of the off-campus online speech cases involved student speech directed at a school staff member. In these cases, the courts have generally held that the school must demonstrate that this speech has or could lead to a substantial disruption in the delivery of instruction or school operations, not merely disruption of a staff member. However, as this chapter is being written, there are two important cases pending before the Third Circuit that directly address this issue (*Layshock* v. *Hermitage School District*, 2006; *Snyder* v. *Blue Mountain School District*, 2010). The resolution to these cases will help to clarify the ability of a school to respond to online speech directed at school staff. The decision may or may not address the issues of a school response to student-on-student speech.

What about speech that has been directed at a student who is now feeling unsafe or is unable to learn or participate in school activities? The most important case addressing this issue is *Saxe* v. *State College Area School District* – a decision that was written by then-Judge Alito whose language from the Supreme Court decision on Morse was quoted above. The State College Area School District's anti-harassment policy had been challenged on the basis that it was overbroad and could impact speech that someone might find merely offensive. The Court did find some of the provisions were overbroad, but in discussing various provisions of the policy, the Court noted:

We agree that the Policy's first prong, which prohibits speech that would "substantially interfer[e] with a student's educational performance," may satisfy the Tinker standard. The primary function of a public school is to educate its students; conduct that substantially interferes with the mission is, almost by definition, disruptive to the school environment.

Note specifically the use of the term "a" student – which leads to the presumption that school officials can respond to student speech that interferes with the rights of any individual student, not the school or school activities. Further, the court appeared to be drawing a close connection between the two prongs of Tinker, essentially stating that speech that substantially interferes with a student's education constitutes a substantial disruption. Further, the Court noted that to establish a significant interference with a student's education requires both the subjective perspective of the student and an objective perspective. This decision is very important from the perspective of cyberbullying, because most often student speech is being directed at one student and the disruption or interference is solely of that student's ability to feel safe at school and learn.

Thus, looking at all of this case law, it appears that school officials have the legal authority to respond to student off-campus online speech in situations where this speech has caused, or there are particular reasons to believe it will cause, a substantial disruption at school or interference with the right of students to be secure. This might involve the threat of violent altercations between students, significant interference with the delivery or instruction, or a situation where, based on both a subjective and objective perspective, there has been a significant interference with the ability of any student to receive an education. However, school officials cannot respond to student off-campus speech merely because they find the speech offensive or contrary to the school's educational mission.

Let's consider this standard from a different perspective. If the off-campus online speech of a student or students has caused, or there are good reasons to believe it could cause, physical violence between students at school, a significant interference in the ability of teachers to teach and students to learn, or is preventing any other student from feeling safe at school and learning or participating in other school activities, would any rational individual argue that school officials should not respond?

From a school administrator perspective, the factors that must be considered include those shown in the following list. School administrators can use this list as a "checklist" when they are considering whether or not their response to a student's off-campus speech is warranted.

- Notice. It is prudent for districts to ensure that their disciplinary policy provides clear notice to students and their parents that the school can and will discipline students for off-campus speech that causes or threatens a substantial disruption at school or interference with rights of any other students to be secure and receive an education.

- School "nexus" or impact. If a school administrator intends to respond, there needs to be a nexus between the off-campus online speech and the school community and an impact that has or is predicted to occur at school. In the context of this, "school" includes school-sponsored field trips, extracurricular activities, sporting events, and transit to and from school or such activities. Therefore, administrators could respond if student speech could lead to violence at a school football game.

- Impact has occurred or is reasonably foreseeable. School administrators must be able to point to a specific and particular reason why they believe a substantial disruption or interference will occur. Timing is an issue. Their formal response needs to be for the purpose of preventing a foreseeable substantial disruption or interference.

- Material and substantial impact. The impact has to be, or it is reasonably foreseeable it will be, significant. This does not include school official anger or annoyance, disapproval of the expression of a controversial opinion, or speech that is contrary to the educational mission of the school. The impact must also be more than simply a situation that requires a school administrator to investigate.

- Disruption of school or interference with rights of students. The speech must have caused, or it is reasonably foreseeable it will cause: significant interference with instructional activities, school activities, or school operations; physical or verbal violent altercations; significant interference with a student's ability to participate in educational programs or school activities. It is necessary to assess the interference with students' education based on the target's subjective response and a reasonable observer perspective. Thus, a school administrator should keep records regarding how the targeted student is responding, so that if there are any questions, an objective third party reviewing this would agree that the student's response was justified.

- Causal relationship. The speech has, or it is reasonably foreseeable it will, be the actual cause of the disruption, not some other factor.

Unfortunately, sometimes when parents contact school officials because their child is being harmed by other students in off-campus postings, the response of the administrator is "off-campus, not my job." The reason for this response is that the legal standards have not been made clear to many administrators. If the off-campus speech is clearly preventing their child from feeling safe at school, parents will need to insist that the school get involved. Parents should make sure that all online material has been provided to the school administrator and that the harmful impact on their child is documented. It will also be very helpful to document or describe all associated on-campus interactions that relate to this online speech. Sometimes, these situations can be very difficult to resolve.

School administrators, parents, and law officers must remember that the primary objective in these situations is to get the harm stopped. While there may be a desire to impose discipline on the student who has caused the harm, decisions in this regard should be measured in response. The reality is that in many cases, simply suspending a student for engaging in bullying or cyberbullying is more likely to continue the harm. This is especially true given that there are many ways in which a vengeful student can anonymously retaliate online. A measured response that is grounded in restorative justice – and directed at ensuring that all students involved get back onto a healthy positive track – is essential.

If you are the parent of a child who has been engaging in cyberbullying, it is important to recognize how your child's reputation, friendships, and even future opportunities are at risk. To put it quite plainly, no one likes bullies. Insist that your child accept responsibility for the harm caused and seeks reparations. It is important to recognize that a child who engages in bullying frequently has significant emotional issues that are not being met. While you should work in collaboration with the school to ensure that your child is held appropriately accountable, also make sure that you seek additional assistance in ensuring that the challenges your child may be facing are also effectively addressed.

Use of Digital Imaging Devices at School

Given that by the secondary school level, the vast majority of students have a personal device that can be used to take pictures or videos of other students or staff, it is necessary for school administrators to establish some standards for this. The ways in which these pictures or videos can be used in a harmful manner include:

- taking and publishing a picture or video in a place where privacy is expected, like in a bathroom;
- taking and publishing a picture or video of a student that is very embarrassing, such as an image of a student whose clothing has become amiss in a manner that others would consider offensive;
- taking and publishing a picture or video of a fight;
- taking and publishing a picture or video of a teacher or other school staff person who is engaged in an embarrassing act – or who could be abusing a student.

Other situations where students may take a picture can be quite healthy, such as a shot of friends together at a concert or athletic event, as long as consent has been obtained and the picture is not published or used in a harmful manner. So trying to prevent this from occurring entirely would be unwarranted, if not impossible. Thus, the focus in a disciplinary policy must be on situations where pictures have been taken and used, likely published, in a way that is harmful.

The general standard for taking pictures of others relates to whether or not taking such a picture violates someone's privacy (Boydston, 2007). Photographers may generally take pictures in a public place. But to take pictures in a private location, consent must be obtained. So is a school a public place or a private place? An argument can be made that a school is a private place, unless the school has been opened for a public activity, such as a concert or assembly. However, it is clearly safest to establish this as an expectation through the use of a written policy to this effect. Therefore, students must obtain consent before taking pictures. Students also should never post online any picture taken at school or send such pictures to someone without their written consent. If a student takes an embarrassing picture and publishes it, a more significant sanction should be imposed.

In the above examples, there are two situations where students should not face discipline for taking pictures or videos – if the pictures or videos are then provided to responsible officials. If a student records a fight or staff abuse and then provides this digital evidence to the school administrator, this can provide an exceptionally effective resource to support appropriate consequences. But if, instead, the student posts this to YouTube, this is not a helpful response. Thus, it is important to advise students to provide these images to an appropriate school official.

Potential District Liability

School officials must also be mindful of potential liability for failure to respond to situations involving cyberbullying. Although there are no cases that have specifically addressed situations involving the harmful impact of the combination of off- and on-campus harmful actions, these situations clearly can result in the creation of a hostile environment at school for the student who has been targeted. If these interactions have created a hostile environment for a student, there appears to be a potential for district liability.

It is important to consider these issues in the context of students' rights to receive an education. As the court said in *Brown* v. *Board of Education* (1954):

> Today, education is perhaps the most important function of state and local governments. Compulsory school attendance laws and the great expenditures for education both demonstrate our recognition of the importance of education to our democratic society. It is required in the performance of our most basic public responsibilities, even service in the armed forces. It is the very foundation of good citizenship. Today it is a principal instrument in awakening the child to cultural values, in preparing him for later professional training, and in helping him to adjust normally to his environment. In these days, it is doubtful that any child may reasonably be expected to succeed in life if he is denied the opportunity of an education.

Schools have a legal responsibility to prevent student-on-student harassment. In *Davis* v. *Monroe County Board of Education* (1999) the Supreme Court allowed a private Title IX damages action against a school board in a case involving student-on-student sexual harassment. To establish a prima facie case of student-on-student harassment, the student must demonstrate each of the following elements:[3]

- The harassment was so severe, pervasive, and objectively offensive that it could be said to deprive the plaintiff of access to the educational opportunities or benefits provided by the school.
- The school had actual knowledge of the harassment.
- The school was deliberately indifferent to the harassment.

Lower courts appear to be increasingly paying attention to the effectiveness of the school response. In situations where the schools had a policy against bullying and did respond in some manner when situations were reported, but neither the policy nor the response were effective in stopping the ongoing harm, the courts have begun to question whether the failure to stop the harm, despite the actions taken, constitute deliberate indifference. For example, in a 2000 case, *Vance* v. *Spencer County Public School District*, the court stated:

> [W]here a school district has knowledge that its remedial action is inadequate and ineffective, it is required to take reasonable action in light of those circumstances to eliminate the behavior. Where a school district has actual knowledge that its efforts to remediate are ineffective, and it continues to use those same methods to no avail, such district has failed to act reasonably in light of the known circumstances.

It also appears that the US Department of Education Office for Civil Rights is getting more active in this area. On October 26, 2010, the Office issued a Dear Colleague letter addressing harassment and bullying. Discriminatory harassment may include harassment or bullying that is grounded in race, disabilities, and gender, including sexual orientation. This document specifically noted:

> ED is issuing the DCL to clarify the relationship between bullying and discriminatory harassment, and to remind schools that by limiting their responses to a specific application of an anti-bullying or other disciplinary policy, they may fail to properly consider whether the student misconduct also results in discrimination in violation of students' federal civil rights.
>
> What are a school's obligations under these anti-discrimination statutes?
>
> - Once a school knows or reasonably should know of possible student-on-student harassment, it must take immediate and appropriate action to investigate or otherwise determine what occurred.

- If harassment has occurred, a school must take prompt and effective steps reasonably calculated to end the harassment, eliminate any hostile environment, and prevent its recurrence. These duties are a school's responsibility even if the misconduct also is covered by an anti-bullying policy and regardless of whether the student makes a complaint, asks the school to take action, or identifies the harassment as a form of discrimination.

Ali, 2010:2

Thus, it is very important that districts have a policy against bullying and cyberbullying that includes reference to the kinds of actions that could also constitute discrimination that is in violation of a student's federal civil rights. This will provide important notice to students and their parents. The aspect of this issue that is most important at this time is a prohibition against bullying and cyberbullying grounded in sexual orientation, which is, unfortunately absent in some district policies.

Effective bullying prevention means more than simply having a policy and responding in some manner when an incident has been reported. It is essential that districts have a comprehensive program to support a positive school climate and prevent and respond to bullying. The most important step a school administrator can take to ensure effectiveness is to routinely engage in follow-up to ensure that whatever actions were taken have been effective.

A recent study of the Youth Voice Project noted that only 42% of students who had been bullied at a moderate, severe, or very severe level actually reported to a school official (Davis & Nixon, 2010). Of significant concern is that in only 34% of these cases did the student report that the situation got better. In 29% of the reported cases, the situation got worse. If a student has reported bullying or cyberbullying to a school administrator and the response by the school only made things worse, that student is unlikely to make a follow-up report. This could lead to school violence or student failure.

Other Legal Considerations

There are additional legal considerations related to cyberbullying that school officials, parents, and law officers should be mindful of. These include potential civil actions that the individual who has been targeted might take against the individual engaging in aggression, as well as potential criminal charges. It is important to understand that in civil or criminal cases involving cyberbullying, the actions have been recorded in electronic form. Therefore, except for the issue of proving identity, which may be somewhat challenging in some cases, all of the evidence is easily available.

Civil Law: Intentional Torts

There are several civil law theories that could provide the basis for a lawsuit for financial damages to be filed against the offending student and his/her parents by the target of the cyberbullying. All of the following legal theories are considered "intentional torts." Intentional torts are offenses that are committed by a person who intends to do an act that results in causing harm – essentially, an intentional "wrongdoing." Civil actions could be filed by a student or a staff member who has been targeted.

In civil litigation, the injured person can request financial damages from the person who has caused harm. In cases where the defendant is a minor, the case is filed against the parents or legal guardians. The financial damages can include loss due to pain and suffering, costs of counseling, and losses related to lowered school performance or school avoidance, and the like. The injured person can also request an injunction, which is a court order requiring certain behavior or the cessation of certain behavior.

The intentional torts that apply to harmful speech and could apply to cyber-bullying include:

- Defamation (or libel) (*§ 558 Restatement of Torts (Second) [1977]*). The cause of action of defamation (or libel) is based on the publication of a false and damaging statement. The statement must identify the target and the statement must harm the target's reputation in the community. It must also be demonstrated that the person committing the defamation intentionally published the statement or failed to prevent its publication when he or she should have acted to prevent such publication. The defense to a claim based on defamation is that the statement is true.

- Invasion of privacy – publicity given to private life (*§ 652D Restatement of Torts (Second) [1977]*). An invasion of privacy claim involves the public disclosure of private facts. Public disclosure of private facts occurs when a person publicly discloses a non-public detail of another person's private life, when the effect would be highly offensive to a reasonable person. Defenses to actions based on invasion of privacy are that the facts are "newsworthy" or that the target gave consent. Activities of young people that are the subject of Internet denigration are unlikely to be newsworthy. Consent must be provided by someone who is considered capable of giving legal consent. Minors are not considered capable of giving legal consent.

- Invasion of privacy – false light (*§ 652E Restatement of Torts (Second) [1977]*). The claim of false light can be made when there has been a publication that was made with actual malice that placed an individual in a false light that would be highly offensive or embarrassing to reasonable persons. Creating and publishing an image that superimposes a person's head onto a nude image would fall under a claim of false light.

- Intentional infliction of emotional distress (§ 46 *Restatement of Torts (Second) [1977]*). The claim of intentional infliction of emotional distress supports a legal action when a person's intentional or reckless actions are outrageous and intolerable and have caused extreme distress. To support this claim, actions must be considered to be very outrageous and regarded as utterly intolerable in a civilized community. Unfortunately, many of the more egregious incidents of cyberbullying would appear to meet this standard.

Sometimes, state laws will support a civil course of action based on acts that are in violation of a state criminal law. For example, in Oregon, ORS 30.198 (Actions for intimidation) provides the basis for a civil action in cases that meet the requirements of the crime of intimidation (ORS 166.155), which is the state's "hate crime" law. The intimidation law prohibits acts that "(i)ntentionally, because of the person's perception of race, color, religion, national origin or sexual orientation of another or of a member of the other's family, subjects such other person to alarm by threatening." ORS 30.198 provides that any person injured by a violation of the intimidation law can file a civil action for damages and injunctive relief. This is in addition to any criminal proceeding and also does not require that any criminal activity even take place. The law specifically provides that parents can be held liable for the actions of their child, in an amount not to exceed $5,000. There is also the potential to recover attorney's fees. Other states or jurisdictions may have similar legal provisions.

Holding Parents Financially Liable

There are two legal approaches under which parents can be held financially responsible for the harm caused by cyberbullying by their child. With the increased attention to cyberbullying and its harms, it is likely that filing a civil action for damages against the parents of the child who has caused harm will become a more attractive option. Thus, parents have yet one other reason to make sure their child does not harm others through cyberbullying.

Under the doctrine of "negligent supervision," parents can be held liable for the intentional or negligent actions of their child. Parents have a duty to use reasonable care to supervise their children when they know, or should know, of the necessity to exercise control or supervision and if they have the ability and the opportunity to exercise such supervision at the time it is needed (§316 *Restatement of Torts (Second) [1965]*). Under the claim of negligent supervision, the parents are considered at fault for their failure to supervise. To prove a claim of negligent supervision in a case of cyberbullying, the injured party will have to show: (1) the parents were aware of or should have been aware of specific instances of harmful conduct; and (2) the parents had the opportunity to control their child.

Parents generally would be considered to have the opportunity to control their child's use of a computer located in their house or their child's use of a cell phone. Whether or not the parents know or should know that their child is engaged in harmful online activities is a question that would be decided differently, depending on the facts of a case. With all of the news coverage about the concerns of cyberbullying, a strong argument can be made that parents certainly should know what their child is doing with respect to harmful electronic activities. School district activities that provide information to parents about these concerns and the need to monitor their children's online activities could also help to establish that parents should have been aware of the potential that their child could engage in cyberbullying and the need to ward against this.

If a child has been identified as having engaged in cyberbullying and the parents are informed that their child is engaging in such behavior by either the school or the parents of the child who is being harmed – and the behavior continues – then the parents clearly know there is a concern and their failure to adequately address the known concern could increase the potential of liability. The increased potential for financial liability could potentially be a "lever" that school officials can use to encourage the proactive involvement of parents in stopping the harm, ensuring the harmful materials are removed to the best degree possible, and that there is no retaliation from their child or his or her friends. Parents whose child is being harmed can also download the material and send it, along with a certified letter demanding that the behavior cease, to the parents of the child(ren) causing the harm, which will also clearly establish notice. An attorney can also send such a letter.

Additionally, states have statutes that are most frequently called "parental liability" statutes. For example, in Oregon, ORS 30.765 (Liability of parents for tort by child) provides that parents can be held liable for damages caused by any tort intentionally or recklessly committed by the child. In most states, there is an upper limit on the financial liability of parents. Under parental liability laws, the focus is on the intentional tort committed by the child. If it is demonstrated that the child committed the tort, the parent can be held liable, regardless of whether or not the parent was negligent – that is, regardless of whether or not the parent knew or should have known that the child was engaged in such activities or had the opportunity to control their child's behavior.

Criminal Laws

Lastly, it is important to discuss how a child's harmful online actions can be so egregious that the child faces the potential of arrest and criminal prosecution. One difficulty in providing general information addressing criminal law is that different jurisdictions and states have different laws that could be applied to cases involving cyberbullying. However, the following are some common kinds of statutes that could be applied to cyberbullying situations:

- Making threats of violence to people or their property. This offense would apply if a young person makes a credible threat to harm someone that is delivered electronically.
- Engaging in extortion or coercion. This kind of statute would address situations where someone was trying to force someone to do something they didn't want to do, like provide a nude image.
- Making obscene or harassing telephone calls. These laws have been updated to include text messaging.
- Harassment or stalking. These statutes frequently are used in situations where a former partner of someone is engaging in continuing actions that place this person in fear.
- Hate or bias-based crimes. These statutes would apply in situations where cyberbullying is based on some type of protected class, such as based on race, religion, or disability, and in some states sexual orientation.
- Creating or disseminating material considered "harmful to minors" or child pornography. This statute might be used in cases that involve cyberbullying linked to sexting – distributing nude images of someone to embarrass and harm that person.
- Sexual exploitation. This statute might also be used in cases involving cyberbullying that is linked with sexting.
- Invasion of privacy or taking a photo image of someone in a place where privacy is expected. This is the criminal level of the invasion of privacy tort.

Conclusion

While the entirety of this chapter has been focused on the legal issues, it must be kept in mind that the end objective of all adults involved – school administrators, parents, and law officers – must be to stop the harm. Yes, the young people who have caused harm must be held accountable, school administrators must take responsibility for protecting the safety and well-being of the children who are under their care, law enforcement must enforce the laws, and parents must both ensure that their child's safety and well-being is protected and that their child does not cause harm to others. However, the overriding objective must be that adults proceed in a manner that will ensure that all the young people who have been involved in a cyberbullying incident, as aggressor or target, remain connected to their school community and feel safe at school and can continue their learning.

BOX 3.1 CHECKLIST FOR POLICY DEVELOPMENT

Cyberbullying

Expand the bullying report and review process to incorporate cyberbullying.

Add cyberbullying to bullying policy with language such as:

Bullying that takes place on or immediately adjacent to school grounds, at any school-sponsored activity, on school-provided transportation or at any official school bus stop, through the use of the district Internet system while on- or off-campus, through the use of a personal digital device on campus, *or off-campus activities that cause or threaten to cause a substantial disruption at school or school activities.*

"Substantial disruption" means:

- significant interference with instructional activities, school activities, or school operations;
- physical or verbal violent altercations between students;
- a hostile environment for any student that impairs that student's ability to participate in educational programs or school activities.

Personal Digital Device Search and Seizure Policy

Develop a policy addressing the search and seizure of students' personal digital devices, including:

- Standards for when a student's cell phone can be seized.
- Standards for when and how a student's cell phone can be searched. Unless there are clearly established exigent circumstances, the parents should be made aware of the situation and be present for, and consent to, any search. This includes the search of a cell phone of a student who is over 18.
- Unless there are clearly established exigent circumstances, if the reasonable suspicion for a search involves possible criminal matter, fully inform the student and parents of their right to refuse consent to a search and to require that the law officer obtain a search warrant.
- Develop a policy that will allow for routine monitoring of certain records on a personal digital device that is used in the classroom for instructional activities that will allow a teacher to check the records to determine if the student is properly engaged in the instructional activities.

Taking Pictures or Videos at School

Develop a policy for students related to taking pictures or videos at school:

- School and school activities should be considered generally not a public place to take pictures or videos of students or staff, except for when the school has been opened up for a public event, such as an assembly, concert, or athletic event.
- Specific permission should be required to take a picture or video of anyone at school or school activities. This would exclude pictures or videos taken as part of an approved school activity or for a specific school-related purpose, student journalism, public events like sporting events or concerts, or recording evidence of an abusive situation.
- Taking a picture or video in a place where privacy is expected, like a locker room or restroom, is generally a violation of state statute and should also be a significant violation of school policy.
- Taking a picture or video of someone at school and publishing it online, unless with permission or as part of an approved student project, should be considered a violation of that person's privacy and school policy.
- Taking a picture or video of someone at school and publishing it online with an intent to harm or harass should be a significant violation of school policy.
- Create means for students to provide pictures or videos of staff or student abuse to appropriate officials.

Extracurricular Activities

Add the "substantial disruption" language to extracurricular activities policy.

- Any on- or off-campus communications with students from other schools, that causes or threatens substantial disruption of any extracurricular activity should lead to restrictions on involvement.

Notes

1. The two-part test was first enunciated in Justice Harlan's concurring opinion and subsequently applied in other Fourth Amendment cases – e.g., *Smith* v. *Maryland*, 442 U.S. 735, 740–741 (1979).
2. These cases are reviewed very extensively in the district court opinion of *Layshock* v. *Hermitage School District*.
3. Based on language from *Soper* v. *Hoben*, 195 F.3d 845, 854 (6th Cir. 1999), citing *Davis*, 526 U.S. at 633.

References

§ 46 Restatement of Torts (Second) [1977].

§ 316 Restatement of Torts (Second) [1965].

§ 558 Restatement of Torts (Second) [1977].

§ 652D Restatement of Torts (Second) [1977].

§ 652E Restatement of Torts (Second) [1977].

ACLU. (2010). *ACLU settles student-cell-phone-search lawsuit with Northeast Pennsylvania school district.* Retrieved from www.aclu.org/free-speech/aclu-settles-student-cell-phone-search-lawsuit-northeast-pennsylvania-school-district.

Ali, R. (2010, October 26). *Dear colleague letter: Harassment and bullying.* Retrieved from www2.ed.gov/about/offices/list/ocr/docs/dcl-factsheet-201010.pdf.

Bethel School District v. *Fraser,* 478 675 (S. Ct. 1986).

Boucher v. *School Board of the School District of Greenfield,* 821 (F.3d (7th Cir. 1998) 1998).

Boydston, J. (2007). Photographers' guide to privacy. *The Reporters Committee for Freedom of the Press.* Retrieved from www.rcfp.org/pullouts/photographers/index.php.

Brown v. *Board of Education of Topeka,* 483 (U.S. 1954).

Davis, S., & Nixon, C. (2010). *Youth voice research project: Victimization & strategies.* Retrieved from www.youthvoiceproject.com/YVPMarch2010.pdf.

Davis v. *Monroe County Board of Education,* 120 1390 (F.3d 1999).

Electronic Communications Privacy Act, 18 U.S.C. § 2510. ECPA Pub. L. 99–508. 100 Stat. 1848. (1986).

Hazelwood School District et al. v. *Kuhlmeier et al.,* 484 260 (S. Ct. 1988).

Katz v. *United States,* 347 (U.S. 1967).

Klump v. *Nazareth Area School District,* 422 622 (E.D. Pa. 2006).

Layshock v. *Hermitage School District,* 412 502 (W.D. Pa. 2006).

Mahling, W. (1996). Secondhand codes: An analysis of the constitutionality of dress codes in the public schools. *Minnesota Law Review, 80,* 715.

Morse v. *Frederick,* 127 2618 (S. Ct. 2007).

New Jersey v. *T. L. O.,* 469 325 (S. Ct. 1985).

Nunnally, D. (2010). Second suit over Lower Merton web cam snooping. *The Philadelphia Inquirer.* Retrieved from www.philly.com/inquirer/front_page/20100728_Second_suit_over_Lower_Merion_webcam_snooping.html.

Saxe v. *State College Area School District,* 240 200, 213 (3d. Cir. 2001).

Snyder v. *Blue Mountain School District* (3d Cir. 2010).

Tinker et al. v. *Des Moines Independent Community School District et al.,* 393 503 (S. Ct. 1969).

Vance v. *Spencer County Public School District,* 253 (F.3d 2000).

4

YOUTH VIEWS ON CYBERBULLYING

Patricia Agatston, Robin Kowalski, and Susan Limber

Although there is a growing body of research about the problem of cyberbully-ing (see especially Chapter 2), there has been relatively little qualitative research highlighting youth's own views of this emerging public health issue. As Mishna, Saini, and Solomon (2009:1222) have noted, qualitative research can assist in "discovering important discourses and nuances of cyberbullying that might be less visible in large scale studies." This chapter provides an overview of youth's perspectives on cyberbullying, drawing largely upon information gleaned from focus groups, individual interviews, and informal discussions with youth.

Prevalence, Seriousness, and Forms of Cyberbullying

Definitions of cyberbullying vary somewhat across studies (Kowalski & Limber, 2007). We have defined cyberbullying as bullying that occurs "through e-mail, instant messaging (IM), in a chatroom, on a Website, or through digital messages or images sent to a cellular phone" (Kowalski, Limber, & Agatston, 2008:1). Because of some conceptual disparities among researchers and because students seem to grapple with understanding when cyberbullying has in fact occurred, focus groups with students are useful vehicles to allow a more in-depth analysis of their conceptual understanding of and experience with cyberbullying.

Toward that end, in 2006, we had the opportunity to conduct focus groups on cyberbullying with middle- and high-school students (Agatston, Kowalski, & Limber, 2007; Kowalski et al., 2008). Approximately 150 male and female stu-dents (aged 12–17) participated in focus groups at two middle-schools and two high-schools in the southeastern United States. Students in these focus groups reported that cyberbullying was a problem that typically occurred outside of school but that often impacted the school day (Agatston et al., 2007). Students shared the following comments when asked by the interviewer if cyberbullying was a problem at their school (Kowalski et al., 2008:124):

- "I think it is a problem but people keep it to themselves." *High-school girl*
- "Yeah, because it happens a lot." *Middle-school boy*
- "Yes. It is a problem specifically at this school." *High-school girl*
- "I remember when I first started using the Internet I didn't know anyone who got cyberbullied, and now it's really bad, it's getting a lot worse as time progresses. I feel like it's getting worse among young people, like young teenagers, like middle school." *High-school girl*
- "Yeah, it's getting a lot worse – even among elementary school kids." *High-school girl*
- "I think it bleeds into the school day." *High-school boy*

At the time that these initial focus groups were held, cyberbullying was a relatively recent phenomenon. Many of the students were unfamiliar with the terminology until the actual behaviors were described to them. Since that time, youth have increased their use of technology significantly. According to the Pew Internet and American Life Project (Lenhart, Purcell, Smith, & Zickuhr, 2010), 93% of teens are online (compared with 87% in 2004), and 63% of these teen Internet users are online every day (compared with 51% in 2004). Three-quarters of teens have a cell phone (up from 71% in 2007), and 69% have a computer (up from 59% in 2007). Nearly three-quarters (73%) of online teens have a social networking page, compared with 55% in 2006. Daily text messaging by teens increased from 38% in February 2008 to 54% in September 2009, a period of just 18 months (Lenhart, Ling, Campbell, & Purcell, 2010). In addition, reports of youth involvement in cyberbullying have received greater media attention as a result of reports of several deaths by suicide attributed at least in part to cyberbullying. (For a review of the relationship between suicidal ideation and cyberbullying, see Hinduja and Patchin (2010).)

During our focus group interviews in 2006, we found that middle- and high-school students were concerned about cyberbullying, but that females were more likely than males to perceive it as a problem (Kowalski et al., 2008). More recently, Mishna et al. (2009) conducted focus groups with students in grades 5–8 who were regular Internet users and found that while the majority of participants agreed that cyberbullying was a problem, males were somewhat more likely than girls to question the seriousness of cyberbullying. These focus group findings support recent research from the Cox Communications Survey (2009), which found that although the majority of teens viewed cyberbullying as a serious problem among today's youth, girls viewed it as more problematic than boys (76% of girls vs. 60% of boys). This survey also noted gender differences in students' beliefs that there should be stricter rules about cyberbullying (80% of girls vs. 70% of boys). The finding that girls appear to be more concerned with cyberbullying than boys is also consistent with research that suggests that girls are more involved in cyberbullying than boys (Hinduja & Patchin, 2009; Kowalski et al., 2008).

Voices from a recent informal discussion group (led by Dr. Agatston) with 30 high-school peer leaders in early 2010 highlight the concerns that teens have about cyberbullying:

- "People can be meaner so much easier now." *High-school girl*
- "It's way more powerful than regular bullying." *High-school girl*
- "It's harder to deal with cyberbullying than face to face bullying. You can stand up to someone face to face and they will back off. If you stand up to someone online it just escalates things." *High-school boy*

While students expressed concerns about cyberbullying in our 2006 focus group, it appeared that both males and females were more inclined to view cyberbullying as a particularly challenging form of bullying during this 2010 discussion group. However, some 13-year-old boys in a recent 2009 focus group (Mishna et al., 2009) did not agree that it was a problem.

- "I don't really think it's that big of a problem. It could become a big problem but I don't think at the moment it's a huge problem."
- "I never thought it was such a big problem. I guess it must be because you are having a focus group about it. But, otherwise, I don't think generally it is that much of a problem." (p. 1226)

However, one of the 13-year-old boys in the focus group indicated that he perceived cyberbullying as rare but that it could still be severe: "When it happens it can be really big and can lead to depression and other things" (Mishna et al., 2009:1226).

Much has been written about the various forms that cyberbullying can take, including harassment, denigration, impersonation, outing and trickery, exclusion/ostracism, and cyber stalking (Kowalski et al., 2008; Willard, 2007). In focus group and interview settings, youth and parents have provided various examples of these forms of cyberbullying that have occurred.

In Dr. Agatston's recent informal high-school discussion group, a student brought up one of the more recent methods for engaging in cyberbullying – the use of applications or websites such as Honesty Box or Formspring.me that allow users to post anonymous questions or comments about the individual who is using the application. As one girl mentioned, "there are apps like Formspring that are easy to use and people use it to say awful things to one another." The students in this discussion group also questioned why someone would use a website or an application that allowed for such posting. This suggests that some youth recognize that using an application or website that allows individuals to post anonymous comments about them may heighten their risk for being cyberbullied.

BOX 4.1 EXAMPLES OF FORMS OF CYBERBULLYING

Harassment

> I've heard of people going into chat rooms and picking on one person.
>
> *High-school girl (Kowalski et al., 2008:125)*

Denigration

> This one girl had the password to her MySpace or Facebook [stolen] and they put up all these bad pictures and stuff on it.
>
> *High-school girl (Kowalski et al., 2008:125)*

Outing and Trickery

Recently one of the authors had a parent share with her that her daughter was pressured to reveal her weight at a sleepover. Her daughter, being overweight, was reluctant to tell. Eventually she yielded to the pressure of the group, only to learn that her supposed friends had posted her weight online for everyone else to see.

Impersonation or Masquerading

> People who know someone's password can pretend to be them and say terrible things to someone else ... my friends would like go and talk to someone that is on my contact list and pretend to be me.
>
> *13-year-old boy (Mishna et al., 2009:1225)*

> Someone knows my friend's screen name and is using it against her. This person is ruining her reputation and says things that my friend would never say.
>
> *(Kowalski et al., 2008:77)*

Cyber Stalking

> I have this one friend and he's gay and his account got hacked and someone put all these real homophobic stuff on there and posted like a mass bulletin of like some guy with his head smashed open like run over by a car. It was really gruesome and disgusting.
>
> *Middle-school girl (Lenhart, 2007:5)*

Another more recent form of cyberbullying involves coercion to obtain nude pictures or videos via webcam, as described by these students:

> [W]hat happened to a friend of mine, they were on MSN and one of the people they thought were friends that was a male, they had told their secrets to and they had friends over and they said, if you don't flash us, we'll tell people your secrets.
>
> *13-year-old girl (Mishna et al., 2009:1225)*

Both quantitative and qualitative data confirm that many youth perceive cyberbullying as a serious problem that can impact them or their peers. In the next section we will look at how youth compare cyberbullying and traditional forms of bullying.

Student Perspectives on the Relationship between Traditional Forms of Bullying and Cyberbullying

Researchers have focused recent attention on the similarities and differences between cyberbullying and more "traditional" forms of bullying. On the one hand, cyberbullying and traditional bullying do share certain key features in common (Kowalski et al., 2008; Raskauskas & Stoltz, 2007). They are both acts of aggression that occur between individuals with different amounts of power. Furthermore, they are both often repeated over time (Dooley, Pyżalski, & Cross, 2009). Kowalski and Limber (2010) found a moderate correlation between traditional bullying and cyberbullying, showing that many children who are involved in more traditional forms of bullying are also involved in cyberbullying. They surveyed 931 middle- and high-school students and, based on their involvement in traditional forms of bullying, classified them as victims, bullies, bully–victims, or uninvolved. Of those students who had not been involved in traditional bullying, 5% indicated that they had cyberbullied others and 9% had been cyberbullied one or more times in the previous couple of months. Thus, youth who are not involved in traditional bullying were unlikely to be involved in cyberbullying. In the same study, the authors found that those who were involved in cyberbullying behaviors had high involvements in traditional bullying. Sixty-one percent of youth who reported that they were cyberbullied reported being traditionally bullied, and 64% of youth who reported that they had been cyberbully-victims (they were cyberbullied and cyberbullied others) reported being traditionally bullied as well. Of those who had not been cyberbullied, 33% reported having been bullied in traditional ways, and 25% said they had bullied others in traditional ways.

Despite the overlap in these phenomena, there are key ways in which cyberbullying and traditional bullying differ from one another. The perpetrator of traditional bullying is a known entity, unlike the perpetrator of cyberbullying, who is often anonymous. Kowalski and Limber (2007) found that almost 50%

of the middle-school-aged victims of cyberbullying in their survey did not know the identity of their perpetrator. Because of their perceived anonymity, individuals may feel empowered to act in ways online that they would not act if their identities were known (Mason, 2008). As a result, anonymity may increase the potential pool of perpetrators of bullying. Individuals who might never engage in face-to-face bullying may engage in cyberbullying.

Students have voiced significant concerns about the anonymity of online aggressors. In their focus groups with fifth through eighth graders, Mishna et al. (2009) noted that most students described cyberbullying as anonymous. As one participant noted, it "can be anyone, even someone next door" (2009:1224). Another painted the image of a cyberbully as one who "hid[es] behind the keyboard" (Mishna et al., 2009). Children reflected on how this anonymity may disinhibit behavior:

> It's easier to say more hurtful comments because sometimes you don't like to say things to people's faces but when you do it for revenge on MSN or something, it might be easier to do because you don't see how much they are hurt by it.
>
> *Mishna et al., 2009:1224*

Although a common theme among the participants in this study was that anonymity was a core feature of cyberbullying, they also expressed some uncertainty about whether the Internet provided actual or simply a "perceived anonymity for the aggressor" (Mishna et al., 2009:1226). Further analysis of the participants' comments demonstrated that the students often discovered the identity of the perpetrator, although this discovery may not occur until some time later, typically from a witness or someone who knew about the incident.

Another difference between traditional bullying and cyberbullying is its pervasiveness in settings that had previously been relatively free from peer bullying. Unlike traditional forms of bullying, which typically occurs during school hours (Nansel, Overpeck, Pilla, Ruan, Simons-Morton, & Scheidt, 2001; Olweus & Limber, 2010), cyberbullying may occur anywhere and anytime (Kowalski et al., 2008). One participant in Mishna et al.'s (2009:1224) focus group coined the term "non-stop bullying" to depict the phenomenon of bullying originating at school but continuing online when the student goes home.

In Dr. Agatston's informal group discussion with high-school students in 2010, the relationships between cyberbullying and traditional bullying were further explored. Students were asked: "Do you see cyberbullying incidents as just happening all of a sudden, or are they reactions to things that happen in ongoing relationships and between peer groups?"

- "It is both."
- "Some start spontaneously online, and some are reactions from relationships among peers at school."

During the group discussion that ensued, a consensus emerged that most cyberbullying incidents occurred in reaction to incidents that happened at school or as part of ongoing relationships between peers. Similar findings emerged from focus groups with middle- and high-school youth that were conducted between February and April 2010 by the Illinois Attorney General's office (Madigan, 2010). Youth in all three high-school focus groups observed that there was overlap between the bullying that originated online or in-person. According to the study's authors, "participants noted that bullying either started online and transitioned into in-person conflict, or vice versa, but there was always overlap" (Madigan, 2010:5).

Even when the bullying primarily takes place off-campus, it is likely to affect peer relationships on-campus if youth attend the same school. This was a common theme voiced by participants in the Illinois study, who indicated that cyberbullying often impacted school life: "Repercussions may not always translate into traditional bullying behaviors, but it is often accompanied by discomfort, dirty looks, self-consciousness, and other forms of intimidation that impact daily life for the students" (Madigan, 2010:4). This has implications for educators, and suggests that we cannot ignore off-campus cyberbullying that is affecting relationships among students.

Middle-school students who were interviewed as part of the Pew Internet and American Life Project (Lenhart, 2007) provide vivid examples of how off-campus cyberbullying can affect students at school.

> I know there's like one of my friends, something happened online and people started saying she said something that she never said, and the next day we came into school and no one would talk to her and everyone's ignoring her. And she had no idea what was going on. Then someone sent her the whole conversation between these two people.
>
> *Middle-school girl (Lenhart, 2007:3)*

> Like I was in a fight with a girl and she printed out our conversation, changed things that I said, and brought it into school so I looked like a terrible person.
>
> *Middle-school girl (Lenhart, 2007:5)*

Cyberbullying can intensify and escalate experiences of on-campus bullying behavior, and on-campus bullying may also occur as an extension of bullying that originated online. Some youth may not differentiate between online and offline bullying – it is just viewed as bullying that is occurring in a variety of venues. As one student in Mishna et al.'s (2009:1224) focus group commented, "[C]yber bullying oh my god! It's another way to bully just over the computer." Fifth through eighth graders in Mishna et al.'s (2009) focus groups viewed cyberbullying and traditional bullying as most similar when they were used to spread rumors and make threats and derogatory comments. But are the effects of online and offline bullying similar?

Effects of Cyberbullying

To understand the effects that cyberbullying can have, one needs only to attend to media accounts of adolescents who have committed suicide in part as a result of being cyberbullied. Although such extreme consequences are rare, other negative physical and psychological effects are not. Similar to the effects of involvement in traditional bullying, involvement in cyberbullying is associated with lower self-esteem, heightened anxiety, heightened depression, a higher number of school absences, aggressive behavior, substance abuse, and greater physical symptomology (Hinduja & Patchin, 2007; Kowalski & Limber, 2010; Patchin & Hinduja, 2010; Wang, Nansel, & Iannotti, 2010). These effects appear to be strongest for cyberbully-victims (those who both engage in cyberbullying and are cyberbullied) – particularly male bully-victims (Kowalski & Limber, 2010). The consequences of cyberbullying also may be magnified relative to those that follow from traditional bullying (Kowalski & Limber, 2010), although additional research is needed to explore these initial findings. One reason may be the anonymity attached to many instances of cyberbullying. Not knowing the identity of the perpetrator may heighten feelings of powerlessness in the target (Vandebosch & Van Cleemput, 2008). Some quotes from focus groups demonstrated students' concerns about how their peers were affected by cyberbullying:

> She would cry a lot. They said mean stuff and she couldn't get it shut down because she didn't have the password. She was really upset for a while.
>
> *High-school female*

> She thought the girls who did it were her friends, so she lost those friendships.
>
> *High-school female*

> The stuff [the cyberbullies] said really affected [her]. I don't know how I could ever say something like that. It was just kind of ridiculous. It made her be mean to people for awhile. [She] didn't want to do anything with anyone; [she] didn't want to deal with it. It affected [her] mood [her] relationships. It affected [her] academically. [She] stopped coming to school for a few days.
>
> *High-school female (Kowalski et al., 2008:125)*

British students surveyed by Smith and colleagues (Slonje & Smith, 2008; Smith, Mahdavi, Carvalho, Fisher, Russell, & Tippett, 2008) perceived some forms of cyberbullying (e.g., picture/video-clip bullying) to be worse than traditional forms of bullying because of the potential audience to whom messages could be distributed and because victims could be identified in videos and pictures (Slonje & Smith, 2008). However, students felt that other forms of cyberbullying had similar or lesser effects than traditional forms of bullying. Similar themes emerged from focus groups conducted by Smith et al. (2008) with students aged 11–16. Many believed that cyberbullying was equally as bad as traditional forms of bullying ("They can both hurt"), some felt that cyberbullying was worse ("You haven't got friends around you to support you"), and several felt it was less harmful ("A text is easier to ignore than something that happened in a specific place" (Smith et al., 2008:381).

Students in focus groups conducted by Mishna (2009) acknowledged the damage that could result from cyberbullying. As one 10 year old boy remarked,

> I think cyberbullying is much worse than verbal bullying because you can't tell anyone about it and then no one really knows what's going on and, the person who's doing it doesn't feel as guilty because they're not saying it to their face.
>
> *Mishna et al., 2009:1224*

Students in these focus groups also noted that because children expect to feel safe from bullying in their own homes, the cyberbullying that they experience at home may feel particularly invasive.

Sharing Passwords and Other Personal Information

Because masquerading as someone else appears to be a common practice, the importance of not sharing passwords can be preventative in nature. Participants in focus groups shared that students frequently provide their passwords to their friends as a "sign of friendship," but that this can lead to impersonation, profiles being altered, and other forms of cyberbullying. One student shared how his friends would masquerade as him in order to bully others. "Some stuff that happens to me is that my friends would like go and talk to someone that is on my contact list and pretend to be me" (Mishna et al., 2009:1225).

One student suggested protecting personal information with the following advice: "Chat rarely and don't give personal information, including gender, race, etc." (Blumenfeld & Cooper, 2010:124). In addition, some youth shared how taking intimate pictures of themselves and sharing with friends or boyfriends can lead to cyberbullying. Once they are posted, "anyone can steal the pictures" (Mishna et al., 2009:1225). Students were also aware that coercion was often part of image sharing. In addition to encouraging youth to avoid posting/sending intimate images, youth would benefit from prevention efforts that discuss how to respond to coercive techniques to share intimate photos.

Do Youth Share their Cyberbullying Experiences with Adults?

Children and youth who are bullied in traditional ways are not inclined to share their experiences with people in positions of authority (Boulton & Underwood, 1992; Olweus & Limber, 2010). The same reluctance to report victimization appears to occur with cyberbullying. Smith et al. (2008) found that victims of cyberbullying (aged 11–16) were significantly less likely than victims of traditional bullying to report the bullying. Kowalski and Limber (2007) found that the most common reaction among middle-school students who had been bullied was to do nothing. Few reported cyberbullying incidents, and, among those who did, most reported the incident to a friend. Among students who were victims of cyberbullying, only 15% reported the incident to their parent. Only 5% reported the incident to a teacher or another adult at school (Kowalski & Limber, 2007). In our 2006 focus groups (Kowalski et al., 2008), concerns emerged about reporting that are unique to cyberbullying. Some youth shared that if they report cyberbullying, the adults in their lives may restrict their access to technology:

> She was afraid if she told her parents she would get restricted, so [she] didn't want to let them know. Or [their parents] would make them quit using [a social networking site].
>
> *Middle-school girl*

> They might be scared to tell their parents, because they might say, "I told you so, I told you not to have that blog."
>
> *High-school girl (Kowalski et al., 2008:92)*

Another reason children and youth say they do not report being cyberbullied has to do with difficulty in identifying the perpetrator. In focus groups conducted in 2007 by Smith et al. (2008), students expressed frustration with the anonymity involved in much cyberbullying: "You can't report it because you don't know who they are" (p. 381). In focus groups conducted by Mishna et al. (2009), participants shared that, in addition to fearing loss of technological privileges, youth are not convinced the adults will have sufficient evidence to address it. As one 13-year-old girl commented, "some people that may be cyber bullied, if they do tell their principals, a lot of people will just lie and be like that wasn't me on MSN. That was someone else" (p. 1225).

Some youth have noted that cyberbullying often is not reported because of a lack of confidence in educators' abilities to appropriately address it. In Dr. Agatston's informal discussion with high-school students, participants reported that they would be reluctant to discuss their cyberbullying with educators, but would be somewhat more likely to share their experiences and concerns with parents. When asked why they were reluctant to share their negative experiences with educators, they responded that doing so often escalated the problem. As one high-school girl noted, "Our administrators did a mediation with some girls who were cyberbullying another student. It just got worse. [The offenders] became more secretive." In addition, students were concerned that they would be blamed for the negative experience if they responded aggressively. Some noted that they did not believe the educators could really help, particularly if there was a lack of clear evidence about what had occurred. Students pointed out that evidence could be altered when it is copied and pasted, and so educators are sometimes reluctant to act.

However, some of the students in an informal high-school discussion group conducted by Dr. Agatston felt that it helped to talk with certain school personnel: "Going to a counselor is better than going to an administrator." Such sentiments lend support to recent research by Davis and Nixon (2010), who found that targets of bullying preferred adult support and advice over other forms of adult intervention that are more punitive in nature. Similarly, participants in the Illinois focus groups noted that punitive consequences such as suspension were not effective and pointed out that suspension might allow a student engaged in cyberbullying to have more time on the computer to engage in aggressive actions (Madigan, 2010).

How Should Adults React?

Youth may be more likely to share their experiences with adults if they have confidence that the adults will keep their confidence and respond in a caring, empathetic, and calm manner. In one study of lesbian, gay, bisexual, and transgendered (LGBT) and allied youth, a teen stressed the importance of treating disclosures confidentially: "Make it easy and confidential to report it" (Blumenfeld & Cooper, 2010:125). Youth in the Illinois focus groups described the following traits that were important in finding an appropriate adult in whom to confide: "trustworthiness; does not exhibit favoritism; shares background or similar youth experiences; and willingness to learn about the circumstances before judging" (Madigan, 2010:7). They also suggested that administrators could designate a staff member who possessed these qualities and have them trained to address cyberbullying and be the primary student contact. A common message from youth in our own focus groups (Kowalski et al., 2008) is "Please don't blame the victim." This advice applies to parents who restrict or cut off their child's technology access, but also to adults who imply that the targeted child is somehow to blame for the cyberbullying.

Many youth wish to try to handle some cyberbullying incidents on their own, as evidenced by this comment from a high-school student in Dr. Agatston's recent informal discussion group: "You should try to resolve it yourself. If that doesn't work you talk to your parents. Schools should be the third/last option." In fact, many of the students believed that they could take steps to address cyberbullying on their own and with their friends' support. However, they were quick to note that a poor response can also escalate the situation. Another student in the discussion group commented about responding aggressively:

> It really does make things worse. And then you have put yourself in a position where you look bad too because you said things back. That's why a lot of kids don't tell because they have said bad things back, and so they can't prove they didn't do anything wrong – that it was one-sided.

A common theme among youth is that ignoring mean or nasty comments posted or sent online is the best reaction: "Basically I just ignored the person and went along with my own civilized business" (Lenhart, 2007). Although such actions may be appropriate in some cases, in more serious instances they may prove ineffective or counter-productive (Kowalski et al., 2008).

Prevention of Cyberbullying: Suggestions from Youth

Elsewhere (Kowalski et al., 2008), we have recommended a number of steps for educators to take to address cyberbullying, including defining cyberbullying adequately, developing clear rules and policies regarding cyberbullying, and encouraging the reporting of cyberbullying, particularly allowing ways for students to anonymously report the problem. We also recommended that schools partner with parents and share resources to help parents feel empowered to deal with social media and the mobile Internet. We stressed spending class time on the issue of bullying and cyberbullying because classroom elements have been found to be a critical strategy for preventing bullying (Olweus, 1993), and this is often the ideal setting to discuss positive bystander behavior when students witness bullying. We stressed that educators and parents work together to educate students on the importance of online "netiquette," protecting their privacy, and monitoring their online reputation. We also noted the importance of training and utilizing student mentors to address these issues in a peer-to-peer model.

Recognizing the importance of youth involvement in effective prevention, we asked teens in our original focus groups (Agatston et al., 2007; Kowalski et al., 2008) and again in our 2010 informal discussion group for their ideas to help prevent cyberbullying. In our original focus groups the teens suggested that parents set age-appropriate guidelines, communicate about appropriate ways to deal with conflict, and monitor their children's use of the Internet – but in a manner that implies supervision, not "snooper vision." In our 2010 discussion group, youth discussed pros and cons of prevention efforts in the school setting. The majority of youth did not feel that a one-time assembly was effective. However, they did agree that hearing real stories about the impact of cyberbullying on others could be effective in preventing cyberbullying behavior: "Students need to hear from real people how it affected them."

Blumenfeld and Cooper's (2010) qualitative study with LGBT and allied youth indicated that the youth participants supported education that informed students and parents about the effects of cyberbullying, as well as consequences for engaging in cyberbullying behavior. One student suggested "hav[ing] sessions for teens in the matter but have it in a fun and active environment" (2010:126). Another teen suggested "rais[ing] awareness by adding it onto student organizations' agendas," while another suggested "hold parent information sessions" (2010:126).

Youth in the Illinois focus groups expressed concerns regarding a need for reports of cyberbullying to be treated confidentially in order to protect against retaliation (Madigan, 2010). In a qualitative study by Stacey (2009), Australian students aged 10–17 suggested improved Internet education for parents and teachers in an effort to reduce fear-based responses by adults.

A theme that has emerged from several studies is the importance of youth leadership and positive bystander behavior to address cyberbullying. Youth in our informal discussion group acknowledged the power of the bystanders to make a difference. As one high-school female noted: "It is easier to be a positive (active) defender through technology than it is face-to-face," suggesting that youth see a role in using technology to support peers who are experiencing cyberbullying. The qualitative data from discussions with LGBT youth (Blumenfeld & Cooper, 2010) stressed the importance of peer leadership to address cyberbullying. According to these teens, youth are more likely to listen to their peers than to adults, whom they perceive as less effective in addressing and resolving cyberbullying: "I don't really think that there is anything that authorities can do about cyberbullying. I think that we as teenagers need to put a stop to it" (Blumenfeld & Cooper, 2010:126). However, while many of the students in this study recommended challenging or confronting the cyberbully, one participant suggested a more reflective approach:

> I think cyberbullying can only be halted if someone is confronted (online or not) about what he/she said and that it is damaging to people. Only with understanding and candor can this be fixed – gentle exposure. Radical reactions are just as bad as the original hateful messages.
>
> *Blumenfeld amd Cooper, 2010:126*

Students in the 2010 informal discussion group were asked to give examples of how they had helped peers work out cyberbullying-related problems. One student shared that he actually did advise the student to talk to his parents about the problem. A female student shared that she "told them not to respond and stay calm." Similar to the participant from the focus group quoted above, students in the discussion group discussed how it is possible to respond if you think through a thoughtful response, but that most kids "just react and make it worse." Thus there is likely a skill set that is needed to confront cyberbullying appropriately, and this could be incorporated into education programs.

Since the suggestions from youth involve multiple strategies to prevent and address cyberbullying, we will likely be well-served when we form partnerships between parents, youth, and educators to address cyberbullying that include educator and parent training, classroom discussion, and peer leadership infused throughout these efforts.

Conclusions

As research on the nature and prevalence of cyberbullying grows, and as efforts are made to more effectively respond to and prevent cyberbullying, researchers and educators alike will benefit from listening to the voices of youth themselves. Quantitative data – such as information gathered through large-scale surveys of youth – is critical, but qualitative data is also important in order to help adults better understand nuances in these data. Asking youth to share their experiences with and attitudes about cyberbullying also signal to youth that we take their views seriously.

References

Agatston, P. W., Kowalski, R., & Limber, S. P. (2007). Students' perspectives on cyber bullying. *Journal of Adolescent Health, 41*, S59–S60.

Blumenfeld, W. J., & Cooper, R. M. (2010). LGBT and allied youth responses to cyber-bullying: Policy implications. *International Journal of Critical Pedagogy, 3*(1), 114–133.

Boulton, M. J., & Underwood, K. (1992). Bully victim problems among middle school children. *British Journal of Educational Psychology of Addictive Behaviors, 62*, 73–87.

Cox Communications. (2009). *Teen online & wireless safety survey*. Retrieved from www. cox.com/takecharge/safe_teens_2009/media/2009_teen_survey_internet_and_wire-less_safety.pdf

Davis, S., & Nixon, C. (2010). *Youth voice research project: Victimization & strategies*. Retrieved from www.youthvoiceproject.com/YVPMarch2010.pdf

Dooley, J. J., Pyżalski, J., & Cross, D. (2009). Cyberbullying versus face-to-face bullying: A theoretical and conceptual review. *Zeitschrift für Psychologie/Journal of Psychology, 217*, 182–188.

Hinduja, S., & Patchin, J. W. (2007). Offline consequences of online victimization: School violence and delinquency. *Journal of School Violence, 6*(3), 89–112.

Hinduja, S., & Patchin, J. W. (2009). *Bullying beyond the schoolyard: Preventing and responding to cyberbullying*. Thousand Oaks, CA: Sage Publications (Corwin Press).

Hinduja, S., & Patchin, J. W. (2010). Bullying, cyberbullying, and suicide. *Archives of Suicide Research, 14*(3), 206–221.

Kowalski, R. M., & Limber, S. P. (2007). Electronic bullying among middle school students. *Journal of Adolescent Health, 41*, S22–S30.

Kowalski, R. M., & Limber, S. P. (2010). *Psychological, physical, and academic correlates of cyberbullying and traditional bullying*. Clemson, SC: Clemson University.

Kowalski, R. M., Limber, S. P., & Agatston, P. W. (2008). *Cyberbullying: Bullying in the digital age*. Malden, MA: Blackwell Publishing.

Lenhart, A. (2007). *Cyberbullying and online teens*. Retrieved June 27, 2007, from www.pewinternet.org/pdfs/PIP%20Cyberbullying%20Memo.pdf.

Lenhart, A., Ling, R., Campbell, S., & Purcell, K. (2010). *Teens and mobile phones*. Retrieved from http://pewinternet.org/~/media//Files/Reports/2010/PIP-Teens-and-Mobile-2010-with-topline.pdf.

Lenhart, A., Purcell, K., Smith, A., & Zickuhr, K. (2010). Social media and young adults. *Pew Internet & American Life Project*. Retrieved from www.pewinternet.org/~/media//Files/Reports/2010/PIP_Social_Media_and_Young_Adults_Report.pdf.

Madigan, L. (2010). *Cyberbullying: A student perspective*. Retrieved from www.illinoisattorneygeneral.gov/children/cyberbullying_focus_report0610.pdf.

Mason, K. L. (2008). Cyberbullying: A preliminary assessment for school personnel. *Psychology in the Schools, 45*, 323–348.

Mishna, F., Saini, M., & Solomon, S. (2009). Ongoing and online: Children and youths' perceptions of cyberbullying. *Children and Youth Services Review, 31*, 1222–1228.

Nansel, T. R., Overpeck, M., Pilla, R. S., Ruan, W. J., Simons-Morton, B., & Scheidt, P. (2001). Bullying behaviors among U.S. youth: Prevalence and association with psychosocial adjustment. *Journal of the American Medical Association, 285*(16), 2094–2100.

Olweus, D. (1993). *Bullying at school*. Oxford: Blackwell.

Olweus, D., & Limber, S. P. (2010, November 5). *What we are learning about bullying*. Paper presented at the International Bullying Prevention Association Annual Conference, Seattle, WA.

Patchin, J. W., & Hinduja, S. (2010). Cyberbullying and self-esteem. *Journal of School Health, 80*(12), 616–623.

Raskauskas, J., & Stoltz, A. D. (2007). Involvement in traditional and electronic bullying among adolescents. *Developmental Psychology, 43*(3), 465–475.

Slonje, R., & Smith, P. K. (2008). Cyberbullying, another main type of bullying. *Scandinavian Journal of Psychology, 49*, 147–154.

Smith, P. K., Mahdavi, J., Carvalho, M., Fisher, S., Russell, S., & Tippett, N. (2008). Cyberbullying: Its nature and impact in secondary school pupils. *Journal of Child Psychology and Psychiatry, 49*(4), 376–385.

Stacey, E. (2009). Research into cyberbullying: Student perspectives on cybersafe learning environments. *Informatics in Education, 8*, 115–130.

Vandebosch, H., & Van Cleemput, K. (2008). Defining cyberbullying: A qualitative research into the perceptions of youngsters. *CyberPsychology & Behavior, 11*, 499–503.

Wang, J., Nansel, T. R., & Iannotti, R. J. (2010). Cyber and traditional bullying: Differential association with depression. *Journal of Adolescent Health, 48*(4), 415–417.

Willard, N. E. (2007). *Cyberbullying and cyberthreats: Responding to the challenge of online social aggression, threats, and distress*. Champaign, IL: Research Press.

5

CYBERBULLYING

How School Counselors Can Help

Russell Sabella

Rapidly evolving technology is affording our world – and certainly our youth – an unprecedented level of power and potential than ever before imagined. Children and adolescents now have in their hands the same tools that, just a few years ago, only large corporations could afford. As Uncle Ben said to Peter Parker (a.k.a. Spider Man), "With great power comes great responsibility." Unfortunately, some children (and adults) are choosing to use technology in irresponsible ways and they are hurting, humiliating, and embarrassing others by cyberbullying.

Cyberbullying involves the use of information and communication technologies (ICT) such as email, cell phone, text messaging, instant messaging, defamatory personal websites, and denigrating online personal polls, to support deliberate, repeated, and hostile behavior by an individual or group, that is intended to harm others (Belsey, 2004; Kowalski, Limber, & Agatston, 2008).

Cyberbullying seems to be even more nefarious than "offline bullying" because the attacks are more intense, frequent, unsuspecting, and difficult to stop. Compared to conventional or traditional bullying, cyberbullies are not restrained by space, pace, or time. They can anonymously attack others at any time, from anywhere, and whenever they want, and they can now do it in front of bigger audiences – much, much bigger. With the power of technology, cyberbullies can be even more cruel than offline bullies because, in addition to words, they can incorporate as part of their attacks a rich array of media, including sounds, altered graphics, text, video, slide shows, polls, and photos (Li, 2007; Sabella, 2008).

Why School Counselors?

School counselors are well-equipped to help children both reduce their risk of cyberbullying and successfully cope with it should a student be subjected to cyberbullying. Professional school counselors serve a vital role in maximizing student success (ASCA, 2009; Bahat, 2008; Lapan, Gysbers, & Kayson, 2007; Stone & Dahir, 2006). Through leadership, advocacy, and collaboration, professional school counselors promote equity and access to rigorous educational experiences for all students. Professional school counselors support a safe learning environment and work to safeguard the human rights of all members of the school community (Sandhu, 2000), and address the needs of all students through culturally relevant prevention and intervention programs that are a part of a comprehensive school counseling program (Bowers & Hatch, 2006; Lee, 2001). School counselors use a variety of approaches to help K–12 students acquire knowledge, skills, and disposi-tions that help them succeed among various domains, including academically, socially, personally, and in their careers. Among the many ways that school counselors provide students with a comprehensive school counseling program, the following approaches can be used to directly impact how a student understands, confronts, experiences, and/or copes with cyberbullying (Bowers & Hatch, 2006):

- *School guidance curriculum.* School counselors provide structured lessons designed to help students achieve the desired competencies and to provide all students with the knowledge and skills appropriate for their developmental level. The school guidance curriculum is delivered throughout the school's overall curriculum and is systematically presented by professional school counselors in collaboration with other professional educators in K–12 classroom and group activities.
- *Responsive services.* Responsive services consist of prevention and/or intervention activities to meet students' immediate and future needs. These needs can be necessitated by events and conditions in students' lives and the school climate and culture, and may require any of the following:
  - individual or group counseling;
  - consultation with parents, teachers, and other educators;
  - referrals to other school support services or community resources;
  - peer helping;
  - psycho-education;
  - intervention and advocacy at the systemic level.

Finally, confronting cyberbullying is an ethical obligation for school counselors. According to Section A.10.e of the American School Counselor Association Ethical Standards for School Counselors (ASCA, 2010:3), school counselors should "Consider the extent to which cyberbullying is interfering with students' educational process and base guidance curriculum and intervention programming for this pervasive and potentially dangerous problem on research-based and best practices."

What Can School Counselors Do?

As leaders and change agents charged with implementing a comprehensive school counseling program, school counselors may confront cyberbullying on at least five fronts. The remainder of this chapter outlines how school counselors can, as part of a collaborative and comprehensive school counseling program, implement policy development, classroom guidance (psycho-education), counseling, consultation and training (e.g., with parents, staff, and others), and peer helper programs.

Policy Development

School districts across the nation and throughout the world are currently working to establish appropriate policies regarding cyberbullying for three primary reasons: (1) to communicate to students the school's belief about the seriousness of cyberbullying; (2) to more effectively and efficiently respond to cyberbullying situations among students; and (3) to be in compliance with new legislation and case law about cyberbullying. Some cyberbullying activities originating or occurring off-campus are causing significant emotional harm to students. When students are emotionally harmed they may present a danger to themselves and to others. According to Willard (2007), if school officials fail to effectively respond to these situations when they are at the "harmful speech" level, there is a risk that they will eventually have to respond at the "school failure," "school violence," or "student suicide" level.

According to the American School Counselor Association's Position Statement about bullying (ASCA, 2005:1), leadership in the form of policy development is an appropriate role and responsibility of the school counselor:

> Professional school counselors collaborate with others to promote safe schools and confront issues threatening school safety. Professional school counselors encourage the development of policies supporting a safe school environment, and they provide leadership to the school by assisting in the design and implementation of school wide violence prevention activities and programs. Comprehensive violence-prevention programs require data-driven decision making, coordination, instruction and evaluation of the program, and they are most effective when incorporated into the academic curriculum by all members of the community.

Every school district is in need of clear, appropriate, and comprehensive policies regarding cyberbullying, both at and away from school (Dyrli, 2005). School counselors can suggest the development of policies as described by Franek (2006), who stated that all forms of cyberspace harassment either during school hours or after school hours should not be tolerated. An anti-cyberbullying policy should include establishing a prevention program and an annual assessment of such a program to determine its effectiveness (Diamanduros, Downs, & Jenkins, 2008). In addition, the following components of an anti-cyberbullying policy have been identified as important for inclusion (see, e.g., FDLE, 2010; Hinduja & Patchin, 2009; Willard, 2010):

- specific definitions of cyberbullying and harassment;
- graduated consequences and remedial actions;
- procedures for reporting, including immunity for reporters;
- procedures for (prompt) investigation;
- a clear statement that students will be disciplined if their behavior (on- or off-campus) is considerably disruptive of the educational environment;
- procedures for educating students, teachers, staff, and parents about cyberbullying;
- procedures for immediate notification to the parents of a victim and protection of the victim;
- procedures for referral to counseling; and
- procedures for publicizing the policy.

Classroom Guidance

School counselors provide psycho-educational training (better known as classroom guidance or school guidance curriculum) as an important part of a comprehensive school counseling program. Classroom guidance that confronts cyberbullying could include recognizing legal and personal consequences of cyberbullying, improving social problem-solving and anger management skills, and increasing the ability to empathize with victims (Hazler, 2006; Limber, Kowalski, & Agatston, 2009). Victims could be offered training in increasing assertiveness skills, developing a more positive self-concept, increasing social skills and reducing social isolation, and practicing positive behaviors that reduce the risk of further victimization (Harris & Petrie, 2003). Hinduja and Patchin (2009) have posted on their website, the Cyberbullying Research Center (www.cyberbullying.us), a one-page document entitled *Top Ten Cyberbullying Prevention Tips for Educators*. It provides specific guidance for those in the school system to reduce the vulnerability of students to online harassment.

Diamanduros et al. (2008) recommend that the following specific components are discussed and emphasized within a comprehensive cyberbullying prevention lesson plan:

- the right for students to feel safe at school and home;
- the definition of cyberbullying;
- how cyberbullying occurs;

- the prevalence of cyberbullying;
- the impact of cyberbullying on the victim and cyberbully;
- understanding that electronic messages can be traced;
- the legal ramifications of cyberbullying;
- the need to take a stand against cyberbullying;
- the need for victims to report incidents of cyberbullying to adults;
- the need for bystanders to protest and report incidents of cyberbullying;
- the need to keep personal information private;
- Internet safety and online etiquette rules; and
- the need to be respectful of others when using the Internet, and being responsible users of technology.

As part of cyberbullying training for students, one school counselor (Sutton, 2009)[1] uses the acronym I DON'T PLAY, which represents:

- IDENTIFY the sender. If a student has another student's identification, it is possible for him or her to pose as that student online. Students using someone else's identification can really hurt other students. Students should have ways to identify a sender, such as asking them questions that only the apparent sender can answer.
- DO not respond to or retaliate for hurtful statements that are directed toward yourself or others. Agreeing with people who make nasty statements about others has a way of getting back to the victims. Retaliating statements are often shared and made public. Words in print are difficult to deny or take back.
- OPENLY communicate with someone in authority or your parents when you receive a damaging message.
- NEVER share your password. When I ask students whether anyone knows their password, they will say no. Unfortunately, when I pursue the matter further, the students admit that they have told only their best friend or a couple of people they trust. Friendship fluctuation is quite common at this age – an old friend can become a new enemy, and then the student's identification is in bad hands.
- THINK carefully before sending messages. Once messages are sent, they cannot be called back.
- PRINT out messages that are threatening. A paper trail will help the authorities stop the harassment.
- LET the provider know about inappropriate conduct.
- ACTIVELY change passwords and screen names on a regular basis. This is easy to do and will help keep students' identification out of the hands of other people.
- YEARN to know more about the Internet and how it can be used. Implement processes and procedures with due diligence, using in-house resources

and a team composed of students and faculty members to teach students about the potential of the Internet. Bring in outside speakers and presenters for help when necessary.

In fact, pieces of cyberbullying and technology safety training learning activities are scattered throughout the Internet among numerous websites. More comprehensive and learning activities and coherent/sequential lesson plans are emerging to help kids with the issues of cyberbullying and Internet safety. Appendix A provides a listing of such helpful resources maintained by the author and also available online at www.guardingkids.com/resources.htm.

Counseling

School counselors provide counseling in a small group or on an individual basis for students expressing difficulties dealing with relationships, personal concerns, or normal developmental tasks (ASCA, 2005). According to Chibarro (2007), school counselors should provide counseling and support to both victims and perpetrators of cyberbullying. Many counseling approaches exist that can be helpful in working with students involved in cyberbullying situations. Following is a brief description of three models that are effective for both victims and perpetrators: solution-focused brief counseling (SFBC), reality therapy (RT), and rational emotive behavioral therapy (REBT). All three models help cyberbullies to take responsibility for their actions and correct their behaviors, while also empowering victims to successfully cope and respond (Davis, 2005).

Solution-Focused Brief Counseling

SFBC is a relatively unique approach that uses a systematic process in which counselors help students to focus on solutions rather than problems. Students are encouraged to think about times when their problems did not exist, how these times contributed to situations that were better, and how to recreate such circumstances in their present situations. The primary focus of this type of counseling model is the student's strengths and abilities rather than their weaknesses. Solutions are derived by the students themselves and therefore not only are they more involved in their success, but the solutions fit their unique lifestyles. Finally, because they find their own solutions that work, often self-confidence is increased. With this emphasis of counseling for solutions rather than problems, counseling is also typically more brief (Murphy, 2008; Sklare, 2005).

For perpetrators, SFBC can assist them in recognizing behaviors and thoughts that are more socially appropriate and effective, especially in response to feelings of anger or vengeance (Young & Holdorf, 2003). For victims, SFBC has great potential for summoning their strengths, skills, thoughts, and dispositions to best cope and effectively respond to their situation (Newsome, 2005).

The SFBC approach is an action-oriented approach to counseling that has five main pathways and six primary techniques. The pathways include:

- *Goaling.* School counselors assist students in focusing on goals – behaviors and/or thoughts – that would demonstrate achievement or success. Goals should meet at least three criteria, which include that they are (1) detailed, (2) in the presence of an action, and (3) in the student's control. For example, a solution-focused goal might be, "When I feel angry, I will write down what I want to say to the person who upset me, check my words for effectiveness, and then ask to speak with the other person"; or "When I feel hurt, I will ask my friend to come with me to talk to the counselor or request mediation."
- *Hypothetical.* This pathway to change helps the student to imagine life as if the goal were already achieved and then to complete small parts of that goal in the present. It is important that the counselor focuses on actions that are in the student's control. So, for example, if a student describes a future where "they are no longer being bullied," the counselor must refocus on a different behavior because this is not in the student's control. They might ask, "And if the bullying were to slow down or stop, how would life be better for you? What will you be able to do or think better as a result?" Then, the counselor begins to help the student do those things even though the bullying may continue (i.e., *act* as if the bullying has stopped). The hypothetical is classically approached in the form of a "miracle question" such as: Suppose tonight, while you are asleep, a miracle happened and your problem was solved. Only you are asleep, so you don't know it happened. Do you wake up and you realize the day is different? What will you notice yourself doing better that tells you that this miracle occurred?
- *Exceptions.* As a detective might do, the counselor helps the student to rediscover clues to solutions by exploring the times that are better. Again, the counselor must stay focused on those actions that, in the past, have led to success. For example, after thinking about it, one student recognized that during her "better days," she coped more effectively with the cyberbullying attacks she experienced by saving the evidence and then reporting to the Youth Resource Officer.
- *Scaling.* The process of scaling has the student decide how they are currently doing on a scale from, say, 0 to 10, with 10 signifying that they are back on track. Then, the student and counselor explore progress already made before finally exploring future progress as it might occur when things get 10% better (Sabella, 2005).
- *The message.* Usually at the end of a meeting, the school counselor will write the student a message that compliments them, summarizes the general wish,

and then assigns specific tasks or goals (see Sutton (2009) for a comprehensive handout about this counseling model).

Among other techniques, the SFBC model also gives the counselor six different techniques for facilitating one or more of the five pathways described above:

- *Reframing* describes the method of changing the way something is said to change direction. The words we use determine our perceptions and our perceptions shape our realities. For example, if a student says, "Some days it's really hard to come to school because of what's happening," the counselor might say, "So, some days you have to muster the strength and courage to come to school."
- *Cheerleading*, also known as *pleasant feedback* or *complimenting*, is just that: letting the student know how their behavior has a positive impact on their lives or the lives of others. For example, "I am very excited that you are standing up for yourself. I'm impressed that you had the courage to report the bully to the principal."
- *Mind mapping* is a process that helps the student to develop a mental image or "map" that helps them to understand how they progressed from bad to better. Mind mapping focuses on the "how," while *goaling* focuses on the "what." One example of mind mapping is pointing out to a student, "So, when you tell yourself that 'this is not the end of the world and that things will get better,' you help yourself to be more calm and rational."
- *Mine fielding*, in a nutshell, helps the student to better understand how they are sometimes able to achieve even in the face of adversity. In this instance, the counselor helps the student to answer the question, "How do you do it even though sometimes it's difficult?" The metaphor is that of a student navigating a mine field of barriers and challenges to progress to a goal or "the other side."
- *Amplifying* uses a three-step process to "amplify" the effects of either exceptions or hypotheticals. In essence, the counselor helps the student to take small steps toward a goal – toward a "tipping point." The three steps include: (1) detailing successful behaviors or thoughts; (2) identifying the positive impact or difference that one's behavior has made on others; and (3) recognizing how the difference in others has positively impacted oneself (Sklare, 2005). In essence, amplifying highlights the positive spiraling effect of success: a student does better, others notice this and experience a positive difference, and that difference comes back to the student and makes his or her life better as well. For instance, a student who was able to confront a cyberbully inspired others to do the same and, as a result, was viewed more as a hero among her peers.
- *Detailing* is when the counselor helps the student describe their goal in more detail. In fact, goals are not fully developed until they are fully observable or, in the case of thoughts, fully describable. Questions that the counselor may

ask to help a student to better detail their goal are: "What will I see you doing that lets me know that you are [*less defined goal such as behaving*]?"; "If I had a video camera and tried to record you being 'good,' what will I see you doing that lets me know it's time to record?"; or "What will your teacher tell me you are doing when she notices you being more on track?"

Reality Therapy

Based on choice theory (Glasser, 1999), RT (Glasser, 1975; Wubbolding, 2000) endeavors to help students reach their goals in ways that are more "right, realistic, and responsible." Students are encouraged to come up with a workable plan that helps them to fulfill their needs without depriving others of the same. Very similar to the SFBC model, RT is an action-oriented approach that holds the focus primarily on the present and future while avoiding a great deal of discussion on symptoms and complaints. RT assumes that people are responsible for their own behavior: human beings – not society, not heredity, not history – determine their own choices. It also assumes that people need not remain victims of external forces, nor do they need to wait for the rest of the world to change before being able to satisfy their own needs (Wubbolding, 2000).

One of the most well-recognized and commonly used frameworks for practicing reality therapy is one developed by Robert Wubbolding (2000), which is known as WDEP. The procedures of RT summarized in the WDEP system define and clarify the student's wants (Wants); examines their total behavior – feelings, effective or ineffective self-talk, and especially their actions (Doing); helps them to conduct a (sometimes uncomfortable) self-evaluation (Evaluation); and culminates in specific and attainable positive plans (Plans) for improvement.

To learn more about choice theory and the WDEP approach to helping students, watch the following videos:

- Bob Hoglund describes the basic reality therapy questioning process that was developed by William Glasser, M.D. (www.youtube.com/watch?v=mZWGzWPqja0).
- Bob Hoglund shares a few of the basic concepts of Dr. William Glasser's Choice Theory (www.youtube.com/watch?v=-2BzLKGx_ng).
- Bob Hoglund demonstrates how asking evaluation questions gets better results than telling people what to do (www.youtube.com/watch?v=_57gtNQfyx4&t=0m44s).
- The schools systems across the United States are learning the "Making Good Choices" phrase, and spreading it along to parents (www.youtube.com/watch?v=FhBwh2Iiw1o).

Rational Emotive Behavioral Therapy

REBT was founded by Dr. Albert Ellis in 1955 as a response to his dissatisfaction with the status quo of counseling approaches at that time (Ellis & Dryden, 2007). The effectiveness of REBT in cyberbullying situations lies in its principles, which include:

- People or events don't make us feel good or bad, it is our perceptions or thoughts (i.e., the meaning) about the situation that determines how we feel.
- Placing dogmatic, unrealistic, illogical demands on ourselves, on others, and on the world is irrational and leads to irrational behaviors/choices
- Irrational thinking produces destructive behaviors and other unhealthy consequences.

> REBT techniques include refuting irrational thinking, helping students to gain perspective from evaluating their situation against other situations considered worse (i.e., catastrophe scaling), playing the "devil's advocate," reframing, using imagery, and "acting as if." Using the principles and techniques of REBT, counselors can help both perpetrators and victims to change the way they think and what they believe about events in their lives to more peacefully interact with others and navigate the painful experience of cyberbullying.

In general, REBT counseling follows the acronym ABCDE. First, the counselor helps the student to describe the precipitating or *a*ctivating event (A), then helps him or her to explore their *b*elief system (B) about the event, and then helps the student to determine the emotional *c*onsequences (C) of both A and B. Next, the counselor begins to *d*ispute (D) the irrational and illogical beliefs that led to the consequence in order to elicit a new cognitive, emotional, and behavioral *e*xperience (E). More reasonable and flexible belief systems can help perpetrators to curb their behaviors and victims to successfully cope with the traumatic experience of cyberbullying. For example, coping with C would be less stressful if more of the targets of cyberbullying switched from telling themselves "I must not be treated this way. It is absolutely horrific that I am treated this way and those who treat me this way should be severely punished," to "What the others are doing to me is awful, although I can handle it; I will work to stop it, and I will know that what they are doing does not reduce my value as a person or diminish my ability to be with others." Similarly, the prevalence of cyberbullying would be diminished if cyberbullies told themselves "I am disappointed in the other person," or "I don't like the other person although nobody said I have to. It's okay. Not every single person that I meet likes me either. That would be unreasonable," instead of "This other person deserves to be cyberbullied" or "How awful and catastrophic it is that this other person does not like me or that they are [doing something that I don't like]. They deserve to be punished and I'm the perfect one to do it."

Consultation and Training with Parents, Staff, and Other Caretakers

Parenting has always been a tough job, although most people today would agree that it is tougher now than ever before. In large part, because of technology, the world is changing, and fast. As parents we want to help our children take advantage of emerging tools in a way that bests advances their development and achievement. And, we want to ward off the trouble that technology can cause our children and families. There are more "bases" to cover in the course of supervising our children. Now, more than ever before, we need to stay focused and goal-oriented in a world that is chaotic and uncertain. We need to help our children realize that "Just because you can, doesn't mean you should." For example, just because you can share information with the rest of the world in the blink of an eye doesn't mean that you should. Granted, much of technology has a high "cool factor" and can be a lot of fun. There are lots of bells and whistles out there, and those bells and whistles can call unwanted attention to ourselves and can easily distract us from other, more important endeavors. We have to make informed choices about the role technology plays in our lives and in the lives of our children. One of the things about effective decision-making is that the quality of the information is key. What you don't know can hurt you (Sabella, 2008).

School counselors can be key players in providing parents, guardians, and school staff with the professional development or training they need to reduce the risk of cyberbullying among students (Bauman, 2011). In collaboration with community groups and the Parent/Teacher Association, school counselors can enhance the way care-takers work with children by providing parents with solutions from both a human/relational and technological perspective (Bradshaw, Sawyer, & O'Brennan, 2007), which is discussed next.

Human/Relational Solutions

According to Sabella (2008), communication and trust are certainly very important processes in the context of overall effective parenting. When it comes to supervising children in a high-tech world, they are critical. There exists a delicate balance between giving children their "space" or freedom to be autonomous and staying informed of what they are doing (i.e., supervising). To know everything that a child is up to is unrealistic and, I think, unnecessary. Yet, at the same time, as parents we fear that, at any given time, our children may be involved in an experience that puts them at risk without our knowledge. To complicate the matter, communication and trust are two relationship behaviors that are interdependent. That is, healthy communication leads to enhanced trust, but without trust, communication is difficult at best. When we engage in meaningful, caring, and positive communication, we experience this as "bonding." Our children believe that we understand them in their world. They perceive us as accepting and non-judgmental. So how can adults facilitate a trusting relationship based on effective and appropriate communication? Tough question! The answer deserves much more space than allotted in this chapter, although I do want to provide you with a few tips that should help.

First, let's take a look at what healthy communication is not. Especially with children, communication is not the same as interrogating, questioning, or lecturing, which typically occur when the interaction stems from anger, suspicion, or guilt. Instead, be curious instead of suspicious. Investigate the situation, not the child. Ask questions that help you learn, not help you to establish a "case against the accused" as if you were in a courtroom. If you find yourself using the word "you" a great deal, it probably sounds like an accusatory lecture, which more often than not is a trust and communication killer. As much as possible, keep the focus on yourself by using the word "I," as in "I am worried about your level of safety when you chat online with others who I don't know," or "I wonder about how having a cell phone might distract you from homework?" Have relaxed conversations about your child's use of technology when the situation is calm, in the absence of any problems or issues. Do this from a point of being interested.

Understanding is also important. Kids need to understand that the rules and precautions their parents establish exist for their own safety and well-being. It would probably be much easier on parents to just let children do whatever they wanted, although this would not be in their best interest. Parents need to explain to children this part of the parenting job in a way they can comprehend and appreciate, using familiar analogies from everyday living. For instance, with middle- and high-school-aged students, you might use helpful analogies such as driving a car – no matter how skilled one is behind the wheel of a vehicle, one must still practice "defensive driving" and following the "rules of the road" to stay safe from the dangers posed by others who use the same roads. In addition, our cars are equipped with safety features such as seat belts, air bags, impact-absorbing structures, and warning sensors. The overall message is, "I trust that you are responsible and cautious, although I still worry about how others can hurt you."

Negotiation

Some things are simply not negotiable, such as letting a child cross a busy street by herself at the age of five. And, even though she may already be a good driver as evidenced by her high scores on the Crazy Taxi™ video game, you would probably just have to say "No" to letting your 9-year-old take the family van out for a spin. What about getting a MySpace or Facebook account? How about watching an R-rated movie or chatting online? Should she really own her own cell phone? These questions are not as clear-cut, as the risks may not be as apparent. Yet, your child may have some logical and compelling arguments for doing these things that may be tough to debate. So when and how much do you give in?

First, don't give in just because it's easier on you. Kids can wear you down, so it's important to stay in the game and continue focusing on what is right. If you are tired, delay your decision until later, catch your breath, and think it over. Make sure your spouse or partner is "on board." If your child continues to engage, explain that asking more than twice is harassment and harassment is against the rules, which results in a default "No" and possible other consequences. If your child is not willing to wait for a decision, then again, the immediate answer is "No." If he is willing to wait for you to "take the decision under advisement," then negotiations may continue.

Second, realize that technology can be very powerful and can extend our capabilities in incredible (and fun) ways. Let's remember, however, that just because you can, doesn't mean you should. It is true that your child can stay in constant touch with his friends and get the latest gossip before it hits the streets. It is also true that he can correspond with almost anyone in the world at any time – but should he? One of the ways to determine this is by evaluating the purpose the technology serves. What is your child trying to achieve by using the technology? For instance, what is the purpose of having a Facebook or similar account? Ask questions such as, "What do you get out of being on Facebook?" If the purpose is legitimate (having fun, for both kids and adults, is legitimate), then ask yourself, "Is this the safest and most secure way to achieve this purpose?" If yes, then okay. If not, then the adult must help the child figure out how he or she can achieve their purpose in a better way. How about calling those would-be Facebook "friends" on the phone? What about a more private email directly to the friend? Could the same goal be achieved by meeting at the park to hang out? Can the child increase his circle of friends in the existing community to enhance his multicultural experience? What about a more secure and personal social network (e.g., www.groupsite.com)?

Perhaps your child's rationale for having a social network account is to avoid being left out (i.e., "Everyone I know has one"). Although not having something that others have can be uncomfortable or unpleasant, it is not fatal. In fact, not having a social network account actually gives your child something the other children do not have – more time and focus for other important things such as studies and family activities. You get the idea … we all need both focus and balance in our lives. The best way to convince kids of this is by actually practicing by providing structure and experiencing the benefits (as opposed to lecturing and trying to convince them that it's true).

What purpose does a cell phone serve for a sixth grader or elementary-school kid? Usually, cell phone ownership can be justified by the peace of mind extended to parents who can communicate with their children almost instantaneously. I agree, this is a wonderful advantage. But what about the potential pitfalls of owning a cell phone, such as cyberbullying, access to inappropriate content, and distraction from school, to name a few? Like all negotiation, this one begs for a compromise, a situation where everyone gets some of what they want but has to give up a little as well. In the case of cell phone ownership, remember, the goal is to give the child the capability of anytime and anywhere communication with a parent/guardian and members of the emergency response community. This can be achieved by a limited-use cell phone, one that restricts the types of outgoing and incoming calls and access to the network (i.e., no data plan).

In the course of negotiations, remember to be objective. Be careful not to allow sensational stories propagated by the media to skew your judgment. Do your homework. Investigate any technology by searching online and asking other parents. There are always both potential benefits and risks to using any technology. Remember that the value of technology is determined by its use, not the technology itself. A hammer can be used to build a house or commit a murder, depending on the user's intentions. Assess the benefits versus the risks, and whenever you deem it safe enough, allow your child their request. Negotiating is never about control or the upper hand. Always keep in mind outcomes that are in the best interest of your child, and also how the negotiations can enhance your relationship.

I would also add that allowing your child to deal with some reasonable risk can be a valuable learning experience and allows her to demonstrate to you that she is responsible. Realize, too, that rarely is anything in technology a black-or-white situation. Instead, technologies can usually be customized, which allows your child to use them with certain conditions. For instance, allowing your child to have a Facebook account only if she shares with you the password or, perhaps at a minimum, "friends" you to allow access to her profile.

Third, as much as possible, focus more on what your child can do instead of what he cannot do. For instance, you may not allow your child to have his own cell phone, but you may allow him to borrow yours now and then for special occasions. You may not allow your daughter to set up a Facebook account, but you may allow her to set up her own blog, which you monitor. Chatting with strangers is a definite no-no, although your kid may chat with school and community buddies using a secure application (e.g., Google Talk, AOL Instant Messenger).

Finally, the same message may be easier to "swallow" if it came from someone else. If you can get another child, a friend, or other respected adult to relay the same message, it may carry more weight than coming from you. The message does not even have to be appreciatively different; it's the messenger that makes the difference. In particular, peers (those perceived to be equal in standing in a particular group) can make a message resonate among their contemporaries.

Teaching Kids the "Rules of the Road"

Increasingly, schools are integrating into their classroom curriculum lessons that give children the knowledge, skills, and attitudes to effectively use technology and to advance their personal and educational goals. Although steady, progress in this area has been slow because technology competencies typically do not have the same priority as the traditional or "core" competencies of science, math, English, and social studies. The focus on high-stakes testing has also made it difficult to make room in the curriculum or otherwise allot instruction time to appropriately give kids the training they need in the area of technology. Parents also have a responsibility to educate their children about safe and responsible use of technology. However, some parents believe that anything related to their child's education should be the responsibility of schools. Such parents have even relinquished some of their parental duties to their children's teachers and other educators. This is inappropriate, unrealistic, and, frankly, unfair. All aspects of a child's education should be the result of a collaborative effort among all stakeholders, including the child.

Early on, our kids need to know that what applies in real life also applies in cyberspace; that online behaviors do have offline consequences. Whether online or offline, sexual predators and kidnappers are good at "grooming" children to trust them and eventually lure them into a dangerous situation. School counselors can help by teaching kids to recognize signs of the grooming process: how predators take their time, determine the child's vulnerabilities, and then say just the right things that appeal to their sense of adventure. Kids must understand how predators reach out to their prey by instilling in them feelings of self-confidence and belongingness – the very same goals that we as parents strive to help our children achieve. In essence, predators became parental figures with a sick motive. Or worse, they use their adult knowledge and resources to gain an unfair (and evil) advantage towards becoming the victim's "boyfriend" or "girlfriend." They follow the same process that rapists follow: first, enter the child's "personal space." They get to know the child and interact in friendly ways to create an illusion of trust. Second, they rely on the child ignoring any improprieties, thus leading to a slippery slope of continued sexual banter and playfulness. Third, when the timing is right, they lure the child into isolation, where there is little chance of others, especially adults, getting in the way. This can begin with a private one-to-one chat in the virtual world, and may end up with a secluded meeting in the real world. Finally, comes the assault. At the same time, however, we must not instill an irrational sense of terror in children by misleading them to believe that all strangers are dangerous. Similarly, we should not allow the issue of online sexual predators to overshadow other issues, such as cyberbullying.

Technological Solutions

Technological solutions to guarding kids are never a replacement for human intervention (Sabella, 2008). We have to help children be knowledgeable about the use (and misuse) of technology, teach them how to make good decisions about how they use technology, and help them to police themselves (and perhaps each other). Technological solutions are an effective complement or backup to how we otherwise prepare and supervise our children.

Teens already exhibit many useful technological tools to respond to cyber-bullies. They commonly block the bully or log-off of their computer temporarily. They also change their screen name or email address (Hinduja & Patchin, 2008). A survey by Juvonen and Gross (2008) also showed that, of the prevention strategies enabled by the technology used, blocking a given screen name was the most common tactic. In the sample, 67% had blocked someone in the past. One-third (33%) had restricted certain screen names from their buddy list. About one-quarter (26%) of the sample had switched a screen name and sent a warning (25%) to someone to prevent cyberbullying.

Blocking/Filtering Software

Software solutions to preventing access to harmful or offensive material falls into two general classes: solutions that (1) block access to certain websites deemed to contain objectionable material (i.e., blocking); and (2) those that remove certain words or phrases in the content being downloaded (filtering). Neither of these approaches is foolproof. Remember, the Web is a dynamic place with content being added, changed, and deleted from all over the world during every second of every day. No person, organization, or robot could ever document all websites that contain objectionable material at any given moment. In trying, some legitimate websites are also screened-out based on the occurrence of certain words or phrases that could very well be written in a daily newspaper or even the Bible. Many types of blocking, filtering (and monitoring) software exist (e.g., see http://getparentalcontrols.org). Here are a few that have been well reviewed and received:

- K9 Web Protection is a free Internet filtering and parental control solution for your home Windows or Mac computer (www1.k9webprotection.com).
- Cybersitter is a feature-rich blocking, filtering, monitoring, and Internet scheduling suite (www.cybersitter.com).
- Net Nanny is a feature-rich blocking, filtering, monitoring, and Internet-scheduling suite which is available for Macintosh, Windows, and some mobile phones (www.netnanny.com).
- Norton™ Online Family allows you to see your kids' online activities at a glance (https://onlinefamily.norton.com/familysafety).

- OpenDNS provides families with blocking, filtering, protection, reporting, and more on one computer or across the entire home network (www. opendns.com).
- Operating system safety features. Microsoft Windows and Macintosh OS X both have robust parental controls as part of their operating systems.

Monitoring Online Activity

Parents have to decide for themselves what the appropriate balance should be between a child's right to privacy and their need to monitor online activity. Factors to consider in making such decisions include the developmental age of the child and the child's track record of responsible decision-making. Parents may use one or more monitoring techniques as part of a continuum of methods that ranges from low monitoring (reviewing a browser history) to high monitoring (e.g., key logger).

- *Reviewing Web browser history.* Each Web browser, such as Explorer, Safari, Chrome, and Firefox, keeps track of a user's history, which can easily be accessed (but also deleted).
- *Google Alerts.* With a free Google account, a parent can use Google Alerts, which allows a parent to enter a phrase, email address, username, real name, or other keywords into the alerts system. Google then provides email alerts when it finds anything online that matches your search terms (www. google.com/alerts).
- *Facebook monitoring.* In addition to the options of accessing a child's Facebook account using his or her password or monitoring his or her activity as a "friend," a parent may also use websites designed to search public Facebook updates using any search term. Several such websites exist, including http://youropenbook.org, http://zesty.ca/facebook, and www.booshaka.com.
- *Automated services.* Some parents may elect to pay for a service to automatically monitor one's Web content that has the potential of hurting or damaging a child's reputation. One such site is www.reputationdefender.com.

Peer Helper Programs

Students are truly essential in the effort to reduce the risk of cyberbullying among their peers, both perpetrators and victims. Ultimately, they alone are in control of their own behavior and must decide to take a stand against cyberbullying. They must "think before they click" and always act as if someone is watching. Also, children stand to be a considerable force in risk-reduction training. Because of their peer status, the messages that have to be communicated to promote understanding of cyberbullying among youth can be delivered more impactfully by peers as part of a peer helper program.

One way school counselors can help students to receive timely support and reduce the overall risk of cyberbullying is to mobilize student resources through peer helper programs. Young people can be trained to work with students who are "at risk," as well as with those who are experiencing typical childhood problems and concerns. They can play important roles in both intervention and prevention programs. Peer helper programs are yet another way that school counselors can help students reach a higher level of maturity and accept responsibility (ASCA, 2008).

Other advantages of using trained peer helpers to facilitate outreach and in educational functions are known. For instance, according to one study by Myrick, Highland, and Sabella (1995), using peer helpers in general included the following advantages:

- Students communicate more effectively and are more positive with each other. They learn more about how to be sensitive to others and how to stand up for their own rights.
- There are more student or peer helpers in the school, which means that interventions can be delivered to a wider audience (i.e., more students are involved).
- Peer helpers can be part of a highly visible, cyberbullying risk-reduction program that brings positive public relations to the school's counseling program.
- Peer helpers can help evaluate the lesson plans, content, or learning activities to provide insight into their effectiveness.
- Students are less likely to resist learning something when they perceive that their help is valued and wanted.
- Peer helpers have the opportunity to act as models for other students. They can help build positive school environments that make school a better place for everyone, including teachers and counselors.

One teacher eloquently described how her students assisted her in developing lesson plans, materials, and ultimately teaching other students about cyberbullying and other technology-related issues:

> When I began implementing this curriculum the next fall, I noticed how much the 8th graders knew and were eager to impart to one another – with almost desperate urgency. As if riding a roller-coaster, students relayed stories and advice to one another, hitting highs and lows at breakneck speed. They were experts in some aspects of online interaction and risks but complete novices in others. I realized that their knowledge and thirst to exchange information provided a rare opportunity. So I charged my 8th grade students with the job of teaching my 6th graders.... As you might expect, every 8th grade student rose to the occasion, even the most

traditionally reluctant participants. Their talks, materials, and activities kept the younger students fully engaged. They asked questions and got their peers to think and reflect, sometimes with creative tactics.

Mustacchi, 2009:80

Summary and Conclusion

School counselors are leaders and advocates who are responsible for developing a comprehensive school counseling program that helps children meet competencies among three domains: academic, personal/social, and career domains. Comprehensive programs are developed, maintained, delivered, and enhanced via a collaborate effort among all stakeholders, including parents, teachers, administrators, students, and community members. Cyberbullying, from both perpetrator and victim perspectives, is antithetical to student achievement in all three of these domains. Because of this mission and the unique training that they receive, school counselors can appropriately take the lead in a five-point approach to confronting cyberbullying: policy development, classroom guidance (psycho-education), counseling, consultation and training (e.g., with parents, staff, and others), and peer helper programs.

Note

1 Reproduced by permission of the author. Also available online at www.guardingkids. com/resources.htm.

References

ASCA. (2005). The professional school counselor and bullying, harassment and violence-prevention programs: Supporting safe and respectful schools (Position Statement). *American School Counselor Association*. Retrieved from www.schoolcounselor.org/content.asp?pl=325&sl=127&contentid=178.

ASCA. (2008). The professional school counselor and peer helping. (Position Statement). *American School Counselor Association*. Retrieved from http://asca2.timberlakepublishing.com//files/PS_PeerHelping.pdf.

ASCA. (2009). The role of the professional school counselor. *American School Counselor Association*. Retrieved from www.schoolcounselor.org/content.asp?pl=325&sl=133&contentid=240.

ASCA. (2010). Ethical standards for school counselors. *American School Counselor Association*. Retrieved from www.schoolcounselor.org/content.asp?contentid=136.

Bahat, C. S. (2008). Cyber bullying: Overview and strategies for school counselors, guidance officers, and all school personnel. *Australian Journal of Guidance & Counselling, 18*(1), 53–66.

Bauman, S. (2011). *Cyberbullying: What counselors need to know.* Alexandria, VA: American Counseling Association.

Belsey, B. (2004). Always on, always aware. Retrieved from www.cyberbullying.ca/pdf/Cyberbullying_Information.pdf.

Bowers, J., & Hatch, T. (2006). *The ASCA national model: A framework for school counseling programs* (2nd ed.). Alexandria, VA: American School Counselor Association.

Bradshaw, C., Sawyer, A., & O'Brennan, L. (2007). Bullying and peer victimization at school: Perceptual differences between students and school staff. *School Psychology Review, 36*(3), 361–383.

Chibarro, J. S. (2007). School counselors and the cyberbully: Interventions and implications. *Professional School Counseling, 11*(1), 65–68.

Davis, S. (2005). *Working with young people who bully others: Tips for mental health professionals.* Retrieved from www.stopbullyingnow.com/Counseling%20young%20people%20who%20bully%20others.pdf.

Diamanduros, T., Downs, E., & Jenkins, S. J. (2008). The role of school psychologists in the assessment, prevention, and intervention of cyber bullying. *Psychology in the Schools, 15*(0), 693–701.

Dyrli, O. (2005). Cyberbullying: Online bullying affects every school district. *District Administration, 41*(9), 63.

Ellis, A., & Dryden, W. (2007). *The practice of rational emotive behavior therapy* (2nd ed.). New York, NY: Springer Publishing Company.

FDLE. (2010). Criteria for district bullying and harassment policies. *Florida Department of Education.* Retrieved from www.fldoe.org/safeschools/bullying_prevention.asp.

Franek, M. (2006). Foiling cyberbullies in the new wild west. *Educational Leadership, 63*(4), 39–43.

Glasser, W. (1975). *Reality therapy: A new approach to psychiatry.* New York, NY: Harper Collins.

Glasser, W. (1999). *Choice theory: A new psychology of personal freedom.* New York, NY: HarperCollins, Inc.

Harris, S. L., & Petrie, G. F. (2003). *Bullying: The bullies, the victims, the bystanders.* Lanham, MD: Scarecrow Press.

Hazler, R. J. (2006, March 18). *Essential techniques for successful intervention and prevention of bullying,* Carrollton, GA.

Hinduja, S., & Patchin, J. W. (2008). Personal information of adolescents on the Internet: A quantitative content analysis of MySpace. *Journal of Adolescence, 31*(1), 125–146.

Hinduja, S., & Patchin, J. W. (2009). *Bullying beyond the schoolyard: Preventing and responding to cyberbullying.* Thousand Oaks, CA: Sage Publications (Corwin Press).

Juvonen, J., & Gross, E. F. (2008). Extending the school grounds? Bullying experiences in cyberspace. *Journal of School Health, 78,* 496–505.

Kowalski, R. M., Limber, S. P., & Agatston, P. W. (2008). *Cyber bullying: Bullying in the digital age.* Malden, MA: Blackwell Publishing.

Lapan, R. T., Gysbers, N. C., & Kayson, M. A. (2007). Missouri school counselors benefit all students. *Missouri Department of Elementary and Secondary Education.* Retrieved from http://dese.mo.gov/divcareered/Guidance/SchoolCounselorsStudy_Jan2007.pdf.

Lee, C. (2001). Culturally responsive school counselors and programs: Addressing the needs of all students. *Professional School Counseling, 4*(4), 163–171.

Li, Q. (2007). New bottle but old wine: A research on cyberbullying in schools. *Computers and Human Behavior, 23*(4), 1777–1791.

Limber, S. P., Kowalski, R. M., & Agatston, P. W. (2009). *Cyberbullying: A prevention curriculum for Grades 6–12.* Center City, MN: Hazelden.

Murphy, J. J. (2008). *Solution-focused counseling in schools* (2nd ed.). Alexandria, VA: American Counseling Association.

Mustacchi, J. (2009). R U safe? *Educational Leadership, 66*(6), 78–82.

Myrick, R. D., Highland, W. H., & Sabella, R. A. (1995). Peer helpers and perceived effectiveness. *Elementary School Guidance and Counseling, 29*(4), 278–288.

Newsome, S. W. (2005). The impact of solution-focused brief therapy with at-risk junior high school students. *Children and Schools, 27*(2), 83–90.

Sabella, R. A. (2005). Scaling towards student success. *Guidance Channel Online.* Retrieved from www.eeducating.com/default.aspx?M=a&index=1326&cat=15.

Sabella, R. A. (2008). *GuardingKids.com: A practical guide to keeping kids out of high-tech trouble.* Minneapolis, MN: Educational Media.

Sandhu, D. S. (2000). Alienated students: Counseling strategies to curb school violence. *Professional School Counseling, 4*(2), 81–85.

Sklare, G. B. (2005). *Brief counseling that works: A solution-focused approach for school counselors and administrators.* Thousand Oaks, CA: Corwin Press (Sage Publications).

Stone, C. B., & Dahir, C. A. (2006). *The transformed school counselor.* Boston, MA: Houghton Mifflin Company.

Sutton, S. (2009). School solutions for cyberbullying. *Principal Leadership (Middle School Ed.), 9*(6), 38–40.

Willard, N. E. (2007). *Cyberbullying legislation and school policies: Where are the boundaries of the "schoolhouse gate" in the new virtual world?* Retrieved from www.cyberbully.org/cyberbully/docs/cblegislation.pdf.

Willard, N. E. (2010). School response to cyberbullying and sexting: The legal challenges. *Center for Safe and Responsible Internet Use.* Retrieved from http://csriu.org/documents/documents/cyberbullyingsextinglegal_000.pdf.

Wubbolding, R. E. (2000). *Reality therapy for the 21st century.* New York, NY: Brunner-Routledge.

Young, S., & Holdorf, G. (2003). Using solution focused brief therapy in individual referrals for bullying. *Educational Psychology in Practice, 19*(4), 271–282.

6

EMPOWERING BYSTANDERS

Stan Davis and Charisse Nixon

This chapter starts with the words of a 13-year-old girl. She wrote this account of being cyberbullied as a participant in the Youth Voice Project, a research project conducted by Davis and Nixon (2010) in schools across the United States. More than 13,000 young people in grades 5–12 answered our questions in winter 2009–2010, about bullying and about what helps youth who are bullied. Here is this young woman's story:

> One of the girls at school who wasn't really a friend but wasn't not a friend [of mine either] said really mean things about one of my best friends, then told her i said them, and she made a fake email account from "me" and sent my friends mean emails from "me." I am no[t] friends with either of these girls anymore. A lot of kids still believe i did all that so i don't relate very well to the popular kids of school anymore.

We know that not all children respond the same way to being bullied. As a result, we thought it was important to ask how *severely* she was affected by this behavior. From a multiple-choice list of options ranging from mild to very severe she chose "Moderate: It bothered me quite a bit." We then asked what she had done about this problem. She wrote that she had tried "telling the other person or people to stop," and *things got worse*. She also tried "telling the other people how I felt" and "pretending it didn't bother me" and "reminding myself that it's not my fault," and that *nothing changed* after she did those things. She reported doing two more things: telling friends and telling an adult at home about what happened. Notably, after doing those two things, she told us *things got better*. She went on to explain in her own words. (Note: the questions asked in the survey are included in brackets before each of her answers.)

[What happened when you did that?] *"I made new friends who have been through what I have been through. They understood my problems better, because unlike the other girls they knew how it felt to be hurt."* As evidenced above, we know that children *themselves* can do things in response to being cyberbullied. We also know from talking with hundreds of children and youth that it matters how *adults* respond to bullying. To inquire about the adults' role in the bullying process, we asked [What was the best thing adults did?]. She wrote, *"The thing that helped me most was that they listened to me. At the time all my friends were friends with the other girls so they would try and defend them, it helped having an adult to talk to.* We then asked [What happened when they did that?]. She wrote *"Nothing happened except that I felt a little more confident about myself afterwards."*

The last group we focused on were *peer bystanders.* Understanding the importance of peer support, we asked [What was the most helpful thing other students did?]. She responded: *"My absolute best friend stayed by me, she was the only one and made me feel good about myself and reassured me that i wasn't as mean as the other girls."* [What happened when they did that?] *"It made me feel more confident that i would be able to keep being myself and not let this ruin my life."*

The last question we asked our respondents was about what they themselves, have done to help *other* students at school: [What have you done to help another student be safe or have friends at school?]. Her response: *"In my first few weeks in middle school, I was able to identify kids who were like me and befriend them. Because my best friend went to another school, I knew what it felt like to be alone now and i could tell that they did too."* [What happened when you did that?] *"I think that they appreciated having someone who they could all talk to and have someone understand them and not try to defend the bully. My friends and I have all been bullying victims, so we all know what it feels like."*

BOX 6.1 WHAT PEER ACTIONS MAKE THINGS BETTER FOR VICTIMIZED YOUTH?

- Spend time with them.
- Talk to them.
- Encourage them.
- Call or message them at home.
- Listen to them.

This young woman's account of what was done to her, how it affected her, and what she and others did to help, reflects the stories of many of the young people who have participated in the Youth Voice Project, as well as many of the youth we have known throughout our careers. In both face-to-face bullying and cyberbullying, there are often many peers who witness or are exposed to mean behavior.

Importantly, many young people participate (either intentionally or unintentionally) in both types of peer mistreatment, often through their silence and inaction. What is most striking to us in the individual responses quoted above and in our survey data is that mistreated young people often tell us that things were most likely to get better when their peers *increased* their social connection to them. For example, youth in our study told us that things got better when peers walked with them, listened to them, phoned or messaged them at home, and encouraged them. This is true for both males and females across a wide range of ages.

We might think social connectedness is only an issue of intense concern for middle-school youth. Yet, a recent meta-analysis revealed that larger social networks were associated with a 50% increase in adults' longevity, even when controlling for age, gender, initial health status, and cause of death (Holt-Lunstad, Smith, & Layton, 2010). These results underscore the importance of social connectedness as a risk factor not only for mental health issues (e.g., depression), but also for physical health issues (i.e., morbidity and mortality rates among adults). Clearly, the benefits of social connectedness are not only reserved for the young! We also examined the relationship between school connectedness and level of *emotional trauma* for victimized children and youth in our Youth Voice Project. We thought it was important to look at children's emotional trauma as a result of their peer victimization (not just the frequency of their victimization), given the important influence that children's *perceptions* have on their adjustment. To assess children's level of emotional trauma, we asked them, "How severe was the impact of what they did on you?" Response options included: Mild (bothered me only a little); Moderate (bothered me quite a bit); Severe (had or have trouble eating, sleeping, or enjoying myself because of what happened to me); Very Severe (I felt or feel unsafe and threatened because of what happened to me; or Does Not Apply. Our results showed that the more connected children and youth were to school, the less emotional trauma they reported in response to peer victimization. Specifically, mistreated young people who described themselves as feeling valued and respected at school and as feeling part of their school reported lower levels of trauma after being mistreated by peers. Our research, along with many other recent studies, found that being connected to other people increases resiliency (Commission on Children at Risk, 2002).

We cannot underestimate the value of social connection!

How can we Encourage Safe Bystander Behaviors that Build Positive Social Connections among Children and Youth?

Our most successful conversations with young people about bystander action start with an acknowledgment that they are not the only ones who face the frequent dilemma of what to do in bystander situations. Eleanor Roosevelt wrote: "It is not fair to ask of others what you are unwilling to do yourself." Before we ask children and youth to stand up for others using confrontational strategies, we first need to be willing to look at our own actions. Adults are often faced with difficult decisions about what to do when we witness mean behavior by other adults. When we see parents yelling at their children in a store, we are often silent because of our fears of being hurt or of making things worse. We might make a distraction, walk near the yelling adult, empathize with the adult about how difficult it can be to take kids shopping. If the parental behavior escalates, we might call store security or the police. Most of us would not walk up to the parent and say angrily: "That's child abuse. Cut it out."

When we hear a friend telling us mean things about another friend behind that other person's back, we have to face another difficult decision. We might listen in silence. We might change the subject. We might say something positive about the person who is being criticized. We might begin avoiding the friend who criticized because we believe that he or she is likely to talk behind our backs as well. We might spread positive rumors about the criticized friend to make up for the negative information that is being spread around. Yet few adults would tell the criticizing friend that he or she is being mean. We have learned that indirect and supportive bystander actions are usually safer and more powerful than confrontation.

BOX 6.2 PEER BYSTANDERS CAN HELP VICTIMIZED YOUTH ADOPT MORE POSITIVE PERSPECTIVES

Peer bystanders have the power to shift targets' victimization experiences from negative, destructive assumptions to more positive and healing assumptions.

Why is it Important to Encourage Positive Bystander Action?

The harm done by any kind of emotional trauma depends in part on how others in the person's social environment react to the negative event. For example, if a child is sexually molested and tells adults, that child will be more severely traumatized if the adults call him or her a liar, refuse to give emotional support, and continue to give the molester access to the child. The child will be less severely traumatized if he or she is believed, supported, and protected from further abuse. Decades of resiliency research (Werner & Smith, 1992) have established that traumatized youth who experience positive peer and adult relationships can grow to be strong, capable, happy adults, and that social connectedness is related to increased physical health. Importantly, *peer bystanders* have the power to shift targets' victimization experiences from the most destructive assumptions (e.g., "I deserve this" and "Everyone hates me and likes what they are doing to me") to more positive and healing assumptions (e.g., "There will always be a few people in any situation who enjoy being mean to others. I should understand that so I don't wind up marrying someone like that. On the other hand, most people like me and want me to be okay").

That last statement should not be interpreted to mean that youth or adults who currently enjoy mistreating others cannot change. It also does not mean that all peer mistreatment is intended to harm. Some harmful behavior is impulsive or done without clear negative intent, though these behaviors have equal potential to do harm and should be stopped. The key element of this statement is that it is important for mistreated youth to understand that the person who mistreated them is fully responsible for his or her own behavior, instead of blaming themselves for the mean actions of others. The young woman whose story began this chapter clearly identified *peer support* as the most effective source of healing in her life. She identified peer support as effective, even though the mistreatment did not stop right away. Her positive connections with peers helped her see herself as a valuable, loved person.

How Do People Decide what to do when they Witness or are Exposed to Mean Behavior?

There continue to be incidents in the news in which we hear about people walking by others who are injured or dying. In April 2010, surveillance cameras captured footage of people walking past a man in New York City who had been stabbed, without calling an ambulance (Associated Press, 2010).

On the other hand, we also hear of people who rescue or support others who need help. For example, the *New York Post* ran a story about two young toddlers who were jumping on their bed and accidently jumped out the window of their Bronx apartment. One little boy survived the five-story fall, while the other little boy held on desperately to a ledge outside the window. Fortunately, a bystander raced up a fire escape, reached over, and pushed the little boy back inside the window (McGurk & Williams, 2005).

What influences peoples' choice of action when they witness situations in which someone needs help? In a uniquely helpful study which was reported in his 2008 book, *Bullying in Schools and What to do About It*, Dr. Ken Rigby surveyed young people in elementary and secondary schools in Australia to determine what they would do if they witnessed mean behavior toward a peer. He was also interested in children and youth's *reasoning* behind their choices (Rigby, 2008). Increasing our understanding of the underlying thinking processes motivating a bystander's decision to positively support a victimized peer can assist us in developing more effective prevention and intervention efforts. Rigby (2008) found that students who said they would help the mistreated person gave several different reasons. Some said it was the right thing to do, while others remarked it was an expression of who they were as a person. Some students said that they empathized with the person being mistreated. Some students hoped that if they helped others, they would receive some benefit for themselves. Other students commented that they would only help their friends, but not anyone else, apparently seeing that action as the limit of their responsibility. Finally, some students said they would help others if they were seen as heroes.

> Telling youth "not to tattle" is one of the most harmful things an adult can do when dealing with peer victimization.

Interestingly, fewer students said they would tell a teacher, with many of these students reporting that telling teachers would be unlikely to help the situation. We would add from our own Youth Voice Project data that the majority of bystanders who saw or heard rumor-spreading, exclusion, harassment based on religion, gender, race, and sexual orientation or who witnessed kicking or other physically aggressive acts did not tell an adult at school. In fact, approximately 80% of students who witnessed peer victimization chose not to tell an adult at school. Listening to thousands of young people, it seems apparent that youth in the United States believe that telling a teacher about a classmate's mean behavior is wrong; in fact, telling often results in disapproval from both adults *and* peers. This current belief system is consistent with students' constant struggle to understand the complex and sometimes unclear difference between *telling* and *tattling*. The teens responding to the Youth Voice Project survey rated being told "not to tattle" as the most harmful thing adults did when youth were dealing with negative peer actions. This adult action, which was reported by one-fifth of middle-school students and one-fifth of high-school students, seems to discourage young people from seeking further help. Instead of focusing on the difference between tattling and telling, our experience and the input of the many youth who took part in our survey tells us that it is important for adults and educators to teach students from a young age that they should always tell an adult when they, or someone else they know may be hurt – either physically or emotionally. In fact, telling an adult when someone is hurt is not tattling, it is responsible behavior. We propose that adults stop trying to make the difficult distinction between "tattling" and "telling," which we see as having the unintended negative outcome of initiating codes of silence in youth. When we welcome young people telling us about their honest concerns and about the potentially harmful actions of others, we make it easier for them to get the necessary support. When young people tell us about unimportant concerns, we can thank them for letting us know and return to our other tasks.

Youth codes of silence may interfere with positive bystander action. This idea that seeking help from adults is a negative action parallels an experience Stan had in the 1970s with a friend from a small paper-mill town in Maine. This friend was dying of cancer. As his workmates and their spouses gathered at this friend's house, the conversation quickly turned to the names of several other paper-mill employees, as well as people living near the mill, who had contracted cancer. As the conversation ensued, Stan learned that the mill employees had stopped leaving their cars in the mill parking lot due to the paint damage resulting from the gases and particulates emerging from the smoke stacks. Instead of continuing to expose their cars' paint to the same air they were breathing at work for 40 hours per week, the employees arranged to be dropped off and picked up when their shifts were completed. These employees certainly had reasons to think that the mill was causing increased cancer rates. Stan wondered aloud if, given their concerns, anyone in the community had called the Centers for Disease Control or the EPA to start an investigation into whether the pollution coming from the mill had caused an increase in cancer deaths. The room became silent. Stan was told in no uncertain terms that no one in town would make such a call.

Over time the community had developed and enforced a standard of silence that was seen as the price of having steady work. The paper-mill was the major employer in town. Mill-workers' wages supported the other businesses and services in town. After repeated threats by the mill to shut down and relocate elsewhere, any action that threatened the mill's profitability in any way had become seen as a threat to the economic well-being of the entire community. The accepted code of silence was in effect. As in many schools, there was a strong, dysfunctional community standard mandating silence. Contrast this code of silence to our community standards about what should be done if we see another driver on a highway weaving erratically from lane to lane at high speed, or if we see smoke or flames coming from a building. Given those scenarios, it is likely that the majority of people would feel an *obligation* to call the police or fire department to report a concern, in order to prevent potential harm. We can use these powerful analogies to help us counteract the current codes of silence in schools regarding bullying. We can also counteract codes of silence by responding effectively to children and youth when we become aware of any kind of bullying behavior.

> It is important to proactively address the current, accepted code of silence with respect to peer victimization.

Consistent with this cultural code of silence, our own Youth Voice Project data revealed that over half (51%) of the victims reported that their peers chose to do nothing about the situation and "ignored what was going on." Not surprisingly, some of Rigby's (2008) youth also said they would ignore the situation. They had several reasons for this action (or inaction). For example, some youth believed that what was going on was not their business. Others believed the person being mistreated was responsible for the negative action because of his or her action or inaction. Some felt that their actions would make things worse or wouldn't help. Other students said they would choose this strategy because they were afraid of the consequences they would experience *if* they did something.

> Over half of the targets reported that their peers chose to do nothing about their situation.

We believe that these last two reactions are most prevalent in youth who are focused solely on one kind of bystander action – *overtly* telling the bullying youth to stop their behavior. The kind of support received by the girl whose story started this chapter may be safer for the bystander than direct confrontation, and more helpful. The empirical data from our Youth Voice Project data confirm this conclusion and show that supporting and spending time with the victim was more effective (in terms of making things better for the victim), than using direct confrontation strategies with the bully. We must point out here that we are in no way advocating that youth not be trained to be assertive and stand up for themselves.

> Supporting and spending time with the target is more effective in making things better than using direct confrontation with the aggressor.

Based on the data and on our own experiences, we believe it is valuable to prepare young people to be assertive and to teach them ways to tell others to stop in a clear, powerful, and non-aggressive way. It is possible that these data also suggest that students may need additional training regarding how to effectively confront others in an assertive, non-threatening manner. Possible explanations aside, these data suggest that it is important for adults to communicate to youth that directly telling others to stop will not always work. By informing and educating youth about the potential downside of relying solely on direct confrontation, victimized students may be less likely to become immobilized if this strategy does not make things better. Given these findings, adults might want to reconsider the common practice of refusing to listen to youth who are reporting mistreatment until that young person tells the mistreating peer to stop directly. Importantly, participants in our Youth Voice Project reported that telling a bully to stop often feels *unsafe*. With these current data in mind, adults should acknowledge that it is not always *safe* to tell others who are mistreating us to stop. In addition, adults should remember their own discomfort when confronting others in bystander situations and understand that youth probably feel the same way.

A minority of students responding to Rigby's survey (2008) said they would support the bullying behavior. Some of these youth said that siding with the bully was safer. Others said they "love to watch fights." Some admired the aggressor, while others said the person being mistreated deserved it. An effective initial intervention to improve bystander behaviors may begin by asking youth who approve of verbal, relational, and/or physical aggression *not* to act on their impulses. Stan remembers giving a student presentation in New Hampshire. A teen, after some thought, said to him, "Do you mean that if I have bigoted thoughts I should [there was a pause here for reflection] … keep them to myself?" Stan agreed with her that she had heard him correctly. She seemed surprised by the idea, and then said she would agree to do that. For today's youth, who are often raised watching reality TV shows featuring impulsive unfiltered behaviors; the idea of keeping negative or critical thoughts to themselves seems to be a novel one. It is nonetheless important.

The reasons cited above for acting or not acting apply in the electronic or virtual world as well as in the physical world. When we see a discussion on an electronic mailing list criticizing someone, when someone texts negative information to a group of people, when negative or threatening statements are made on Facebook or other social networking sites, or when we become aware of any of the myriad evolving group of negative actions that have been, and will be invented in the cyberworld, we are influenced by the same thoughts and concerns that Rigby's students expressed in deciding which action to choose in the classroom. How can we help youth make the difficult decisions involved in choosing positive bystander actions?

How Can We Help Ourselves and Others (Including Youth) Find, Create, and Choose *Positive* Bystander Actions?

We framed this question in this way because it is tempting, although inaccurate, to view cyberbullying as something that is done only by and to *young* people. Adults, however, have also been the targets of cyberbullying for quite some time – starting with what was called "flaming" in the early days of USENET discussion groups. Flaming typically involves sending or posting hostile, angry, or mischievous messages intended to "inflame" the emotions and sensibilities of others. These comments or messages do not productively advance or contribute to the discussion at hand, but instead attempt to wound another person socially or psychologically and to assert authority over others. Even in those early days, before the World Wide Web, when very few people had email accounts, and when cell phones were clumsy and rare, there were electronic discussion boards on which people would post ideas and comments. Inevitably, a few people on those boards would gang up on others (a term often referred to as "alliance building") and post negative, obscene, and threatening comments for all to see. If the target of these comments reacted by asking the aggressors to stop, it was likely that these new citizens of the virtual world would *increase* the venom of their attacks, in the apparent belief that they had struck a nerve. If online bystanders asked the aggressors to stop, those bystanders would likely become the targets of new attacks. Like digital citizens of today, these cyberbullies may have been emboldened by what Nancy Willard at the Center for Safe and Responsible Internet Use calls the "you can't see me, I can't see you" principle. This principle is supported by decades of social psychological research exploring the effects of anonymity on behavior (e.g., Phillip Zimbardo's work at Stanford University). We tend to erroneously think of ourselves as "anonymous" when we hide behind a computer screen. That sense of anonymity decreases our inhibitions (Zimbardo, 1969) and, as a result, we tend to use less self-control and are less concerned about accountability. However, the truth is that every time we interface with the computer, we do leave a digital footprint behind and thus can (and should) be held responsible for our part in the hurtful communication. Children and youth need to understand that they are responsible for their actions (or inactions) online and offline.

Recent data suggest that people still believe they are protected by their own anonymity as they hide behind invented usernames/screen names. They feel empowered to say cruel things because they do not see the effects their actions have on the targeted victim. In the past, flaming often escalated into realistic and believable threats. These days, cyberbullying has sometimes tragically escalated into suicides. Cyberbullying is not solely a youth problem. If we are still not convinced of this, all we need to do is read the comments section of any newspaper's website. It is on those websites where we will see people who are clearly adults, at least as defined by age, engaging in vicious personal attacks against others. Cyberbullying can affect everyone. Building positive bystander behavior is a concern for people of all ages.

The "you can't see me, I can't see you principle" is also consistent with the social-psychological concept referred to as de-individuation, which is the loss of self-awareness and evaluation that takes place in group situations, often promoting a "follow the crowd" mentality (Festinger, Pepitone, & Newcomb, 1952). Applying this concept to the virtual world, participating in groups on social networking sites (e.g., Facebook) can and does diffuse individual responsibility and decreases feelings of individual accountability: "I didn't write the post, I only forwarded it!" Moreover, classic research studies have shown that as the size of the group increases, the more one is likely to lose self-awareness and accountability (e.g., Darley & Latane, 1968; Diener, 1976). This social-psychological phenomenon has became known as the "bystander effect." Again, we can apply this concept to the electronic world. For example, when reading a public post available for all to see on a social networking site, where several people are clearly involved, an individual is *less* likely to act responsibly compared to reading an individual email from one person.

Given the power of these social-psychological principles, it is important to brainstorm effective ways to *increase* individuals' self-awareness and accountability when using the computer. For example, in an effort to increase self-awareness [and reduce shoplifting], many stores have chosen to use mirrors and cameras. The use of name tags and bright lights have also been shown to increase individuals' self-awareness (Ickes, Layden, & Barnes, 1978). Importantly, when we increase an individual's self-awareness, he or she is more likely to engage in responsible behavior. It is our job as adults to educate others about the grave bystander responsibilities that come with using a computer, cell phone, smartphone, etc.

> Most people of all ages, including youth, want to make the world around them a better place and benefit from opportunities to think about ways to do that.

According to Rigby (2008), an important factor that influences positive bystander action is an individual's level of *empathy*. The more we understand and feel the suffering of others, the more we are likely to feel an obligation to help them in some way. So many of our youth have told us after the fact that they would never have continued the harassment (or forwarded the text, etc.) if they knew how much harm they had done. Effective prevention and intervention work is, in part, contingent upon our ability to effectively communicate to others the victim's hurt and devastation. It is important for adults to create safe contexts for victims to tell their story. Rigby (2008) also states that "recognizing that it is generally in one's personal interest to help [others]" is a key factor in encouraging positive action. There have been many other researchers (many working in social psychology) who have addressed these issues. In separate research, both Stanley Milgram and Philip Zimbardo found that kind people might do cruel things if they are directed to do so by people in authority or if they are assigned roles in which cruel behavior is expected. We can use the same principles learned in those studies to promote children and youth's positive behavior by communicating clear expectations about what they can do when they become aware of injustice or cruelty. Children and youth are more likely to follow through on this expectation if they have a wide range of safe and effective options to choose from and if they see themselves as making a real difference when they act.

Preparing youth for positive bystander action begins with an understanding of two basic principles of human behavior. First, *any behavior we expect people to use in threatening situations needs to be extensively practiced beforehand.* Without enough practice to establish automatic reactions, people often become immobilized in response to fear. This principle is illuminated when we look at the amount of time schools spend in fire drills each year, preparing for an extremely unlikely situation. We know that without fire drills, youth and adults are likely to panic in a real fire, moving around chaotically, and subsequently preventing others from escaping danger. Similarly, positive action is unlikely in any bystander situation in which bystanders feel at all threatened unless that action has been practiced over and over. Limber, Kowalski, and Agatston's (2009) curriculum about cyberbullying offer opportunities to practice positive reactions to a wide variety of negative digital situations. In addition, two good resources to help us develop practice scenarios are *Cyberbullying – Activities to help Children and Teens to stay safe in a Texting, Twittering, Social Networking World* (Rogers, 2010), and *Cyberbullying Investigated* (Jacobs, 2010). Some of these scenarios are written to provide opportunities to practice reactions by the target of the cyberbullying. However, any scenario can easily be refocused to allow practice for the bystanders who become aware of the bullying behavior.

> Practice is a key element in building positive bystander behaviors.

The second principle comes from the pioneering work of Myrna Shure (from 1972 to the present) and highlights the value of generating many possible solutions to any given problem. According to this principle, a key skill for people of all ages is to *find as many solutions to a problem as possible, and then think about what would happen next following each solution.* It is important to note that youth are more likely to internalize and use solutions and strategies that they develop themselves. Those strategies are more likely to be safe and realistic. In addition, every time young people or adults go through the process of finding five or more possible next steps in solving a problem, they build their capacity to generate diverse solutions to problems in the future. We can also ask youth to pay attention to solutions that often work for them and those that rarely work for them. By training students to pay attention to the personal efficacy of using different strategies, they can then begin to identify specific solutions that fit their own personality and situation. As young people see that giving emotional support to mistreated peers makes those peers feel better, they will choose to give this support more often. When they realize that they made things better by choosing not to forward a negative post or text to others, they are more likely to avoid doing so in the future. When teens realize that waiting before sending angry or mean messages helped them avoid doing harm, they are more likely to wait.

There are many positive actions people can use if they become aware of cyberbullying, either in the planning or the actual execution stage. They can refuse to participate when asked to find out someone's username or password. If that direct refusal doesn't seem safe, they can "attempt" to find out and fail to do so. They can refuse to participate in the mean behavior in other active or quiet ways. They can do supportive things with and for the target. They can encourage others to do kind things with and for the target. They could speak up about how they feel about the planned actions if they feel safe doing so. We will not attempt to generate an exhaustive list because we will be most effective when we ask young people to generate such a list and assess outcomes for a range of different scenarios, and then practice the outcomes they see as having the most value.

Our data clearly shows that telling adults (at home and at school) is an effective bystander strategy, particularly for children and young adolescents. Our students in the Youth Voice Project, for example, told us that when bystanders came *with them* to tell adults, outcomes were more likely to be positive than when they told adults about the bullying themselves. The same was true when bystanders told adults about bullying behaviors. Mistreated youth are often relieved when a witness to mean behavior tells an adult about what is happening, so they can get help without having to tell anyone themselves. There are situations in which adult assistance is invaluable, especially when there is a need to communicate with a hosting company, social networking site, or with law enforcement.

Although the data demonstrate that telling an adult is often an effective bystander strategy, the truth is that the majority of youth currently do not tell adults about incidents of cyberbullying. It is possible youth fear that if they tell adults, they will then be cut-off from access to the digital world in the adult's effort to protect them. Many young people see their access to their friends in the digital world as a crucial part of their social network. This can be especially true for youth who are socially isolated in the physical world, and for whom their social relationships are primarily digital. For this reason, adults can be a more positive resource if they accept the central role that digital socialization has on many youth. In his book, *The Second Family* (published before the term "cyberbullying" was in widespread use), Ron Taffel (2001:70) wrote insightfully about the delicate balance adults need to find between preventing digital access and allowing harm. Seeing trends in the making, he wrote,

> The second family offers endless rituals of connection and belonging. Kids always check in with members of their core group, whether it's by electronic means or by finding time during the school day to say hello and catch up. I've heard from many teenagers that they call each other before bedtime and often fall asleep with their receivers in their ears. Many modern kids go on line every night to share with one another the vagaries of the day.

Since 2001, new layers of technology and new social networking sites have made this connectedness more complex and richer. The result of this added technology has made connectedness seem even more essential to youth than ever before. Taffel (2001:70) goes on to write: "I hope to encourage adults to provide a balance, which consists of the understanding, support and sustenance their teens get from the second family, as well as the guidance that only compassionate, experienced, and knowledgeable grownups can provide."

How Do We Move Youth Past a Narrow Concern For Just Their Friends?

We do well by helping students think of school as their workplace and other students as their colleagues. In a productive workplace, employees commit to supporting their colleagues' work because a business/institution is most successful if all employees do good work. This ethic leads to a school expectation that we are all responsible to look out for each other and to help others feel safe so they can learn. In addition, as youth reflect on the effects of their positive behaviors on others who are not their friends, they can develop workplace habits that will serve them and others well throughout their lives. To make this point clear, we would like to end this chapter with a range of statements from our Youth Voice Project. We asked our 13,000 survey respondents what they had done to help someone who was mistreated or socially excluded. More than 9,000 students took the time to write to us about what they did and about what happened next. A few wrote that they had not and would not do something so strange as help others. Yet, the vast majority of our respondents wrote of things they had done to help others and of the subsequent positive outcomes. Youth who help others, and see the positive effects of those actions, are likely to develop a lifelong ethic of service to others. They will be able to make their communities better places. Here are some of their stories. We hope these accounts inspire youth and adults to take action to support others who are mistreated, both in the physical world and the digital one.

> I always talk to kids that don't seem to be talked to so much. I don't think they're as weird as everyone says they are. I think everyone should be treated equally, or at least have a friend to turn to. I think it makes them feel better.
>
> *An eighth-grade female*

> I just kinda be nice to them. I think that's all we can do. They smiled at me and said thanks or said "hi."
>
> *A seventh-grade student who did not indicate gender*

> A friendly word. It lifted their spirits, usually, and I got a friend.
>
> *A tenth-grade male*

I wasn't mean to him. He had more friends.

A tenth-grade female

I have stuck around them so no one else would hurt them. Nobody came and beat them up.

This student gave no identifying information about age or gender

I just include someone if they feel or look left out. I am also nice to everyone, so they know they have at least one friend to hang out with. Everything was just fine, the person was happier than they were before and my friends don't mind that, they help make people feel comfortable too.

A seventh-grade male

Well once there was this girl and no one really liked her and I felt really bad for her because she was sitting all alone and stuff so I went over there and sat down with her and we talked and when my friends saw me they came over and asked me what I was doing and I told them I was hanging out with my new friend ... anyways after a few days of hanging out with her I came out one day and there was a lot of new kids with her so I was pretty pleased to see that plus it made me happy because like well I don't know I guess knowing that I helped her get a lot of really cool friends made me feel good about myself.

A sixth-grade female

Sometimes, if I'm in class with some one who doesn't have a lot of friends, then i would be partners with them even though I would rather be partners with some one else. She looked happy that some one asked her to be partners, so I felt pretty good about myself afterwards.

A seventh-grade female

I have tried to get them out of trouble, calmed them down if they were upset, and gave them advice. They felt better, walked away, sometimes they listened to my advice, and they ignored the people that were making fun of them.

A seventh-grade female

Well once someone was the butt of a rumor so we tracked them down through all the people who told some one else the rumor until we found the person that started the rumor and told them to stop and take the rumor back. The person stopped telling rumors.

A seventh-grade male

Well a friend was being picked on and I am not the bravest person in the world so really after the bully left I came up to my friend I said are you ok is there any thing I could do. She said ohh its ok. I don't let people being jerks put my life at a stop. We grabbed our bags and went to the buses and we were just talking like nothing ever happened.

A sixth-grade female

I made a bunch of new friends with people that had a small friendship circle. They found that they shouldn't only have one friend, they should "expand the horizon."

A sixth-grade female

I have stayed with them and helped them out and I introduced them to my friends. Things actually got alot better.

An eighth-grade female

Well my friend had a rumor going around about her and wasn't eating, so I helped her out and now she is better. I was scared but I knew that i had to do something about it so I did! I helped by saying don't listen to this stuff cause its not true – you're really cool.

A sixth-grade female

References

Associated Press. (2010). Why did passersby leave homeless Good Samaritan to die on NYC street? *Syracuse.com*. Retrieved from www.syracuse.com/news/index.ssf/2010/04/why_did_passersby_leave_homele.html.

Commission on Children at Risk. (2002). Hardwired to connect: The new scientific case for authoritative communities. *A Report to the Nation from the Commission on Children at Risk*: YMCA of the USA, Dartmouth Medical School, and Institute for American Values.

Darley, J. M., & Latane, B. (1968). Bystander intervention in emergencies: Diffusion of responsibility. *Journal of Personality and Social Psychology, 8*, 377–383.

Davis, S., & Nixon, C. (2010). Youth voice research project: Victimization & strategies. Retrieved from www.youthvoiceproject.com/YVPMarch2010.pdf.

Diener, E. (1976). Effects of prior destructive behavior, anonymity, and group presence on deindividuation and aggression. *Journal of Personality and Social Psychology, 33*(5), 497–507.

Festinger, L., Pepitone, A., & Newcomb, B. (1952). Some consequences of deindividuation in a group. *Journal of Abnormal and Social Psychology, 47*, 382–389.

Holt-Lunstad, J., Smith, T. B., & Layton, J. B. (2010). Social relationships and mortality risk: A meta-analytic review. *PLoS Medicine, 7*(7), e1000316.

Ickes, W., Layden, M. A., & Barnes, R. D. (1978). Objective self-awareness and individuation: An empirical link. *Journal of Personality, 46*, 146–161.

Jacobs, T. A. (2010). *Teen Cyberbullying Investigated*. Minneapolis, MN: Free Spirit Publishing.

Limber, S. P., Kowalski, R. M., & Agatston, P. W. (2009). *Cyberbullying: A prevention curriculum for grades 6–12*. Center City, MN: Hazelden.

McGurk, J., & Williams, B. (2005). Miracle of the "window" tots. *New York Post*. Retrieved from www.nypost.com/p/news/item_W7TubDBVd2Wb2kJRSI0ncP#ixz z19iktV959.

Rigby, K. (2008). *Children and bullying. How parents and educators can reduce bullying at school*. Boston, MA: Blackwell/Wiley.

Rogers, V. (2010). *Cyberbullying: Activities to help children and teens to stay safe in a texting, Twittering, social networking world*. Philadelphia, PA: Jessica Kingsley Publishers.

Taffel, R. (2001). *The second family: How adolescent power is challenging the American family*. New York: St. Martin's Press.

Werner, E., & Smith, R. (1992). *Overcoming the odds: High risk children from birth to adulthood*. Ithaca, NY: Cornell University Press.

Zimbardo, P. G. (1969). The human choice: Individuation, reason and order versus de-individuation, impulse, and chaos. In W. J. Arnold & D. Levine (Eds.), *Nebraska symposium on motivation*. Lincoln, NE: University of Nebraska Press.

7

YOU MEAN WE GOTTA TEACH THAT, TOO?

Mike Donlin

"What about that mean stuff kids do with their email?" This became a persistent question in the early years of the 21st century as my colleague and I were training schools and staffs in Seattle Public Schools on bullying prevention and intervention. "Some of that stuff gets pretty nasty," people would add. It came from school after school and staff after staff. The email focus, per se, is now outdated. Although email is still a part of the electronic lives of students, it has taken on a different role for many. Other types of social networking are now more prominently used for electronic forms of harassment, intimidation, bullying (HIB), and threats. However, even back in "the old days," we realized that we needed to be able to address a growing concern and to offer educators something which they could use in their bullying prevention and intervention efforts. We also realized that the educators themselves were going to be less aware of and less comfortable responding to cyber situations than they were recognizing and responding to real-world, bricks-and-mortar bullying.

With the Megan Meier case, cyberbullying became headline news (Hinduja & Patchin, 2009). Awareness grew, both of the reality of cyberbullying and of the need to formally address it. In 2007, the legislature in my home state of Washington revised the State's anti-harassment legislation. The old 2003 law was revised to include "electronic" forms of bullying and harassment. Cyberbullying was now officially recognized and specifically included in Washington state law. Currently, many other states have written and continue to write or revise their statutes to require the implementation of programs, training, and resources to prohibit HIB (Hinduja & Patchin, 2010). Most – if not all – have also included electronic forms of these behaviors, or cyberbullying, in their state HIB language.

In October 2008, the United States Congress passed the Broadband Data Improvement Act (Protecting Children in the 21st Century Act, 2008). On the surface, with its broad name and stated focus of increasing the availability and deployment of broadband access throughout the nation, the Broadband Act does not *sound* like something having a direct and immediate impact on the classroom. However, Title II of the Broadband Act is the "Protecting Children in the 21st Century Act." The Protecting Children Act *does* have a direct impact on school districts, schools, and classrooms around the country.

The Protecting Children Act requires schools and districts, as part of their school board Internet use policies, to "educate minors about appropriate online behavior" (Protecting Children in the 21st Century Act, 2008). The Act specifically speaks to education around social networking and chatrooms, and recognizing and addressing *cyberbullying*. When this information is presented to educators – from school board members to classroom teachers – it gets some pretty strong reactions! However, when educators further realize that this mandate is connected to E-rate compliance, jaws drop. This basically means that if schools don't figure out a game plan to focus on this subject matter, they will miss out on funds they previously received to purchase their own telecommunications services and Internet access. Questions then fly: "You mean we gotta teach that now, too?"; "Who's going to do it?"; "How are we going to squeeze it into our already packed school year?"; "How are we supposed to do this?"; "Got any training for my staff?"; "What do we have to work with?" And finally, referring to context-setting conversations I often have with my audience on the digital divide between adult "digital immigrants" and youth "digital natives," a principal will usually say, "Remember, Mike, my staff pretty much falls into that 'digital immigrant' group we just talked about" (Prensky, 2001).

The realization that a *board policy* has to be either written or revised is another challenge all by itself. Bottom line, in answer to the question, "You mean we gotta teach that now, too?" the answer is, "Yes, we gotta teach that, too."

During the last several years I worked with Seattle Public Schools, I had a unique position. My functions were split 50–50 between Prevention and Intervention and the district's Department of Technology Services (DoTS). I was thus half on the Learning and Teaching and half on Operations sides of the house. Within the technology department, I managed a variety of technology grant programs. One I oversaw was the district's Federal Title IID Enhancing Education Through Technology (EETT or E2T2) program. Within Seattle Public Schools, these EETT dollars funded an Educational Technologists program. Fundamentally a professional development initiative, the dollars funded stipends for site-based certified teachers and librarians, known internally as the "ETs," in each school. The ETs function as point people who participate in and help lead classroom-focused technology-infusion professional development efforts throughout the schools. Between Prevention–Intervention and DoTS, I thus had regular contact with administrators, bullying prevention teams, counselors, librarians, and ET point people in every school. This was unique. It provided an intersection between Prevention–Intervention and technology training efforts at a time when cyberbullying – and indeed the larger picture of online safety – was becoming a recognized issue to be addressed.

> It is clear that the definition of "youth online safety" has broadened and become more complex in the past 10 years, as have the roles of the online user and the inter-connected devices today's user takes advantage of when consuming, socializing, producing, and connecting.
>
> *Nigam & Collier, 2010:4*

The 5 Cs

Let's begin to look at questions arising from the requirement to educate minors about appropriate online behaviors. For all practical purposes, this essentially amounts to a broad and complex new "discipline." Within many discussions of online safety, the "3 Cs" are often identified and discussed. The 3 Cs generally include *cyber-safety*, *cyber-security*, and *cyber-citizenship*. Cyber-safety involves my personal safety while interacting with others online; cyber-security includes specific technologies (e.g., hardware, software, networks) that protect my equipment as well as personal and private information; cyber-citizenship includes both the freedom and the responsibility I have within my various online communities. One might also consider adding a fourth C: *cyber-literacy*. Cyber-literacy speaks to my power; if the pen is mightier than the sword, I am even more powerful with all the tech tools and toys at my disposal.

Within this chapter, we are focusing on yet another C: *cyberbullying*. It is important to remember, though, that online safety includes the whole range of cyber-citizenship, cyber-safety, cyber-literacy, and cyber-security issues. These weave in and out of each other to form a rich tapestry of social-emotional/educational issues, all of which have grown out of new and "creative" uses of everyday technologies. The issues overlap like circles in a complex Venn diagram (Figure 7.1).

There are those who have asked why we, in Seattle, created curriculum which focused on cyberbullying when cyberbullying can be seen as a threat woven throughout all aspects of online/Internet safety. It could easily be infused into each segment of the Venn diagram shown in Figure 7.1. My response has always been that, although cyberbullying can very much be seen as a part of cyber-safety, cyber-citizenship, cyber-literacy, and cyber-security, it has also come to be recognized as a critical piece of 21st-century HIB. It is the greatest danger young people face online (Palfrey, boyd, & Sacco, 2009). As if to underscore that point, it is specifically mentioned by name in legislation at all levels as an issue to be addressed in its own right.

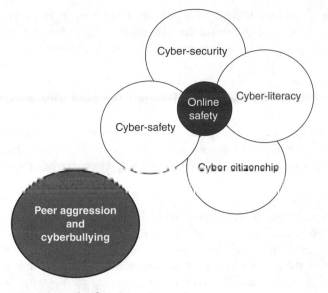

FIGURE 7.1 The five Cs.

Cyberbullying awareness, prevention, and intervention education is required as part of a school's ongoing bullying prevention and intervention efforts. Furthermore, although it can be found within all other components of online safety, so to can it also be used as a springboard for discussion and education around those other components.

> By way of an analogy, imagine if there were no organized sports programs in schools or communities. Kids would still play "ball" in the streets, their backyards and in parks but they would have no formal training in rules.... In many ways, that's exactly what is happening with teens' use of social media. They're playing, but there are very few coaches to help them avoid unsportsmanlike conduct and learn to slide home without skinning their knees.
>
> *Nigam & Collier, 2010*

Seattle Public Schools Cyberbullying Curriculum and Development

With all that as a backdrop, we began working on the "what-do-we-have-to-work-with" question in 2007–2008, even prior to passage of the Broadband Act. Over time, we developed the Middle School Cyberbullying Curriculum (Donlin, 2009). How we did it makes an interesting story. I learned very quickly that "curriculum" means very different things to different people.

By way of illustration, about the time of our initial awareness of an increasing cyberbullying problem, I was discussing this new phenomenon of cyberbullying with a friend and colleague in law enforcement, a Seattle Police Department detective. At the time, the detective was working with the Seattle Internet Crimes Against Children division. She, in turn, had an SPD colleague who was working closely with the police chief of a different jurisdiction. That chief was working with a deputy superintendent from a local school district. All of us had a common interest in cyberbullying. There was what seemed to be an instant network of people with different interests, geographical connections, and areas of expertise. As it turned out, all of us had also come to recognize the need for cyberbullying materials for classroom use, and to also realize that any such materials would have to be created. We decided to meet and join forces. There would be strength in numbers, increased brainpower, diversity of backgrounds, and greater potential to secure funding for the work. Collaboration sounded like an excellent idea. We planned to meet, brainstorm, and plot out a course of action.

From the outset, the group talked about collaboration. The overarching goal was the collaborative development of *curriculum* to address cyberbullying. With the police chief as our de facto lead, the group had several meetings. Initially, our meetings were informal brainstorming sessions. Separately, we had contacted potential funding sources and were waiting to hear about the different funding opportunities. As a collaborative development group, however, our meetings had no agendas; we created no bank of follow-up notes. We also had neither budget nor specific time frame for our work. There was talk, but no substance. Two of the law enforcement officers began to gather documents and data with which to build the curriculum. There was conversation around using youth for input; an excellent idea. However, even though there were two professional educators in the group, there was no consistent talk about involving other educators.

At one of our meetings, I shared a copy of a first-draft funding proposal I was preparing for submission to the Qwest Foundation (Qwest, 2010). If funded, the award would help support development of a cyberbullying classroom curriculum. At our next meeting, I shared a more refined, more nearly complete version of that proposal. I also shared a set of resources for consideration to supplement the curriculum which we were ultimately planning to develop. Finally, I distributed a PowerPoint presentation I had developed which I had been using for staff and parent training.

At that same meeting, two of the law enforcement officers told the group that they were planning an upcoming vacation in Hawaii. They said that they were going to pack up documents they had gathered and write the curriculum while on that trip. While others played on the beach, they planned to sit beside their hotel pool with a laptop and crank it out. They further planned to roll the finished product out to schools within a month to six weeks of their return. I was dumbfounded.

As I drove back to my office after that meeting, I received a call from one of the officers who was very upset by the things I handed out: the grant proposal and the PowerPoint, in particular. She was particularly upset because, as she put it, 85% of the curriculum development work they planned to do in Hawaii was in the staff training PowerPoint I had shared. She made it clear that I had stolen their thunder, gone off and done my own thing, created the curriculum, written a grant to fund my work – and not worked collaboratively with them. We did not meet again.

I relate this story not to speak ill of our law enforcement partners, nor to poke fun at a less-than-professional approach to curriculum development. Rather, I tell it to underscore the needs to understand "curriculum" and what curriculum development entails, and to have educational professionals fully engaged in the process. We will revisit this concept from a slightly different perspective later in this chapter as we consider the resources available on the Web, and some criteria to keep in mind when choosing materials.

With that experience as background, and before beginning actual curriculum development work, I realized that three very important components needed to be in place: a working understanding of *curriculum*; a solid, *credible* development team; and, of course, secure funding.

Taking these in reverse order, to fund the work we completed the application for and was very fortunate to have secured a grant from the Qwest Foundation. The funds were to be used in the development of middle-school cyberbullying curriculum materials. The curriculum would be made freely available to other districts and schools which wanted to use them. The Qwest dollars were then supplemented with additional funds from the Seattle Public Schools Prevention–Intervention program.

Next came the team. As the focus of our efforts was the development of *curriculum* to address *cyberbullying*, the development team required people with experience, specific skill sets, and areas of expertise. Recognizing that cyberbullying and indeed all aspects of Internet safety are not specifically "technology" problems, but that they are social-educational issues involving uses of technologies, the skill sets necessary to create curriculum to address these issues included expertise in curriculum development, and in bullying prevention and intervention. In addition, since the new discipline was highly technology-involved, there was a need for technology expertise, more specifically *educational technology*. That is to say, the need was less for a "techie" type, per se, as it was for someone with expertise in the effective classroom implementation of technological resources. In dealing with sensitive issues of bullying and harassment interventions, counseling and home–school connectivity were also important aspects of the issues. We recognized that the processes and impacts of cyberbullying directly relate to 21st-century media and new media literacy. Finally, we needed a Web presence and someone to maintain that presence as materials were continually created and updated.

After a brief, rocky start, a team fell into place. It consisted of people with project management, bullying prevention and intervention, curriculum development, educational technology, writing skills instruction, school counseling and technology backgrounds. All the key areas of expertise were in place. Once in place, the team considered the issues of curriculum, what topics to address, and how to go about addressing them.

We asked ourselves the purpose of the proposed curriculum. What need was it going to address? Our obvious answer was the need to provide easily accessible, teacher-friendly classroom materials to address a new and growing issue: cyberbullying.

What were our expected outcomes? What were our goals around the awareness, prevention of, and intervention in youth online peer aggression? What educational standards would such a curriculum help students meet? Our goal was to increase awareness of and provide tools to address cyberbullying through teacher-friendly materials which would fit into a well-implemented, evidence-based bullying prevention program. These new materials would help students recognize online bullying behavior and provide them with tools to refuse to participate in it.

Although we had secured funding, that funding was not unlimited. We approached our task realizing that we could not create materials for all grade levels, K through 12. Given the parameters of our grant, the focus was the middle-school/junior-high grades. Within the Seattle Public Schools, most of the middle-schools implement the Olweus Bullying Prevention Program. Elementary schools are encouraged to implement the Second Step (Beland, 1992; Sylvester & Frey, 1994, 1997) and Steps to Respect (CFC, 2001; Frey, Hirschstein, Snell, Edstrom, MacKenzie, & Broderick, 2005), all recognized evidence-based programs. Training coordination among these tested and effective programs helps ensure a common K–8 recognize–refuse–report vocabulary for bullying prevention efforts. New technologies provide both power and freedom; social responsibility is often forgotten. Therefore, the concepts of freedom, power, and responsibility were also embedded throughout. As we progressed, shared draft materials, and received initial feedback, we were happy to receive teacher feedback that the materials were easily adapted up or down a grade level or two from the middle-school grade band.

Perhaps the biggest question was just "what" the new curriculum would include. And insofar as this was essentially a new discipline, what background knowledge would teachers and other staff need to successfully implement the new material? The adult audience – teachers and other educators tasked with implementing curriculum – would likely be learning along with the students. This consideration was especially appropriate since it was teachers who had first brought cyberbullying to our attention.

An Overview of the Cyberbullying Curriculum

For the "what," we developed a list of topics which expand on the notions of recognize, refuse, and report. The topics grew into the nine "lessons" included in the curriculum. The current version of the Middle School Cyberbullying Curriculum can be found on the Seattle Public Schools website (www.seattle-schools.org/area/prevention/cbms.html).

BOX 7.1 THE NINE LESSONS

Lesson 1: Respect and Responsibility – This Lesson helps put cyberbullying into a real-world, interpersonal context.

Lesson 2: What is Cyberbullying? – As with bricks-and-mortar bullying, students – and adults – need a working definition to use throughout future discussions.

Lesson 3: Cyberbullying Across Devices and Services – Students begin to see "how" it is perpetrated and to better recognize it in its many forms.

Lesson 4: Cyberbullying Impacts and Consequences – Within a cyberbullying situation, all the usual players are present: bully, target, and bystander. Each is affected by the bullying.

Lesson 5: Cyberbullying Techniques and Scenarios – Students take a deeper look at how cyberbullying is accomplished and learn to understand that it does hurt and does have consequences.

Lesson 6: What To Do If You Are Being Cyberbullied – The conversations begin to address refusal skills. Students often tell us that they do not know what to do when bullied. Being cyberbullied is even worse as it is outside the understanding and ability of adults to intervene.

Lesson 7: What To Do If You're a Bully – With a focus on the ones who bully, students begin to better understand some of the dynamics and impacts of being a bully, and how this impacts everyone.

Lesson 8: Standing Up for Others – Bystanders, social responsibility, and reporting are discussed. A major consideration of a well-implemented bullying prevention program is helping "bystanders" understand that they can be proactive in helping the target of bullying. This is both more challenging and more important in the context of cyberbullying.

Lesson 9: Serious About Getting Help – Targets, and all players, realize that they do not have to go it alone. Young people understand who they can go to for help and how to create a safety plan for themselves.

Although there are suggested time frames for each lesson, all nine lessons are designed to be flexible in time and delivery. Each is designed to be "chunked" so that it can fit neatly into a variety of time/class/period options. As a component of an ongoing Olweus Bullying Prevention Program which is being implemented with fidelity, each lesson can be segmented to fit into the program's classroom meetings, which generally occur during a Homeroom, Advisory, or other shortened time period.

However, in reality, not all schools implement a bullying prevention program. Some districts have junior high-schools, others have middle-schools. Regardless of grade configuration, there is very little time available throughout the school year to implement something new. If there is no ongoing bullying prevention program being implemented, or if there are no advisory-type classes, how, where, and when might this new curriculum – units and lessons – fit into an already busy school schedule? To fit the variety of school and program settings, the lessons are designed to be flexible enough to be taught in full-length class periods, a single lesson likely running longer than a typical, single 50–55 minute class period. If they are used in longer classroom settings, they fit nicely into existing Health, Language Arts, Social Studies, or Technology classes. They can also be taught as standalones within an exploratory-type setting.

Along with the "what" of content, the "what" also includes classroom-ready, teacher-friendly "stuff" teachers need in order to be successful when implementing the curriculum, especially given the nature of the content.

Located in one, easily accessible location, the curriculum has a complete Teacher Manual. Each lesson contains preparation and background information. Teachers will find a suggested time needed to complete each lesson, classroom resources and materials, and lesson goals. They will also find links to the Washington State Essential Academic Learning Requirements (EALRs) and Grade Level Expectations (GLEs) addressed in each lesson. These educational standards, although Washington state specific, transfer easily to standards in most other states. There is also general and technical vocabulary, which is useful for understanding the concepts. Finally, realizing that the issues may well be very new, there is teacher background information to bring the adults up to speed on the topic quickly.

Within the preparation information, the lessons provide teachers with discussion topics, activities, and homework assignments. Teaching resources provide teachers with additional classroom materials and information to support the concepts being taught. They include Student Activity sheets designed to guide students in learning and internalizing key concepts.

Journal writing is an exercise where students are given a topic to write about. Journals are ungraded but build writing stamina and broaden students' context and thinking. Journals often lead into a culminating writing project. Throughout the lessons, students are frequently asked to write about what they have learned that day. A typical entry might consist of a brief paragraph around specific questions and key points from the lesson.

BOX 7.2 SAMPLE JOURNAL WRITING PROMPT

Describe a situation where you know there is bullying going on. This situation might be real or fictional; it might be real bullying or cyberbullying. Can you help? Why or why not? Explain how this makes you feel.

In addition to journaling, more formalized Writing Extensions have been suggested within lessons. These writing focuses are designed as mini-lessons to teach facets of the writing process where students are encouraged to follow the process to extend their thinking skills through dialogue with their peers. The Writing Extensions also address Washington State EALRs. Again, these requirements should transfer easily to the writing standards in most other states.

Throughout the lessons, students are asked to reflect on statements, questions, a video segment, or other focuses on cyberbullying. Creating small group teams allows them to discuss, question, and pursue clarity with their peers before they present their thoughts and conclusions in a whole-class setting. Interpersonal interaction around the topic is also a powerful device for helping develop understandings, empathy, and a sense of community, all important aspects of bullying and harassment prevention.

One of the most important activities students can do to help stay safe online is to talk to a trusted adult. Students are encouraged to share what they learn with parents or other family members and to talk about cyberbullying. To facilitate this, there are take-home resources for parents with the key concepts and vocabulary from many of the lessons. Parent Resources also provide for consistent home–school communication about the cyberbullying focus the student is experiencing.

Each lesson contains a set of supplementary, motivational materials created to enhance the lesson and extend the learning beyond the classroom into the home. These materials take the form of letters, written by junior high-school-level school counselors and are intended to motivate, inspire, and personalize this curriculum. Each lesson has three such letters: one to the student, one to the teacher, and one to the parent/guardian.

To help assess the materials, their implementation, and the background knowledge needed to implement them, there is a semi-formal feedback process to ensure continuous refinement of really new curricula. To help us assess the actual impact on students, specific cyberbullying-related questions were built into a biennial Olweus Bullying Prevention survey. Interestingly enough, the addition of cyberbullying questions into our survey process was, in itself, problematic. Given the fluid nature of cyberbullying, the first set of questions which were developed were essentially out of date by the second time they were included in the survey two years later. We were faced with the situation of having either irrelevant or revised questions. This would provide either irrelevant data or a useless baseline against which to compare progress.

The middle-school cyberbullying curriculum discussed here is complete and useable. However, that said, it is not *done*. Given the ever-evolving nature of the issues, no curriculum which addresses cyberbullying will never be really *done*. Things change too much and too fast for that to happen. Although the core remains steady, continual updating is critical.

BOX 7.3 KEY FEATURES OF THE SPS MIDDLE-SCHOOL CYBERBULLYING CURRICULUM

1. The lessons were designed by a team of educators, with teachers in mind.
2. They were designed to be compatible with and incorporated into ongoing tested and effective prevention–intervention programs.
3. The Teacher's Manual is designed for teachers who think of themselves as less than tech savvy.
4. Washington state EALRs and ISTE NETS standards, in particular, NETS Standards 2, Communication and Collaboration, and 5, Digital Citizenship, are referenced.
5. It contains a growing list of online and print resource materials.
6. Lessons are specifically designed to be incorporated into ongoing bullying prevention programs but are flexible enough to fit nicely into existing Technology, Health, and Language Arts units, or can also be used in a middle-school exploratory-type setting.
7. The materials are free and available to anyone.
8. There is an evaluation/feedback component to help ensure ongoing input from administrators, classroom teachers, and parents.

Other Considerations for Educators

Let's revisit the concept of curriculum from that slightly different perspective mentioned earlier. With all the resources out there on the Web, what are some other things to keep in mind when choosing materials for schools, programs, and classrooms? There is, in fact, a wide array of "stuff" available to educators, parents, students, and others involved in prevention–intervention and online safety education. These materials can be found on any number of sites across the Internet. The materials run the gamut of quality, accessibility, age appropriateness, usability, and cost. There are some wonderful resources which teachers can use or adapt to be usable and classroom-friendly. There are others which they would want to avoid. A matrix of useful classroom resources is provided in Appendix A. When looking for resources for classroom use, some critical questions and considerations come to mind.

Education around issues of cyberbullying and online safety is still new. Educators are generally required to find and implement tested and effective, evidence-based, best-practice programs for their classrooms. At this point in time, there are no programs which meet that requirement. So how do we address the question of tested and effective? We work with it and around it. We look for information, resources, curricula and other materials that have been developed by credible people and which come from reputable sources; we look for materials which have been developed based on best practice. For example, the Seattle Public Schools Cyberbullying Curriculum is modeled after the evidence-based Olweus Bullying Prevention Program. The Committee for Children's cyberbullying lessons are designed as components of their Steps to Respect curriculum. When looking for resources for teachers to implement, know the source of those materials.

Adults, whether in the role of educators, parents, or simply digital immigrants, must remember that cyberbullying prevention and intervention – and indeed all aspects of online safety education – are *not topics for independent study*. Cyberbullying and all other components of online safety require – demand – adult involvement in delivery and follow-through. This may seem like a given; however, as Harvard scholar Dr. Carrie James recently noted while speaking on the subject of "digital ethics," there is "a dearth of ethical supports for youth in social media" (Nigam & Collier, 2010). This is not to say that there are not good, educational resources available to youth. On the contrary, the Internet is full of materials, games, videos, and other resources designed to help young people understand the issues, to stay safe and to live their online lives safely. Many, though, take an independent study approach to the issues. One such example is *A Thin Line* (www.athinline.com), a youth resource site developed and promoted by MTV. The site is included in the resource list provided with this chapter, and the information given is excellent, well done, and valuable. However, it is geared toward youth alone. There is no apparent nexus between the young people who access this site and their parents, teachers, or other trusted adults in their lives. As well-intentioned and well-crafted as this resource may be, it is designed to be accessed, engaged with, and used by youth – without the guidance of an adult. This approach, however well-intentioned, deepens the division between the online worlds of youth and adults – digital natives and digital immigrants.

I am often inclined to make an analogy to sex education. Think: condoms. Condoms readily available and easily accessible. Adults could tell teens to go get some and read the package. They could then say, "Phew! The kids are safe now." When their young people return home from their dates, they might ask,

"Did you use the condom tonight?" If the answer is "Yes," does the parent say again, "Phew! The kids are safe"? If the answer is "No," does the parent say the same thing? There is a need for conversation, for a deeper understanding of sex and sexuality. Just as sex education is not an independent study, and just as it does not rely solely on "technological protection measures," neither does cyberbullying or other online safety prevention and intervention.

Within an educational setting, an additional resource question asks how easy the materials are to find. Once found, how accessible are they? Can staff easily get to them and download them? Are there roadblocks – technological or otherwise – in the way? How off-the-shelf useable are they? In other words, how much time and effort will it require for staff to find and adapt these materials to their own teaching needs? How age-appropriate are they? Are the language, graphics, and content suitable for the grade level in which they are going to be used? Who is going to do the actual searching, accessing, evaluating, and adapting of materials. Who is going to train others to use them effectively? And, of course, how much will planning, selection, acquisition, adaptation, training, and implementation cost? In the end, these are questions of *buy-in* and *sustainability*. Will school staff be willing and able to buy into the online safety and cyberbullying prevention efforts, and will that buy-in be sustainable? Can and will online safety become a regular and ongoing component of the educational program?

Another – perhaps one of the more subtle – considerations relates to the underlying message of the materials that are found. They may be engaging, but are their messages and the content correct, clear, and current? By way of a very simplistic example, there is the old warning to parents to always locate computers in open spaces where they can be easily seen. When I hear this advice, I ask, "Where is your Blackberry (or iPhone, or...)?" The answer is generally "In my pocket [or purse]." At one point, keeping a computer in an open area of the house may have been sound advice, but that point is long gone.

As additional considerations when planning to address cyberbullying and the mandates of the Protecting Children Act, when searching for material with which to "educate minors," and when implementing activities, programs, and curricula, avoid the following pitfalls to cyberbullying prevention and intervention efforts.

The ostrich approach: Otherwise known as the head-in-the-sand approach, the ostrich approach to issues of cyberbullying and online safety says, "That doesn't happen here, not with *our* kids." Since it doesn't happen, there is no compelling need to address it. Understand that *it does happen here*. No area, group, age, grade, or school is immune. As long as the youth you work with have cell phones, play online games, search the Web, blog, have email addresses, or otherwise access the Internet, it happens. They may not tell you about it. They may fear losing access to their toys and tools, reprisals from perpetrators, or an over-reaction from adults. But it does happen. Here.

One-shot inoculations: Schools may want to send home a note with the opening-of-school packets which says "We don't tolerate bullying or harassment" and call it good. I have visited schools in which the second week in October, or any other day, week, or month, is the anti-bullying week for that year. I have walked into schools with "Bully Free Zone" posters at the front door. However, no one ever talks about what that means.

On the other hand, I have never walked into a school in which students were taught math once and were done. Or science. I have never heard an adult tell a student to brush his teeth … on Saturday … as that would be enough. Unlike flu shots, one-shot, quick fixes do not get the cyberbullying prevention job done. As with any instruction, introduction, repetition, reinforcement, and review are necessary. As with a well-implemented bullying prevention program, cyberbullying prevention, online safety, and all related issues require consistent, ongoing, on-the-spot, classroom, school-wide, and community efforts. They need to be addressed both through direct instruction and infused throughout the curriculum.

A variation of the one-shot approach is the *Guest Expert*. An outside expert – perhaps a police officer, an attorney, a noted consultant, a tech industry representative – is invited to the school to do an assembly or perhaps visit designated classrooms. Although this may well be a very good idea, there are questions which must also be addressed within the school. What is the purpose of the visit, the assembly? Is it a kick-off event? Is it a component of an ongoing unit – in a Health class, perhaps? If the answer to questions like these is "Yes," then, excellent. The guest is not a one-shot standalone. Relative to buy-in and sustainability, then, what preparation did the classroom teacher and the rest of the staff have for the guest's message? What follow-up is provided? How will the message be sustained?

Scare tactics: Scare tactics do not work. This is not news. We have known for years that approaches which rely on messages of fear and which try to prevent youth risky behaviors through scare tactics are not effective (Colorado Department of Education, 2009). Rather, such messages are not believed and the adult presenting the messages loses credibility. Within the context of online safety and cyberbullying, such messages fall under the heading of techno-panic. In the end, it is the adults who are scared while the youth, the intended recipients of the message, are not (Thierer, 2009).

As a corollary to this, and as an important consideration in planning to address online safety issues throughout schools, students are not "scared" because they are much more comfortable and familiar with their technologies than most adults. In the end, they are resources to the adults. Use them in crafting programs which meet the needs of your school community. Use them to carry credible messages among peers. Use the credibility, the cool factor, of older students to carry messages of safety and bullying awareness to students in younger grades.

Just say no: Like scare tactics, this does not work. Just say "no" to "just say no." Young people live in a 21st-century world of technologies where the line between what is bricks-and-mortar real and what is cyber-online is blurred, as best. That world cannot say "no" to the technologies, nor can they rely on old anthems which were recognized as ineffective in the past.

PCP approaches: This one can be tricky. It is a response to the "who is going to teach this?" question. In some schools, the library-media specialist is given the task of teaching online safety. In some schools, counselors run anti-bullying/cyberbullying programs. Sometimes these topics fall to Health educators. This is excellent. The caution, though, is when cyberbullying and online safety become *somebody else's issue*. When this happens, *I*, the regular classroom teacher, don't have to deal with it. I don't have to learn about it, understand it, or face it. When this is the mindset and when a student approaches me in need of help, I am unprepared to intervene and support that student. He or she will both suffer unnecessarily *and* lose faith in my ability to help. As noted above, everyone needs to be onboard at some level or another.

"This is a tech issue" – our filter will take care of it: The Children's Internet Protection Act (CIPA) (2000) requires that districts and schools with Internet access for their students must also provide a filter for that access. It also requires that educators monitor their students when they go online. Without getting into the whole range of questions and issues that arise out of the requirement to filter, and without defining just what "monitor" means in this context, suffice it to say that simply having a filter which blocks unwanted sites does not constitute monitoring. Nor does it ensure the safety of students. Cyberbullying, online harassment, threats, and intimidation are not technological issues. Tech solutions – filters, firewalls, and other online security measures, helpful and useful as they may be – are not solutions to the educational, social, developmental, and emotional situations in which young people find themselves. Remember the condom analogy.

"Go it alone": Just us – no parents, no law enforcement, no outside experts. Earlier, we talked about online resources for educators. Many of the resources were created without the direct input of educators. There are many reasons for this; by and large, this is a new field and many educators are unfamiliar with the content, processes, and technologies. Just as materials cannot be created in a vacuum and given to teachers to teach, neither can educators go it alone. Educators must involve all the key stakeholders as they implement programs. Within the school setting, that would mean that, at a minimum, administrators, teachers, counselors, prevention–intervention and ET staff, parents, and students all need to be included in the conversations. In the larger community, educators, law enforcement, the legal community, the tech industry, and other educational service providers should all be involved.

How: A Three-tiered Approach

So, how do we do that? How do we ensure that everybody is involved? As noted earlier, we are talking about what amounts to a new discipline. We have been addressing a lot of the practical questions which often arise in conversation, especially in light of the mandate of the Protecting Children in the 21st Century Act, requiring that we educate minors about appropriate online behaviors, including addressing cyberbullying. Who is going to do what? When? How? With what materials? Consider answering these questions in the context of a tiered approach which includes prevention, intervention, and instructional support (see Figure 7.2).

In such a model, all students receive the Tier I, universal prevention education. Specific to bullying prevention, cyberbullying is incorporated into existing, ongoing program implementation. It becomes part and parcel of the school-wide and classroom program; staff are prepared to address on-the-spot situations which will most assuredly arise. Some of those situations – and some of the students involved – will rise to a second, Tier II, more focused level of *prevention and intervention* strategies. Tier II moves beyond the classroom into more targeted counseling, student intervention teams and multidisciplinary teams, tapping into all those strategies and resources which a site has in place to address needs and situations which call for more in-depth support. Moving up the pyramid, Tier III interventions are those which require additional, targeted support from counseling, law enforcement, the legal office, the medical community, or others, as appropriate. This three-tiered approach underscores the fact that none of the stakeholders can go it alone.

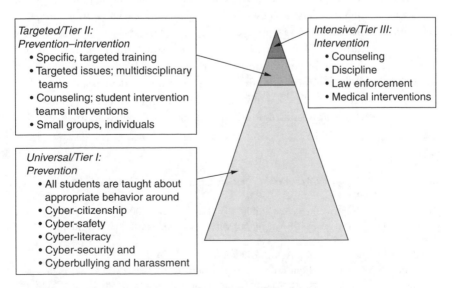

FIGURE 7.2 A Three-tiered Approach to Online Safety.

Concluding Comments

As a final comment, we have been discussing cyberbullying within the context of schools and classrooms. We have looked at considerations for selecting appropriate classroom materials and have taken a close look at one such set of material. Out of this experience, and after speaking with hundreds of educators, parents, and students, several "lessons learned" have arisen. These lessons are not really new at all, but they need to be expressly stated. They include the need for targeted background training for all stakeholders: (1) awareness training for administrators and classroom teachers; (2) legal and policy issues for administrators in particular; and (3) clear, non-techie "what" and "how" information for classroom instruction.

Along with training comes the need for ongoing collaboration and communication among educators, parents, law enforcement, the tech industry and, of course, youth. This is easy to say, but less easy to do. A part of the communication component is the need for common vocabulary and the understanding, as noted above, that cyberbullying and Internet safety are not solely nor specifically technology issues, but rather are social/educational issues. Included in that conversation is the understanding that cyberbullying and online safety, as educational issues, are moving targets, like the technologies themselves, limited only by the creativity of their users.

As a concept and as a set of actions, cyberbullying requires a much more encompassing response than merely setting up filters and firewalls. In fact, a school's filters and firewalls are all but useless. Tech-savvy students easily get around them, and cell phones and other handheld devices are outside them in any case.

Our digital natives are now and will continue to be several steps ahead of us, the digital immigrants. These "new lessons," if used as teachable moments, can help inform the actions and approaches of educators and other stakeholders locally and nationally. They can help ensure successful implementation of our mandate to educate our youth about cyberbullying and other areas of online safety. They will help inform our efforts as we continue to develop, disseminate, and train around issues of cyberbullying, and as we work to educate our youth to be safe, secure, ethical, and responsible in their 21st-century online lives.

References

Beland, K. (1992). *Second step: A violence prevention curriculum for grades 1–5*. Seattle: Committee for Children.

Broadband Data Improvement Act, Public Law No: 110-385 (2008).

CFC. (2001). *Steps to respect: A bullying prevention program*. Seattle: Committee for Children.

Children's Internet Protection Act, Pub. L. 106-554 (2000).

Colorado Department of Education. (2009). *Don't do it! Ineffective prevention strategies*. Retrieved from www.cde.state.co.us/cdeprevention/download/pdf/Don%27tDo_It_Bibiographic.pdf.

Donlin, M. (2009). Middle school cyberbullying curriculum. *Qwest Foundation.* Retrieved from www.seattleschools.org/area/prevention/cbms.xml.

Frey, K. S., Hirschstein, M. K., Snell, J. L., Edstrom, L. V. S., MacKenzie, E. P., & Broderick, C. J. (2005). *Reducing playground bullying and supporting beliefs: An experimental trial of the Steps to Respect program.* Paper presented at the Persistently Safe Schools 2005, Washington, DC.

Hinduja, S., & Patchin, J. W. (2009). *Bullying beyond the schoolyard: Preventing and responding to cyberbullying.* Thousand Oaks, CA: Sage Publications (Corwin Press).

Hinduja, S., & Patchin, J. W. (2010). Cyberbullying: A review of the legal issues facing educators. *Preventing School Failure, 55*(2), 1–8.

Nigam, H., & Collier, A. (2010). Youth safety on a living Internet. *National Telecommunications and Information Administration.* Retrieved from www.ntia.doc.gov/reports/2010/OSTWG Final Report 060410.pdf.

Palfrey, J. G., boyd, d., & Sacco, D. (2009). *Enhancing child safety and online technologies: Final report of the Internet Safety Technical Task Force.* Durham, NC: Carolina Academic Press.

Prensky, M. (2001). Digital natives, digital immigrants. *On the Horizon, 9*(5), 1–2.

Qwest. (2010). *Communications + community.* Retrieved from www.qwest.com/about/company/community/index.html.

Sylvester, L., & Frey, K. (1994). *Summary of Second Step pilot studies.* Seattle: Committee for Children.

Sylvester, L., & Frey, K. (1997). *Summary of Second Step program evaluations (all grade levels).* Seattle, WA: Committee for Children.

Thierer, A. (2009). Against techno-panics. *The Technology Liberation Front.* Retrieved from http://techliberation.com/2009/07/15/against-techno-panics.

8

A "TOOLBOX" OF CYBERBULLYING PREVENTION INITIATIVES AND ACTIVITIES

Jenny Walker

Today's youth spend a growing part of their lives on a "cyber island" where adults generally are not invited (Shariff & Hoff, 2007). Moreover, because youth so quickly and easily assimilate rapid changes in technology, there is a growing digital and communication "disconnect" between adults on the "mainland" and youth on their "island." While many young people experience their cyber island as a positive and productive place, use their cyber "tools" wisely, and demonstrate that they are "remarkably capable of dealing with Internet problems" (Nigam & Collier, 2010:17), other young people have a more negative experience. For example, some engage in cyberbullying, which harms those who initiate it, those who witness it, and those who are the targets. In response to cyberbullying, a rapidly growing body of prevention initiatives and activities (and more broadly, digital safety tools) is available to help teach young people about appropriate online behaviors. As a result, today, educators and parents with busy schedules and limited resources may be saying, "At first, I thought I could not keep up with the kids and their digital world, now I cannot keep up with the prevention tools either!"

In order to help, this chapter provides a "toolbox" of carefully selected resources which can be used to help bridge onto the "cyber island" and communicate with children and young people about appropriate online behaviors. It is a "toolbox" because research informs us that when it comes to cyberbullying prevention initiatives and activities, "one size does not fit all," and the use of multiple tools increases effectiveness of prevention efforts (Emmens & Phippen, 2010; Levinson & Socia, 2010; Nigam & Collier, 2010). There is no one single "solution" which will once-and-for-all prevent cyberbullying. Simply blocking or limiting access to technology is not an effective long-term approach, either. Rather, a recent report to the United States Congress noted that what is needed is a "comprehensive 'toolbox' from which parents, educators, and other safety providers can choose tools appropriate to children's developmental stages and life circumstances, as they grow" (Nigam & Collier, 2010:5). The "toolbox" presented in this chapter provides parents and educators with a selection of exemplary prevention initiatives and activities currently available in order to get you started. The inclusion criteria is based not on what are the most "popular" resources, but rather those which appear to match what current research suggests may be most effective in prevention.

This chapter cannot be the "forever" guide because technology is changing very quickly and new prevention initiatives are emerging rapidly. It will, however, seek to help parents and educators understand how to *intentionally* evaluate and select effective tools using solid research rather than merely responding based on what is most popular or to the loudest promotional plea. To aid in organization, understanding, and selection (and to encourage a mix-and-match approach to meet specific circumstances), prevention initiatives are categorized into nine broad, sometimes overlapping, sections shown in Box 8.1.

BOX 8.1 TOOLS FOR YOUR TOOLBOX: THE NINE TYPES OF TOOLS REVIEWED IN THIS CHAPTER

1. Books, reports, manuals, and guides;
2. Quick-summary tools: fact sheets, safety tips, brochures, and family use agreements;
3. Filters, blockers, and other technology safety features;
4. Presentation materials, webinars, tutorials, school curricula, and lesson plans;
5. DVDs and videos;
6. Interactive media and activities, including social networking;
7. Youth-driven prevention initiatives and activities;
8. Websites, blogs, and e-newsletters; and
9. "Conversation starters" (ways to engage children and young people in discussions about cyberbullying).

The chapter concludes with a "wish-list" for the direction of future prevention efforts. It also includes some "what ifs" that might change the landscape of prevention for all of us. For example, what if policy-makers mandate (and fund!) widespread prevention efforts in all schools? Or, what if large corporations and digital service providers, whether motivated by "citizenship" or economic interest, suddenly decide to invest significant resources to help develop and fund research-based prevention initiatives?

Research-Based Parameters for Cyberbullying Prevention Initiatives and Activities

Many people have had the experience of using a coin or knife point to twist in a screw, or grabbing a rock to pound a quick nail in a board because the rock was close at hand and no screwdriver or hammer was readily available. Contrast this to the image of a surgeon with an expert assistant handing her tool after tool uniquely designed for specific tasks. In cyberbullying prevention, we hope stakeholders thoughtfully and intentionally choose tools using selection criteria based in research, rather than merely the tools that are "handy" or that someone "pushes" them to use.

What does research tell us about cyberbullying prevention initiatives and activities? While cyberbullying has been a focus of research for a number of years, and the field is said to be "maturing in both sophistication and rigor," it is still considered a "young field beginning to take shape" (Mishna, Cook, Saini, Wu, & MacFadden, 2009:10). Moreover, there is not yet a strong body of empirical research measuring the effectiveness or "success" of cyberbullying prevention efforts (Emmens & Phippen, 2010; Jones, 2010; Mishna et al., 2009). A number of recent key research-based articles and reports, however, identify emerging factors which appear *most likely* to generate success in cyberbullying prevention. For example, we know that there are no "quick fix, silver bullet, one-size-fits-all" types of solutions (Emmens & Phippen, 2010; Levinson & Socia, 2010; Nigam & Collier, 2010). We also know that while frequently sought after resources such as summary sheets and checklists are helpful and certainly have a place in the "toolbox," merely identifying risks or disseminating a list of practical online safety tips for children to memorize have not been sufficient (Berson & Berson, 2004). What is needed is a *range of age-relevant prevention resources* that *connect* with the experiences of children and young people online (Berson, Berson, Desai, Falls, & Fenaughty, 2008), and which provide them with the information and skills they need to stay safe online and to be "digitally literate and savvy users" (Byron, 2010:1).

Current research suggests several criteria to look for when selecting cyberbullying prevention initiatives and activities tools (Box 8.2).

BOX 8.2 RESEARCH-BASED SEARCH CRITERIA FOR PREVENTION INITIATIVES AND ACTIVITIES TOOLS

- Be grounded in theory and based upon high-quality research that is rigorous and thoughtful (Jones, 2010; Mitchell, Wolak, & Finkelhor, 2010). A research basis allows for measurement of true effectiveness, whether initiatives and tools are developmentally appropriate, and whether they are "able to evolve with the rapidly changing technological environment" (Mitchell et al., 2010).

- Target "actual" versus "perceived" risks, i.e., be fact-based rather than fear-driven efforts (Emmens & Phippen, 2010; Jones, 2010; Nigam & Collier, 2010). Prevention efforts which focus on the most terrible but least frequent risks can "skew debate in a direction that sends out negative and fear-based messages to children, young people and families" (Byron, 2010:1). For example, while online sexual predation of children by adults is a concern, it is statistically rare, and "bullying and harassment, most often by peers, are the most frequent threats that minors face, both online and offline" (Emmens & Phippen, 2010; Palfrey, boyd, & Sacco, 2009:4).
- Preserve and encourage the positive uses of technology for youth, which far outweigh the negative, rather than focusing on blocking access to technology. As Byron (2010:8) notes:

If we are to get this right, we must remain proportionate, balanced, and evidence based in our thinking and debating so that the issue of child digital safety sits within the broader context of child digital engagement and all of its associated benefits.

- Include interactive programs with skills training offered over *multiple* sessions rather than passive, static, lecture-based, "one-time" approaches (Jones, 2010).
- (Curricular cybersafety tools) must be fully integrated into school content, implemented consistently, and delivered by trained educators, rather than as an ad hoc "bolt on" (Byron, 2010; Jones, 2010; Nigam & Collier, 2010).
- Encourage creative and multi-faceted, multi-strategy approaches to reach youth. For example, choose tools which involve peer-led programs, bystander education programs, public awareness campaigns, parent education, and multi-session school-based programs (Jones, 2010).
- Where budget permits, actively engage young people by using digital media, with high-quality visual animation, real-life video, and representational cultural icons which research suggests are highly effective in influencing behavior (Berson et al., 2008).
- Promote a team approach involving all stakeholders: "providers of services and devices, parents, schools, government, advocates, healthcare professionals, law enforcement, legislators, and children themselves" (Nigam & Collier, 2010:5).
- Keep children and young people at the heart of the initiatives (Byron, 2010; Nigam & Collier, 2010), help youth learn appropriate behaviors, the skills necessary to protect themselves and their friends, and make responsible choices so they can become "stakeholders in their own well-being online" (Nigam & Collier, 2010:5).
- Encourage open lines of communication between youth and adults, and especially parents (Nigam & Collier, 2010).

The next section, the "toolbox," uses these research-based criteria to select a variety of cyberbullying prevention "tools."

A "Toolbox" of Cyberbullying Prevention Initiatives and Activities

If some of you skipped the background above and flipped to this section with an "Okay, just tell me what tools to use," that is fine. We are trying to do some of the "leg-work" and filtering for you and point you to good tools. Keep in mind, however, that the criteria above are important because new cyberbullying tools are emerging every day. This cannot be a "forever" guide. By the time this book is in press, there will be many more tools available. Also, the face of cyberbullying changes rapidly with changing media, culture, and technology. Some of the prevention tools that are effective today may adapt well to future changes and some may not.

The "toolbox" includes not only tools which can be used for short-term, "here-and-now" activities, but also tools to address the need for more complex, longer-term systemic prevention. We hope you will put many tools in your "toolbox," not only to get some immediate results, but also to address long-term solutions involving all stakeholders in a team approach (parents, educators, students, and community partners). The nine sections follow the list of categories set forth in this chapter's introduction. Mix-and-match from the various categories to create your own personal "toolbox" that best fits your specific needs and those of your students or children, as the case may be.

Books, Reports, Manuals, and Guides

With the time pressures many adults are under today, why would anyone take the time to read a book or download a mid-length report? Indeed, one recent study showed that the majority of parents wanted materials that were "brief and to the point," accessible, easy to use, and retrieved quickly, with "considerable support for the use of 'small card' or 'fridge magnet type' resource" (Australian Communications and Media Authority, 2010:9–11). Raising awareness is key in prevention, and while not everyone may have time for in-depth understanding, returning to the analogy of the skilled surgeon with specific tools, we hope there are at least some among each stakeholder category (some administrators, some teachers, some parents, and some youth) who take the time to go "deeper." We hope that others will invest in some of these books to have available as a reference. There are numerous books, reports, manuals, and guides available on the topic of cyberbullying, and we cannot provide an all-inclusive list in this short chapter. Listed below are six of the best books currently available, authored by some of the top researchers and practitioners in the field of cyberbullying, which provide a comprehensive, research-based resource of practical information on this topic. These are all great resources either to read in their entirety, or to have available for reference as time allows.

Books

- Bauman, S. (2011). *Cyberbullying: What Counselors Need to Know*. Alexandria, VA: American Counseling Association. This book gives practical advice and guidance on responding to cyberbullying in the school setting. It is particularly useful not only for counselors, but also for school administrators and teachers, who ready or not, may find themselves having to deal with a cyberbullying situation.
- Hinduja, S., & Patchin, J. (2009). *Bullying Beyond the Schoolyard: Preventing and Responding to Cyberbullying*. Thousand Oaks, CA: Corwin Press. Hinduja and Patchin are two of the top researchers in the field of cyberbullying. You need to know what they are saying about this topic. Deep, research-based, comprehensive content, practical guidance and applications, all in an easy-to-read, user-friendly format. Includes a number of useful appendices.
- Jacobs, T. (2010). *Teen Cyberbullying Investigated: Where do your Rights End and Consequences Begin?*. Minneapolis, MN: Free Spirit Publishing. This book is written to a youth reader. It uniquely communicates to youth the legal and other consequences of cyberbullying, sexting, and other similar behaviors. Adults will find the vocabulary and language tracks useful as they try to communicate these concepts in a way that young people understand.
- Kowalski, R. M., Limber, S. P., & Agatston, P. W. (2008). *Cyber Bullying: Bullying in the Digital Age*. Malden, MA: Blackwell Publishing. While the authors of this book are leading researchers and report on their own studies, they also provide a good overview of other research. In addition, the book is a practical, comprehensive manual on many facets of cyberbullying, such as gender and age differences, motivations, and more.
- Shariff, S. (2008). *Cyber-bullying: Issues and Solutions for the School, the Classroom and the Home*. New York: Routledge. Shariff, like no one else, helps the reader see the "big picture" of policy, causes, culture, trends, and responsibilities. If you want to know "why" and what could be driving cyberbullying, and what we need to be thinking about, you need to read this book.
- Willard, N. (2007). *Cyber-safe Kids, Cybersavvy Teens: Helping Young People Learn to Use the Internet Safely and Responsibly*. San Francisco, CA: Jossey-Bass. Willard is a lawyer who has extensive hands-on experience with many educators and administrators in resolving "real life" cyberbullying and sexting incidents. Her book is filled with helpful advice for administrators, teachers, and parents who are trying to protect the youth in their lives, and doing so amid the practical pressures of budgets, legal threats, and changing technologies.

Reports, Manuals, and Guides

All of the following resources can be downloaded at no charge from the websites indicated.

- *A Parents' Guide to Facebook* (www.connectsafely.org/Safety-Advice-Articles/facebook-for-parents.html). A complete guide for parents. It explains what Facebook is, how it works, and how to parent one's children who are using it, and is filled with pictures of actual Facebook pages showing how to identify the components they are describing. After reading this guide, when faced with the often-heard, "Mom/Dad, you don't understand Facebook," you can now reply, "Oh yes I do!"
- *Guidelines and Resources for Internet Safety in Schools* (2007), Virginia Department of Education, Division of Technology & Career Education (www.doe.virginia.gov/support/safety_crisis_management/internet_safety/guidelines_resources.pdf). A comprehensive resource for schools, including: information for school divisions; students, parents, grandparents, and caregivers; teachers; school administrators; and school boards. It also includes a helpful, extensive list of Web-based resources on Internet safety.
- *Youth safety on a living Internet: Report of the online safety and technology working group* (2010) (www.ntia.doc.gov/reports/2010/OSTWG_Final_Report_060410.pdf). Commissioned by the Congress of the United States, this key document serves as a base-line study on Internet safety prevention efforts and is sure to be cited in future legislative and policy efforts. The list of influential contributors is a veritable "who's who" of experts in the field of Internet safety. Administrators who are seeking funding for programs may want to cite this study in their requests as it represents the highest level authoritative recognition of need for programs in the United States. The annotated List of Internet Safety Education Links (Addendum A) is very useful.

Quick-summary Tools: Fact Sheets, Safety Tips, Brochures, and Family Use Agreements

We know that many adults are under tremendous pressures today, and have limited time, if any, to read in-depth articles and research reports on the topic of cyberbullying. Help is at hand, however, because a number of top websites provide easy-to-access, well-presented, easy-to-read, quick-reference-type materials (often limited to one page) of the "key facts" or "key activities" with regard to cyberbullying. These resources are a great place to begin to learn about cyberbullying because they introduce this complex topic in a manner which neither overwhelms nor intimidates, and which allows readers to have concise, well-researched, and up-to-date information at their fingertips.

Fact Sheets, Safety Tips, and Brochures

- Cyberbullying Research Center (www.cyberbullying.us). Probably the best selection of research-based fact sheets, handouts, reference materials, activities, "top 10" lists, and prevention materials available online. It is almost assured that a principal, counselor, teacher, or parent visiting the site will download and use one or more of the many free tools offered which they can immediately apply to their situation.
- *Cyberbullying: A Whole-School Community Issue* (www.digizen.org/resources/cyberbullying/overview). Produced by the Department for Children, Schools, and Families in the United Kingdom, this eight page summary provides key safety advice for children, young people, parents, and caregivers. It promotes shared responsibility and encourages the positive uses of technology. (There is also an excellent full-guidance report available at www.digizen.org/resources/cyberbullying/full-guidance.aspx.)
- *Cyberbullying: Bullying in the Digital Age* (www.cyberbullyhelp.com). Concise, relevant advice from three of the top researchers in the field of cyberbullying. It includes a two-page, quick reference guide for parents, help tips for reporting offensive profiles to social networking sites, links to longer (but still "reader-friendly") guides/reports, and useful advice for teens.

Family Internet Use Agreements

These tools allow parents and youth to avoid misunderstandings, and establish family expectations and "rules" for using cyber-tools such as the Internet or cell phones. To encourage acceptance and "ownership" of an agreement, it is advisable to include young people in the discussion and creation of the agreement's terms. A selection of family use agreements can be downloaded from the following websites:

- *Family Online Internet Safety Contract* (www.fosi.org/resources.html). Contracts for both parents and children to sign, acknowledging their rights and responsibilities.
- *Family Internet Use Contract and Cell Phone Use Contract* (www.cyberbullying.us/cyberbullying_internet_use_contract.pdf and www.cyberbullying.us/cyberbullying_cell_phone_contract.pdf). Agreements outlining expectations of both parents and children with regard to Internet and cell phone use.
- *Family Contract for Online Safety* (www.safekids.com/family-contract-for-online-safety). A pledge for parents and kids which provides a set of criteria for use of the Internet.

For help in initiating the discussion that leads to contracting, see "conversation starters" at the end of this chapter.

Filters, Blockers, and Other Technology Safety Features

While filters, blockers, and other technology safety features have a place in the "toolbox," reliance on these features has a number of shortcomings: Youth inevitably find a way around them; their use does not address the social relationship issues of online safety; and they can block positive uses of technology (Nigam & Collier, 2010; Walker, 2009). Of course, above all, no filter, blocker, or technological device is a shortcut for maintaining a positive parent–child relationship with regard to online safety issues. For young children, and for youth with identified problems, blockers and filters have their place on a temporary basis, but should be only one line of defense, and are best used in conjunction with other prevention tools and activities. Understanding these limitations, parents may still choose to use blockers and filters, given the ages and circumstances of their individual children.

With regard to technology use in schools, there is a "growing consensus among Internet-safety experts that blocking social media might actually have a negative effect on student safety" (Nigam & Collier, 2010:24) because it might lead to missed opportunities to teach Internet safety in context. In addition, a report from the United Kingdom found that students were "more vulnerable overall when schools used locked down systems because they were not given enough opportunities to learn how to assess and manage risk for themselves" (Byron, 2010:5). Thus, if you use blockers and filters, use them *wisely*, *intentionally*, and *appropriately*, and do not solely rely on them to "do the job." Here are a few sites to get you started:

- *Getnetwise* (www.getnetwise.org/videotutorials). As the website notes, it "contains the largest online repository of instructional how-to video tutorials that show parents and users how to keep their family's online experiences safe and secure. Instructional videos range from setting your search engine to filter pornography in its search results to activating your computer's security settings."
- *GetParentalControls.org* (http://getparentalcontrols.org). This website aims to provide "accurate, comprehensive, and unbiased information about parental control technology." See especially the up-to-date and extensive "Parental Controls Product Guide," which includes a detailed evaluation of software/apps for parents to install on kids' cell phones; monitoring and tracking devices offered by cell phone service providers; and a vetted list of child-friendly sites with an explanation of safety protections.
- *On Guard Online* (www.onguardonline.gov/topics/kids-privacy.aspx). This site provides plenty of useful information on "how to protect your kids' personal information when they are online."

Presentation Materials, Webinars, Tutorials, School Curricula, and Lesson Plans

Schools which accomplish long-term prevention will most likely be those which take up the task of creating new social norms (Nigam & Collier, 2010). This path includes raising awareness of all stakeholders through presentations, webinars, and tutorials, and introducing and integrating curricula and lesson plans. Schools committed to a safe environment where children and young people are free to learn without the danger of being cyberbullied must have a multi-faceted plan integrating prevention and online safety into their overall curriculum. Schools need concerted, intentional strategies so that all (students, teachers, administrators, parents) view cyberbullying as unacceptable behavior, or they will not succeed in the long-term work of systemic change of social norms. The message needs to be loud and clear that it is not "cool" to cyberbully others or to stand by and watch while that is happening to peers.

BOX 8.3 NOTES TO KNOW

In creating a safe school environment strategy, schools should consider the following:

- Establish a cyberbullying "task force" composed of teachers, counselors, students, parents, and community members.
- Appoint cyberbully "trustees" or "experts" whom students, parents, and teachers know are the "go to" people for prevention and reporting.
- Establish (and keep up-to-date if already in place) school policies, including a school harassment policy that clearly defines and prohibits cyberbullying.
- Ensure protocols are in place for reporting cyberbullying, intervening, and collaborating with law enforcement agencies.
- Consider establishing clear rules regarding the use of computers and other technological devices, and install filtering technology as appropriate.

For a more in-depth discussion of creating safe school environments, see Hinduja and Patchin (2009) and Shariff (2009).

Presentation Materials

"One off" assemblies and "one shot" presentations alone will not be effective as a prevention initiative. However, in order to "kick start" or "revitalize" a larger cyberbullying prevention program, and to provide an overview and motivate all stakeholders, schools should consider holding one or more general assemblies with students and other interested parties. It is important, however, that adults avoid talking *at* the students and focus on talking *with* them in order to encourage interest, engagement, and participation in the topic. It is also advisable to consider actively including youth in the presentation, perhaps through creating a "youth panel" or using break-out or focus groups, in order to ensure that youth have a vehicle through which they can participate, share their own insights, and feel a valued part of the process. Educational presentations for teachers and parents are also advisable. Ideally, the presentations should also include media and video clips to capture attention. Some of the best presentation materials can be found at:

- *Center for Safe and Responsible Internet Use* (www.cyberbully.org). Leading expert Nancy Willard's excellent site for downloadable professional resources, including a video presentation and notes on "Cyberbullying and Cyberthreats: Responding to the Challenge of Online Social Aggression, Threats, and Distress."
- *Guarding Kids* (www.guardingkids.com). Leading expert Dr. Russell Sabella's PowerPoint and related files for use with elementary, middle- and secondary-school students.
- *iKeepSafe* (www.ikeepsafe.org/iksc_educators). Assembly presentations for students (elementary, middle-, and high-school) and adults, "created in collaboration with Harvard's Center on Media and Child Health and Penn State University."

Webinars and Tutorials

A tutorial-style learning resource can be a great way for parents and educators to learn more about the topic of cyberbullying in a relatively short period of time. Several sites host webinars and short video clips on the topic of cyberbullying.

- *iKeepSafe* (www.ikeepsafe.org/PRC/videotutorials/index.php). A selection of helpful videos and tutorials, including "What You Need to Know," which "covers social networking, cyber-bullying, online harassment and more."
- *Cybersmart* (www.cybersmart.org/workshops). CyberSmart hosts five "SMART" online, facilitated professional development workshops on topics such as safety and security online, and manners, bullying, and ethics.
- *The Ophelia Project* (www.opheliaproject.org). The Ophelia Project regularly hosts online webinars (some free, some for a nominal charge) on topics such as "Ten Ways for Parents to Prevent Cyberbullying," and "The Five Critical Steps for Addressing Peer Aggression." See also their series on cyberbullying on YouTube (www.youtube.com/user/OpheliaProject).

School Curricula and Lesson Plans

Choosing a curriculum which is grounded in research and addresses cyberbullying as part of a long-term systemic change can be a good start toward creating new social norms in a school. In addition to the general research criteria mentioned above, the better curricula focus not only on teaching new technical "skills" for handling cyberbullying but also include the elements listed in Box 8.4.

BOX 8.4 SOME ELEMENTS TO LOOK FOR IN CYBERBULLYING PREVENTION CURRICULUM

- Emphasis on relationship issues and the importance of changing behaviors;
- Applications across the K–12 continuum;
- Links to national standards, including teaching 21st-century skills such as communication and collaboration;
- Emphasis on the crucial role bystanders/witnesses play in cyberbullying;
- Encouragement of young people to be leaders of positive change;
- Inclusion of peer mentoring as a strategy to address cyberbullying;
- Creation of cross-generational learning between students and adults.

Apart from the obvious vocabulary, age, and cultural distinctives for young children versus older students, a key factor for materials for younger children is to lay a positive foundation and habits at an age when they are just beginning to engage with technology. Exemplary (and free) curriculum materials can be found at:

- *Commonsense Media Digital Citizenship Curriculum* (www.commonsensemedia.org/educators). Curriculum for grades K–5 and 6–8, designed to "help educators empower their students and school communities to be safe, responsible, and savvy as they navigate this fast-paced digital world."
- *CyberSmart* (http://cybersmartcurriculum.org). K–12 materials which "offer schools the opportunity to begin a dialogue with students and build a sustained cyberbullying prevention campaign to continually remind the school community about safe, ethical online use."
- *Seattle Public Schools Cyberbullying Curriculum* (www.seattleschools.org/area/prevention/cbms.html). A curriculum of nine lessons for middle-school/junior-high students, which also includes an excellent range of introductory materials for educators/counselors, such as template letters for parents, students, and teachers; evaluation and feedback forms; and further Internet safety resources.

Another helpful list of available curriculum or lesson plans for helping children with knowledge, skills, and attitudes about cyberbullying can be found in Appendix A at the end of this book.

DVDs and Videos

Not surprisingly, many young people engage better with visual media than with printed material. Additionally, research informs us that the use of "high quality visual animation, real-life video, and representational cultural icons seem to be effective in influencing behavior" (Berson et al., 2008:239). When choosing visual resources, consider the following: Make sure the message is on-target (i.e., age- and content-appropriate) for the audience; and use media in different settings (large groups, classrooms, small groups, and even one-on-one by counselors and parents). Used carefully, thoughtfully, and age-appropriately, these media can jump-start an ongoing dialogue with young people and engage young people in thinking critically, collaboratively, and constructively about cyberbullying and online safety.

Short Videos (10 Minutes or Less) to Capture Attention, Initiate Discussions, etc.

- *At-a-Distance – Standing up to Cyberbullying* (www.cyberbullying.org.nz/at-a-distance-film). Produced by New Zealand's NetSafe for children ages 8–10, this 10-minute video clearly illustrates the important role of bystanders in preventing cyberbullying.
- *Cyberbullying* (www.brainpop.com/technology/computersandinternet/cyberbullying). A five-minute animated, informative message for younger students about cyberbullying and how to respond to it.
- *Let's Fight It Together* (www.digizen.org/resources/cyberbullying/films/uk/lfit-film.aspx). An eight-minute "real-life" depiction of cyberbullying which covers a lot of important ground. Suitable for middle- and high-school students.

Longer Videos (40–45 Minutes) For a More Comprehensive Viewing Session

- *Clicking with Caution* (www.nyc.gov/html/nycmg/nyctvod/html/home/cwc.html). A 42.35-minute four-part DVD created by youth for youth and featuring Gossip Girl star Jessica Szohr to raise awareness of Internet risks and teach preventive measures.
- *Sexting in America: When Privates Go Public* (www.mtv.com/videos/news/483801/sexting-in-america-when-privates-go-public-part-1.jhtml). This 40-minute film explores the dangers of sexting and the repercussions for the people who electronically send and receive sexually explicit photos/videos.

Interactive Media and Activities, Including Social Networking

Due to the "cyber island" phenomena, it is critical that adults have tools in their "toolbox" that help them communicate and connect with youth – tools that help adults become a part of youth's experience, build bridges of communication with youth, and remind youth that they are not alone on the cyber island. Youth may think they do not need help from adults as they rapidly assimilate new technologies, but without adult involvement, they often are learning only the "technology" skills, and not the critical "social relationship" skills that adults are more familiar with and which come with greater maturity.

A positive note is that some of these new sites are being created in consultation with digital safety professionals. Of course, youth will always have the ability to "vote with their feet" on a parallel basis and go "underground" (whether their parents know it or not) to other sites not created with digital safety concerns in mind. This is one reason why adult stakeholders (administrators, teachers, and parents) should place more emphasis on channeling youth to positive Internet tools rather than emphasizing the barriers to access (which have very limited effectiveness, as noted above).

In sum, get some "educational fun" in your "toolbox" with some of the following:

Interactive Media and Activities

The following activities do not include social networking features, which are covered in the next section.

- *Cyber Café* (www.thinkuknow.co.uk/8_10/cybercafe/Cyber-Cafe-Base/). An online animated website where children age 8–10 can learn how to stay safe using technology. Very fun and attractive.
- *Hector's World* (www.hectorsworld.com). A first-class, research-informed, interactive, fun, educational website for children aged nine years and younger. Perhaps the best interactive site currently available for younger children. Produced in New Zealand.
- *Smokescreen* (www.smokescreengame.com). A "cutting-edge" game from the United Kingdom about life online. Teens take part in 13 "missions" involving various aspects of life online.

Social Networking Sites

Knowing that social networking appears to be the inevitable "new world order" for coming generations, it will behoove adults to provide children with good training and the skills necessary to "practice safe social networking" through sites created with safety in mind, such as:

- *Superclubs Plus* (www.superclubsplus.com). A UK-based, protected social networking site for children age 6–12 and their teachers. Schools from 45 countries participate in building their own community websites and in learning how to stay safe in online communities.
- *Togetherville* (http://togetherville.com). A social online community where children (under 10 years) learn how to "use technology to connect with the important people in their lives – safely and responsibly."
- *WoogiWorld* (www.woogiworld.com). An "online virtual educational platform that fosters peer-based, social interactive learning for today's students." See especially the Woogi Cyber Hero program. Suitable for K–6 students.

While we think these are currently among the best, Bauman (2011:41–47) provides a useful overview of others which parents may hear about or see their kids experimenting with, including *Club Penguin*, *Kidsworld*, *Webkins*, *Imbee*, and *Kidswirl*.

Youth-driven Prevention Initiatives and Activities

Research informs us that youth need to be integral to designing the future of their own online safety efforts (Byron, 2010; Nigam & Collier, 2010). As adults work to create effective online safety prevention initiatives and activities, let us not work with an "empty chair," and effectively overlook and forget to include the ideas of the very children and young people who are on the receiving end of our efforts. A good example of keeping young people at the heart of an initiative is MTV's "Draw Your Line" website (www.athinline.org/drawyourline), which collects and categorizes notes by visiting youth of actions they have taken to protect themselves and help others online. Other exemplary initiatives which keep children and young people at the heart of the matter include:

- *Adina's Deck* (http://adinasdeck.com). An award-winning DVD series about a group of teens who belong to a fictional detective agency, Adina's Deck, and who help solve challenges relevant to young people today (for example, cyberbullying). There is a nominal cost for the DVDs.
- *Cyberbullying 411* (www.cyberbully411.com). An excellent website which provides "resources for youth who have questions about or have been targeted by online harassment." This site is very visually attractive, has a message that is "on target," and teens will likely want to engage if led here.
- *Cyber Mentors* (http://cybermentors.org.uk). A UK website where young people are trained to listen to and help other young people who are being bullied and/or cyberbullied. Amazing effort involving (supervised) trained children taking telephone calls and responding online to other kids.

Websites, Blogs, and E-newsletters

The interactive sites reviewed above were for adults and children to learn together. The sites in this section are informational for adult stakeholders to learn and to connect with other likeminded stakeholders. Some of the websites also include sections for children and young people. All the websites noted contain research-based and well-presented information on cyberbullying. The websites are easy to navigate and relevant information can be accessed quickly. Adults are encouraged to use these websites to (re)connect, collaborate, and get involved with young people in learning about cyberbullying and the related aspects of online safety and digital citizenship.

Websites

*   *BnetS@vvy* (www.bnetsavvy.org/wp). "Tools and resources which help promote safe social networking and Internet safety for parents and teens." Includes an "Ask the Experts" section which links to some of the top experts in the field.
*   *Bullying. No Way!* (www.bullyingnoway.com.au). A very impressive Australian site with resources for parents, teachers, and students. Comprehensive treatment of many issues surrounding cyberbullying. Particularly notable is the "deeper issues" section which looks at how cyberbullying affects the larger school community.
*   *Digizen.org* (www.digizen.org/resources). An excellent UK site with "booklets, films, leaflets, games, interviews and lesson plans designed to encourage people to become more responsible digital citizens and address negative online behaviours such as cyberbullying."

A more extensive list of Internet safety websites can be found at Connect Safely (www.connectsafely.org/Directories/internet-safety-resources.html), and in Addendum A of the *Report of the Online Safety and Technology Working Group* (Nigam & Collier, 2010).

Blogs and E-newsletters

Blogs and e-newsletters are great ways for *busy parents and educators to keep up-to-date with information provided by some of the leading professionals in this field.* The following blogs and e-newsletters provide relevant and timely information in a concise format.

*   *Net Family News* (www.netfamilynews.com). If you want to know how youth are using the latest technology, this is the site to visit. Anne Collier can always be counted upon to provide an up-to-date, well-informed, and

helpful perspective. She blogs five days a week and sends out a helpful "weekly summary."

• *Creating Cultures of Dignity* (www.rosalindwiseman.com). Rosalind Wiseman, a well-known author and educator, focuses on the social challenges young people face, including bullying and cyberbullying. She is frequently called upon as an expert by the media when there are prominent bullying/cyberbullying cases. Her advice is always informed, rational, practical, and helpful.

• *Cyberbullying News – Summary Site for Busy Educators* (www.cyberbullying-news.com). This is my site and has much the same purpose as this chapter (that's why I mention it). Rather than primarily giving independent advice, my site specializes in summarizing the research and materials of *other* experts in the field, both nationally and globally. This is a good site for busy educators to "check in," stay up-to-date on what's going on in the world of cyberbullying, and then click on links to primary sources if they want to read further.

Conversation Starters

Research shows that young people *do* want to speak with their parents and other adults about cyberbullying and online safety issues, but they often do not because they feel adults do not understand (Nigam & Collier, 2010; Walker, 2009). We know that often it is not easy for adults to start these conversations with young people: Parents may feel disconnected from, even shut out of, the online lives of their children, and the children may feel their parents "just don't get it" (Walker, 2009) Some of the top researchers and leaders in the field of online safety have considered this challenge and have created some helpful "conversation starters" for you.

• *Cyberbullying Research Center* (http://cyberbullying.us). Two of the top researchers in cyberbullying have put together several useful "scripts" for parents to use to promote dialogue and discussion with young people on this issue. There is also a "Cyberbullying Scenarios" sheet with "starter questions."

• *Net Cetera: Chatting with Kids About Being Online* (www.onguardonline. gov/pdf/tec04.pdf). "What you need to know, where to go for more information, and issues to raise with kids about living their lives online."

• *Start the Talk* (http://us.norton.com/familyresources/resources.jsp?title=ar_start_the_talk). Useful suggestions from Marion Merritt of Norton for starting the talk on online safety.

To conclude this section, before you close the lid on your "toolbox," make sure it has lots of interesting tools in it, not just the ones that attract *you*. Like skilled surgeons with an array of tools at their disposal, you too will want to have multiple tools, from those that raise general awareness, to those that touch specific needs. Also, you may find yourself in a resource role with others. Imagine three students, three teachers, or three parents in your office together. If you offered to allow them to "borrow" one of the many tools in your toolbox, chances are, given their different personalities, backgrounds, learning styles, and needs, they may each choose something different. So make sure your toolbox is filled with an assortment of tools to reach a wide variety of recipients and uses.

Conclusion and "Wish List" for Cyberbullying Prevention Initiatives

This chapter has been designed not only to point you to some of the best available tools for cyberbullying prevention efforts, but also to walk you through a research-based selection process to give you a framework for selecting new tools in the future as tools and technology change. While we cannot predict the future of technology, we can "guess" at the tops of new waves that appear to be coming soon, and new areas that will need to be addressed. This short section presents a few "wish-list" items of shifts in perspective, gaps to be filled, and future initiatives we would like to see.

One quantum shift in perspective we wish for: Viewing the digital online safety challenge as an opportunity of infinite potential. Shariff (2008:257–58) says:

> cyberbullying, as currently defined, is not a battle, but a plea for improved and increased attention to education, dialogue, bonding and engagement with our young people. In that regard, it is an *opportunity with infinite potential* [emphasis added], to address ignorance, overcome orthodoxy and undertake the challenges of our shared knowledge society through ethical, educational, digital-bonding and legally defensible policies and practices. Our children and society, as a whole, deserve no less.

We need a "quantum shift" from viewing cyberbullying and digital online safety issues merely as "problems" to be feared, to one which sees the need for adults and youth to "come together" on technology as one of the greatest intergenerational communication opportunities of our time. The real issues are not about technology. The real issues are about relationships and working with youth to create a new cyber world of social responsibility in their use of technology. (For an excellent discussion on youth relationships, social maturity, and technology, see Strom and Strom (2009).)

Gaps to be filled: Following many of the recommendations of the Online Safety and Technical Working Group (Nigam & Collier, 2010), gaps to be filled include those listed in Box 8.5.

BOX 8.5 GAPS TO BE FILLED

- The need to start educating children at an early age about online safety and digital citizenship. In England, for example, the new primary curriculum, which will come into force in September 2011, includes strong references to digital safety (Byron, 2010:17).
- Create national and global partnerships with colleagues around the world (notable efforts are under way in Canada, Australia, New Zealand, the United Kingdom, and Europe).
- Ensure we educate our teachers and school administrators by requiring that digital citizenship and online safety be an integral part of pre-service training for teachers (Nigam & Collier, 2010:25).
- In the United States, leadership in digital safety and citizenship has arisen from many sectors, including foundations, universities, and some states. However, there is a need for a unified, national, all-encompassing, high-profile campaign to demonstrate that it is a national priority and to raise awareness (Nigam & Collier, 2010). This has been accomplished in other countries, such as the "Zip It, Block It, Flag It" campaign in the United Kingdom (Byron, 2010:13).
- On an international level, see two or three youth-driven initiatives promoted at a high level, to help children and young people work with adults on taking ownership for the issue.
- Create and showcase a few "Stage 5" (successful) schools that are living, breathing models of high-level digital online safety (Levinson & Socia, 2010:5–6). We need real-life examples to point to and say, "This is worth emulating."

A final wish: break through the "no money" and "no influence" barriers. Researchers, digital safety experts, top educators, and others concerned about this area are tired of hearing "there is no money" to address this issue, and that cyberbullying prevention needs to "get in line" behind other pressing issues in tough economic times. Many national and local governments, regulators, and educational policy-makers are increasingly acting to require prevention policies, programs, and other efforts. They do not always fund such mandates, which can create frustration for educators. On the other hand, public funds are often scarce.

We note that major corporations and particularly digital industry providers have, in recent years, been very interested in education, and many examples exist of notable corporate generosity to get technology into classrooms. "Crossing the line" from providing technology to taking stands on the complex behavioral and social maturity issues involved in digital online safety, however, is a very *different* commitment and investment for such companies, and often represents a *different* level of risk for them. Some have ventured out bravely and are pioneering great efforts (for example, those joining forces with the Family Online Safety Institute). We need to support such corporations and digital service providers to continue to use their leadership and influence base, together with a portion of the substantial resources created from youth digital media use, to work collaboratively with researchers and educators in order to break through the "no money" and "no influence" barriers and quickly bring digital safety to a very high international resolution level.

The cyber island and toolbox revisited: We hope this chapter has not only been a good initial overview, but can serve as an ongoing resource in the future as you build bridges to diminish the digital and communication disconnects between the adults and youth in your circles of influence. We hope you have also captured, in a small way, a vision for a future where youth and adults work together to create a more interconnected and mutually satisfying new cyber world.

Note

There are certainly other great materials available which are not referenced herein. I have reviewed many for this chapter that space does not permit to include. The chapter merely attempts to highlight some of the very best. While the author is acquainted with some of the creators of these materials, the author has no personal or financial relationships with them, except for a short reference to the author's own summary (and free) website, www.cyberbullyingnews.com, which performs a similar purpose to this chapter – keeping people up-to-date on emerging materials of others in the field. Please also note that a great number of the non-book materials listed in this chapter are free, or distributed by their creators for a nominal charge.

References

Australian Communications and Media Authority. (2010). Cybersmart parents: Connecting parents to cybersafety resources. *Commonwealth of Australia*. Retrieved from www.acma.gov.au/WEB/STANDARD/pc=PC_311301.

Bauman, S. (2011). *Cyberbullying: What counselors need to know*. Alexandria, VA: American Counseling Association.

Berson, I. R., Berson, M. J., Desai, S., Falls, D., & Fenaughty, J. (2008). An analysis of electronic media to prepare children for safe and ethical practices in digital environments. *Contemporary Issues in Technology and Teacher Education, 8*(3), 222–243.

Berson, M. J., & Berson, I. R. (2004). Developing thoughtful "cybercitizens." *Social Studies and the Young Learner, 16*(4), 5–8.

Byron, T. (2010). Do we have safer children in a digital world? A review of progress since the 2008 Byron Review. *United Kingdom Department for Children, Schools and Families*. Retrieved from www.dcsf.gov.uk/byronreview/pdfs/do%20we%20have%20safer%20children%20in%20a%20digital%20world-WEB.pdf.

Emmens, T., & Phippen, A. (2010). Evaluating online safety programs. *Berkman Center for Internet and Society, Harvard University.* Retrieved from http://publius.cc/evaluating_online_safety_programs.

Hinduja, S., & Patchin, J. W. (2009). *Bullying beyond the schoolyard: Preventing and responding to cyberbullying.* Thousand Oaks, CA: Sage Publications (Corwin Press).

Jones, L. M. (2010). The future of Internet safety education: Critical lessons from four decades of youth drug abuse prevention. *Berkman Center for Internet and Society, Harvard University.* Retrieved from http://publius.cc/future_internet_safety_education_critical_lessons_four_decades_youth_drug_abuse_prevention.

Levinson, M., & Socia, D. (2010). Moving beyond one size fits all with digital citizenship. Retrieved from http://publius.cc/moving_beyond_one_size_fits_all_digital_citizenship.

Mishna, F., Cook, C., Saini, M., Wu, M. J., & MacFadden, R. (2009). Interventions for children, youth, and parents to prevent and reduce cyber abuse. *Campbell Systematic Reviews, 2.*

Mitchell, K. J., Wolak, J., & Finkelhor, D. (2010). Online safety: Why research is important. *Berkman Center for Internet and Society, Harvard University.* Retrieved from http://publius.cc/online_safety_why_research_important.

Nigam, H., & Collier, A. (2010). Youth safety on a living Internet. *National Telecommunications and Information Administration.* Retrieved from www.ntia.doc.gov/reports/2010/OSTWG_Final_Report_060410.pdf.

Palfrey, J. G., boyd, d., & Sacco, D. (2009). *Enhancing child safety and online technologies: Final report of the Internet Safety Technical Task Force.* Durham, NC: Carolina Academic Press.

Shariff, S. (2008). *Cyber-bullying: Issues and solutions for the school, the classroom and the home.* New York: Routledge.

Shariff, S. (2009). *Confronting cyber-bullying: What schools need to know to control misconduct and avoid legal consequences.* New York: Cambridge University Press.

Shariff, S., & Hoff, D. L., (2007). Cyber bullying: Clarifying legal boundaries for school supervision in Cyberspace. *International Journal of Cyber Criminology, 1*(1), 76–118.

Strom, P., & Strom, R. (2009). *Adolescents in the Internet age.* Charlotte, NC: Information Publishing, Inc.

Walker, J. L. (2009). *The contextualized rapid resolution cycle intervention model for cyberbullying.* Arizona State University.

9

RESPONDING TO CYBERBULLYING

Advice for Educators and Parents

Elizabeth K. Englander

Introduction

As with all social upheavals – large and small – cyberbullying and cyber misbehaviors confound and confuse us. That the modern child demonstrates such effortless and marked ease with electronic devices stymies adults even further. Despite their evident comfort with electronic devices, children today are *not* in fact particularly knowledgeable about the prudent and effective use of electronic communications, and thus all parties involved in cyberbullying may find themselves at a loss as to an effective response.

The responses of school administrators and parents must differ. While the first concern of educators is to ensure that all children in the school are able to learn, parents must consider issues such as their child's development, health, social skills, and family life. Our research and fieldwork around the issue of cyberbullying have enabled us to offer the following guides in responding effectively. This chapter will review responding to cyberbullying *as a School Administrator*, *as a Parent if your child is the victim*, and *as a Parent if your child is the cyberbully*.

Responding as a School Administrator

The Problem

Unlike traditional bullying, cyberbullying frequently takes place off-campus, most typically in the child's home. The fact that cyberbullying takes place predominantly *off-campus* means that the behavior potentially falls into a different legal category. While behavior that takes place on the school campus is clearly under the jurisdiction of educators, behavior that takes place at home is usually viewed as being under the jurisdiction of parents.

BOX 9.1 WHERE'S THE FOCUS WHEN IT COMES TO SCHOOL INTERVENTIONS?

The issue of discipline, and whether or not off-campus behavior is subject to discipline by school administrators, is a thorny one that has been repeatedly litigated and is in fact being litigated at the current time. Yet, is it appropriate for schools to focus (perhaps exclusively) on whether or not they can discipline a cyberbully? I would argue that the focus is somewhat misplaced, and that many other steps are even more important. Schools should probably never take the attitude that in the case of an off-campus victimization, they have absolutely no role to play. For one, they will always have a role to play in supporting a victim, and this is true for any off-campus victimization that is significant enough to impact the child's emotional well-being. In addition, schools can always take part in the education of a child who is engaging in risky behavior online. Finally, it appears that online incidents often also involve in-school activities – an obvious place where schools can help!

One important exception to this rule is off-campus behavior or speech that causes a "real threat" or "substantial disruption" to the school climate. Exactly what a "substantial disruption" means is not clear. Different courts have used different definitions for this term. For each cyberbullying case, school administrators must decide (often with the help of the school's counsel) if the cyber-behavior is making, or will make, a *substantial disruption* before they decide to discipline a cyberbully. The legal issues inherent in disciplining off-campus speech, including cyberbullying, are covered in much more detail in Chapter 3 of this volume. However, even if a school decides that cyberbullying is *not* making a substantial disruption to the school environment, there are still important steps that all schools can make to help cope with and resolve cyberbullying incidents.

Seven Action Steps

Here are seven actions that could be taken *regardless* of the disruption to the school environment (or lack of it):

1. *Have an educational discussion with the cyberbully and with cyber-bystanders.* Ideally, this should take place in the principal's office. It may be important to point out that this discussion is *not* discipline; it is educational, about the dangers of cyberbullying and the fact that everyone is now aware of the situation. If relevant, discuss future legal problems the child may incur if they continue with these behaviors. You can involve a school resource

officer (SRO) or other police officer in the discussion (see Chapter 10 for more details of the role of school law enforcement), and the child's parents, if possible. Teachers who hear students discussing cyberbullying will, of course, want to follow their school's protocol in reporting and responding, but should consider strongly contributing to the education of their students by discussing the issues with them as well.

2. *Immediately inform cyberbullies and cyber-bystanders about the consequences for bullying or cyberbullying in school.* Although schools may often lack disciplinary jurisdiction for off-campus speech, they can certainly discipline students for bullying or cyberbullying that happens on-campus. Recent research at the Massachusetts Aggression Reduction Center (MARC) suggests that many digital bullying events involve events during the school day (Englander, 2010b). Thus, a cyberbully or cyber-bystanders should be warned that any continuation of the bullying or cyberbullying during the school day can result in immediate consequences.

3. *Be sure that a victim has a Safety and Comfort Plan.* The victim's sense of safety may be compromised both online and in school. One result of this is that the victim may require a "safe person" in school – someone who the child likes and can go to, and the child's teachers must be told that this child has the freedom to go see their safe person at any time. Initially, do not be concerned if a victim appears to exploit their safe person as a way to avoid class time or schoolwork. Focus instead on the child's sense of safety and comfort. Eventually, when the situation appears to be resolved, you can address a child who exploits the situation (if necessary).

4. *Inform all relevant adults – teachers, coaches, counselors, and bus drivers – about the situation between all the children involved.* Don't assume that online problems are not the business of school personnel. Remember that social problems online frequently find their way into school, and vice versa (Englander, 2010a). Ensure that the adults are aware of the potential for bullying and that they keep a very sharp eye open. Have a checklist of relevant people and check-off each adult as they are informed.

5. *Have a plan for less structured areas, such as buses and the lunchroom.* It's in these areas where online problems are most commonly discussed among students. The victim should never be left to hope that they find a safe seat. For example, in the lunchroom, a seat could be reserved in advance near friends; on the school bus, the seat behind the driver could be reserved. Playground activities can be pre-planned. Care may be taken to keep target and bullies physically apart, to minimize opportunities for abuse. The general principle is to plan ahead for unstructured areas, where bullying is likely to occur. The target can identify those areas where problems have occurred in the past.

6. *Follow up with parents, especially parents of victims.* Do not wait for them to call you; call them to let them know that the above actions are being taken.

Taking the initiative conveys your attention and concern about the matter at hand; waiting until parents contact you might suggest that perhaps you are less interested. Many parents want, or even demand, to know what disciplinary actions are being taken against a cyberbully; you may need to educate them about confidentiality laws (Englander, 2006). Be sure that they understand you are not merely refusing to furnish information because you personally wish to protect a bully (that is, do not assume that they understand this, but state it explicitly). When speaking to parents of a child who may be engaging in bullying behaviors, the goal is to emphasize *concern* (versus frustration) and if discipline is warranted, to emphasize that the goal of any discipline is to help their child *learn* that such behaviors are unacceptable.

7. *Consider creating a "response team" to implement all these responses.* The response team should consist of counselors, SROs, administrators, and teachers. The team can also handle communications with parents and document that all above steps have been taken. Response teams are valuable for tracking children who are frequently involved as either bullies or victims.

BOX 9.2 DOES IT HAPPEN ONLINE OR IN SCHOOL?

As adults, we have a tendency to think of social problems, like bullying, as happening either in school or online (electronically). But that dichotomy may be a false one. Kids today seem to often regard electronic communications and online interactions as just another way to interact and talk with one another – not as a separate, different event. In our current research, 80% of 140 college freshmen characterized most fights or bullying as happening in both venues – that when a social problem begins, it involves both online and in-school behaviors – not one or the other. This suggests, from a practical point of view, that when we are coping with a bullying episode, we always need to ask about both electronic and in-school contributors and incidents.

Parental Responses

Responding as a Parent When Your Child is the Victim

"Responding" as a parent really involves two different issues: how to respond once cyberbullying has happened and, separately, how to avoid cyberbullying in the first place. Clearly, avoiding the problem is preferable. Cyberbullying is somewhat like toothpaste; once out of the tube, there is no going back. What I mean by that is that while bullying is a trauma that children can certainly recover from, it is better to avoid experiencing it altogether. This type of social problem is definitely one situation where an ounce of prevention is worth even more than a pound of cure. With that in mind, here are some common-sense tips that may help parents *avoid* cyberbullying victimization.

Avoid telling your child that online activities are worthless, no big deal, unimportant, etc. It's fine to emphasize the value of *non*-online activities – indeed, most kids today need some encouragement to go offline! But avoid language that may just convince your child that you don't "get it" and are not the person to talk to about online life. For kids today, online socializing is neither worthless nor unimportant. Imagine your parents telling you, as a teenager, that talking on the phone with your friends is pointless – I'm sure most of us would have vehemently disagreed!

Discuss social networking sites with your child. Social networking websites (such as AIM or Facebook) are where most cyberbullying occurs, according to research (Englander, 2010a). Does your child have an account on one of these websites? Talk to your kids about how social networking sites can be fun but, consider the following:

- Profiles are *never* truly private, no matter what settings are active. Any online page that multiple people can view can be copied and distributed very easily; and just because your child has limited the people who can access it, doesn't mean that those people are obliged to keep information on it confidential.
- Because profiles are never truly private, be sure that anything you put on your profile is fine for *everyone* to see – parents, teachers, anyone. Private items, photos, comments, or jokes don't belong on a social networking profile.
- Online, it's easy for users to fake an age, photo, comment, or even an emotion. You may have read or heard about predatory adults pretending to be kids in order to lure unsuspecting teens into very dangerous situations; while these news stories are usually true, they are also relatively rare online. However, what's *not* so rare is for kids to fake the online expression of emotions (e.g., pretending to be romantically interested when they're not) or for kids to pretend to be someone else online (e.g., pretending to be a target they're mad at, and then leaving comments or messages online which will get the target in trouble with others). These entries are technically forbidden because they are fraudulent, but they're not rare or unusual. The lesson for kids is: you may *feel* that something you read online must be true, but that feeling is not always correct. Also, be skeptical when something odd happens online (like receiving a sudden, out-of-the-blue message, supposedly from your best friend, telling you that he or she has always hated you and everyone hates you) (Hinduja & Patchin, 2009b). Keep in mind that your best friend's identity may have been hijacked by someone else.

Make sure that online life still follows the rules. Adults routinely discuss behavioral rules with children for a variety of different settings. We talk with kids about how to behave at school; how to behave in church; and how to behave at home. But unfortunately we don't often think to talk about how to behave online, and kids, as a result, may form the strong impression that online interactions are one area where there are no rules. Because kids often tend to think that online interactions are somehow exempt, it's very important to emphasize that the rules for everyday life also apply when you're online. Consider your family's rules, such as:

- No cheating or lying. If you have to lie about your age or anything else to set up a social networking profile, it's not okay.
- Watch your use of language. Written, online language is even more sensitive than spoken language, because there is always a record of it.
- Treat others politely and with respect. Even online, even when chatting.
- Nothing online is "private" (except for finances and banking, which most kids don't do) so please don't argue that you "need your online privacy" – there is no online privacy!

Make sure the kids know the facts about cell phone use. When your child gets their first cell phone, discuss and compile a list of rules for using a cell phone. Your rules might include issues such as: texting of cruel or inappropriate comments or photos; using the camera illegally (e.g., recording video of someone without their permission,[1] or recording them without clothes on); and how they would feel and respond if they were pressured into providing inappropriate photos. In our research, about one-quarter of the kids who sexted (that is, used their cell phones to take and send nude or semi-nude photos of themselves) did so because they were pressured, bullied, threatened, or coerced into doing so. (Other reasons for sexting included attempts to convey romantic or sexual interest and curiosity.) The findings from our 2010 data suggest that kids pressuring or coercing each other into providing nude photos may not be rare or unusual. Again, the best approach is *prevention*. Make sure your kids know that sexting can be prosecuted and that they shouldn't give in to pressure to send inappropriate pictures to anyone (Snell & Englander, 2010). If they wouldn't rob a bank with their friends or partners, they also shouldn't send nude photos because their friends or partners want them to. Texting and cell phone Internet access are powerful technologies that your child may or may not be ready for – many young adolescents are not yet able to fully understand the impact of what they can do with these technologies. At the MARC at Bridgewater State University we do recommend that parents of children under 15 years old should consider carefully whether the benefits of these technologies outweigh the risks – of course, children can still have cell phones which enable them to make phone calls, which is often the primary reason parents want them to have cell phones in the first place. Teens themselves want, of course, unlimited and unmonitored texting and Internet access on their cell phones; this desire is totally understandable. The difficult judgment that parents need to make is to decide if their child's understanding of the potential misuse of the technology is sufficiently mature to warrant that level of electronic communications power and freedom. The age of 15 is just a guideline for parents, who may feel that their 13-year-old is sufficiently mature, or that their 17-year-old is still not ready for unfettered cell phone usage.

BOX 9.3 SEMANTICS MATTER: LET'S THINK ABOUT THE WORDS WE USE

New communications and devices develop so quickly that it's sometimes challenging to use the right words, but doing so is very important. For example, because we've characterized limited-access profiles on social networking sites as "private," kids (and adults, for that matter) tend to think of them as, well, private. In fact, these profiles are almost never truly private, in the sense that they do not have controls that would prevent any content on them from being made public fairly easily. Many teens have hundreds of "friends" online, often with full access to all of their content, and content can be easily copied and posted elsewhere. Another example in which semantics matter is the designation of mobile devices as "cell phones" when, in fact (according to both our research and the Pew's), kids rarely use them to make voice calls; they are primarily used as mobile computers and by terming them "cell phones" we may be confusing parents who think of them as voice-calling devices. Perhaps we should adopt the term "mobiles" instead.

Responding if Your Child is Victimized

If your child is cyberbullied on a website – such as on a social networking site – that activity usually constitutes what is known as a Terms of Service violation. When anyone sets up an account on a website like a social networking site, they agree to a set of legal terms called the Terms of Service. These terms usually forbid cyberbullying activities (e.g., humiliating people, abusing people, etc.). How to respond to a cyberbully event?

- Look up and review the hosting site's policy. Send them a copy of the webpage and a copy of their own policy. Demand that they remove the page. Use the "Report Abuse" link if the site has one. If not, look in the "Contact Us" area, or send an email to "abuse@" (whatever website the abuse occurs on) (Willard, 2007b).

- If it's spilling over into school, notify the school immediately.
- Keep the evidence. Even if this appears to be a one-time event, this may in fact be the first in a series of events – it's hard to know for certain. Keeping the evidence may be done by either printing out the webpage, or taking a screenshot of the webpage (that is, creating a static copy of the webpage that you can save as an electronic picture) (Hinduja & Patchin, 2009a).
- Have your child block screen names. Talk to them about the possibility that blocking the screen name may make them worry about "missing something." On most social networking sites, there is a button or link that is usually labeled "block" that permits the user to block communications and access for a particular person. The "help" feature can guide you to these blocking features if they're not apparent.
- Consider having a discussion with your child about the impact of messaging on their social life. Although young teens almost universally feel that everyone on the planet has messaging and that their life will be ruined without it, it's worth introducing the idea that these technologies are not always a one-way street: they may enhance socializing, but they may also hurt friendships and romantic relationships (Hinduja & Patchin, 2008). Not every young teen is ready for messaging, and despite what your child may tell you, not every teen has it. If they do, a problem that they experience with messaging may be a learning opportunity for them, and a chance to view the issue in a more even-handed manner. As teens mature and move into high-school, they often are more prepared developmentally to see both the ups and downs of a situation. What you want to avoid is conveying to a child who has reported cyberbullying that you're now punishing them for reporting by peremptorily removing their messaging capability without discussion and consideration, including their opinions and input (Willard, 2007a). As I've noted before, this is much easier to address from a prevention point of view, right before or immediately when a child first receives a cell phone.
- Never give out proprietary information (about yourself or your friends) (Patchin & Hinduja, 2010a, 2010b). Kids may understand very well that they should not post their cell phone number, but they may forget that they should not post their friend's cell phone number or tag a person in a photo who does not want to be tagged.[2] This is not about stranger danger; this is about respecting the privacy of others.
- Although Facebook permits users to join their online friends to groups without the friend's permission, this is not really a good idea. Users should only join themselves to groups. ConnectSafely.org has posted on their website a comprehensive, detailed guide for parents which can help with understanding its settings and policies (Collier & Magid, 2010).
- Never respond to abusive messages. This may seem easy, but it's worth reiterating; kids are often tempted to shoot off a quick response, but it helps if they understand that this is just feeding the fire.

- When should you consider involving the police? Most of the time, cyber-bullying does not involve illegal or criminal behaviors, although it's import-ant to keep in mind that statutes vary significantly by state. A good rule of thumb is that communications that threaten or promise violence or danger should be reported to the police, who may be able to help advise you as to the legality or illegality of the communication (Shariff, 2008).
- As with most things, prevention is easier than reaction! Just talking about these issues will help your child.

Responding as a Parent when Your Child is the Cyberbully

Begin by understanding that children make mistakes, and these days, they make mistakes online. The first step in effectively addressing this mistake is to accept that your child made a mistake, and that you are the adult responsible for responding appropriately and ensuring that the mistake doesn't happen again. It's hard for parents to acknowledge their own children's mistakes, but as others have noted in previous chapters of this book, a significant proportion of teens have admitted to cyberbullying others. This is a problem many parents are going to have to learn to address.

The content of cyberbullying communications can be very upsetting for parents to read. However, it's important to keep in mind that MARC fieldwork in Massa-chusetts has found a great deal of anecdotal evidence suggesting that children (and adults) are significantly more willing to "go further" and to type very shocking things that they would never say in person. The fact that these communications occur in type, and online, greatly reduces their *perceived* impact. Kids believe that online statements simply "don't count" because they're not being said to some-one's face. Indeed, the number-one reason that our research subjects told us they preferred bullying online was because they didn't have to see their victim's face.

Most parents react by immediately limiting their child's social networking access temporarily on computers, cell phones, and mobile tablet devices (such as the iPod and iPad) (the length of limited access would depend, of course, on the problem behavior that you're responding to). That's a fine place to start; but I would add one additional piece. Your child is going to have to learn how to use these com-munications appropriately, and to do that, they need to practice. So I would also emphasize to your child that: (1) here are your expectations; and (2) if they want to continue doing social networking *in the future*, they'll have to earn their way back to it by demonstrating consistently that they understand the rules, understand why they are important and can be relied upon to follow the rules.

By adding these provisions, you're giving them some hope that they can regain their toys, but also underlining the importance of your rules. You can also let them know that regaining this privilege will occur only in stages; for example, the second stage might be letting your child use a new Facebook account, but only with parental control software that (1) lets you see every single thing they type – no exceptions, and (2) limits the time they can spend on a site such as Facebook. As they progress through the stages with no problems, you can ease up.

That's the *doing* part. Now here's the *talking* part.

When a child has cyberbullied, odds are that he or she doesn't understand what all the fuss is about. So the first goal of talking is to help him or her understand why cyberbullying is so hurtful. Have your child read about, and discuss, the stories of Tyler Clementi, Phoebe Prince, and Megan Meier. Read newspaper stories and commentary online, and talk about the power of words. Don't be totally stern and judgmental – it is fine to acknowledge that it can be tricky to know how writing is taken, and that sometimes one means to be funny or look "cool." Ask your child to reflect upon *why* he did what he did, how he was feeling at the time, and what his motive was. Ask her to reflect upon the impact on her victim, and ask if this has ever happened to her. (Odds are it has.)

Emphasize that a willingness to talk about this problem in a lengthy and meaningful way is part of how your child is going to show you that he or she is reliable and can be trusted online. Give your child a timeline, saying, for example, "If you really take a lot of time to talk about this with me, and talk about it seriously, then in one month I'll reassess whether or not you can have limited access to Facebook." Note that this type of statement gives you a lot of "outs": the responsibility is really *theirs* to demonstrate a willingness to explore this issue. Don't worry if you sense that cooperation is being faked at first – it's not likely that after doing all this research, anyone could be truly unaffected by all the damage and trauma surrounding this problem.

A final step would be to consider reparations, which take into account the other family. I'm not a lawyer, and you should consult one if you think any contact with the victim's family could have legal repercussions, but I'll consider this issue from a psychological point of view. You may feel that apologizing to the parents is the right thing to do, but don't expect them to be gracious about it, and let them know that you're not expecting that they'll just instantly forgive your child. Rather, let them know that you're calling to say that you're very sorry and that you are taking serious actions about the situation, and that you take it *very* seriously. You might pose this apology and explanation to them in a letter, which might be easier for both you and them. I would hesitate, however, to advise you about having your child apologize to the target immediately. A victim of bullying can experience an apology as a veiled threat, even if it's not intended that way.

Should I Monitor Everything My Child Does Online? Will That Reduce Cyberbullying?

Monitoring children online – that is, using software to see what they do online – is usually a vigorous debate characterized by two positions. The parents protest that they pay the bills and they are responsible for their child's actions, while the children protest that they deserve their privacy online and should be trusted. In my opinion, neither argument is relevant. Children should be monitored online by their parents for one very good reason: they will, in essence, be monitored online for their entire lives by their friends, employers, families, and communities, and childhood is an important opportunity to teach them to stop and think before they send or post something.

News stories today abound with cases of young adults who post or send foolish messages or pictures and rapidly lose jobs, careers, or both. Clearly, learning to stop and think *before* posting or sending something is a critical skill. We would like to assume that people naturally develop this ability as they grow, but it is apparent by now that if that does happen, it does not happen for everyone. Your time as a parent with your child is your opportunity to ensure that your child does learn this skill. By telling your child, "I will see everything you do online," you are in essence training him or her to stop and think, "What will mom think about this?" before anything is sent or posted. Several years later, having had that thought thousands of times, the habit will be set and your child can go on to adult life having learned electronic prudence from you. That is the best and most sensible reason I know for monitoring your children's online behavior. Of course, it requires you to be honest and candid with your children and for them to know that you will be monitoring them; but that is good parenting anyway. The argument that you will almost certainly hear from your child about their privacy "rights" is an opportunity for education too: Any child who argues for online privacy rights has not learned that *there is no privacy online*.[3]

Will monitoring your child reduce cyberbullying? Not by itself. If your child complains, grumpily, to his or her friends that their mom or dad is watching their Facebook page, then others are less likely to post anything truly egregious. Likewise, knowing that their parents will see what they type will almost certainly reduce the disinhibiting effect of the Internet!

The Internet has made being a parent today more challenging, for certain, but it doesn't necessarily pose a serious problem. Although much has been made of the "dangers" of the Internet, including cyberbullying, it's important to remember that on balance, electronic communications have greatly enhanced our lives. The difficult issues for parents seem to focus on quantity and access to technology, and the necessary decisions that have to be made on a case-by-case basis. How much do your children use electronics versus other types of communications? How can we encourage a variety of developmental experiences in a positive way (versus disdaining their electronic preferences)? Exposing children to other media that they will enjoy may be key – e.g., choosing books based on their interests versus books on topics others may approve. Encouraging experimentation is challenging with many children, but a strong focus on their personal styles and tastes can be very helpful. And accepting their interest in, and strong draw to, electronics needs to be part of that.

Notes

I am *not* a lawyer. For legal facts and advice on when and how to respond to cyber-bullying, be sure to consult a qualified attorney.

1 Different states have different laws regarding the legality of making a video of an unaware subject. In some states, you must have the permission of the subject being video recorded, or you have committed a wiretapping violation. In other states, you don't need their permission. Individuals should check the laws in their own states.

2 "Tagging" someone in a photo simply means identifying them, so that if you search for "John Smith" you would find not also text references to that name, but also photos in which that person has been tagged. Usually the person who posts the photo tags the people in the photo, who may or may not wish to be identified in that photo.

3 The exception to this is banking and financial sites, which typically have no viewers except their account owners, and also have good security, and are thus at low risk of being copied and distributed. However, my experience is that kids generally don't do their banking and financial portfolios when they are online!

References

Collier, A., & Magid, L. (2010). A parent's guide to Facebook. *ConnectSafely.org*. Retrieved from www.connectsafely.org/pdfs/fbparents.pdf.

Englander, E. (2006). Why is it confidential? Understanding your school's limits on sharing information. *Massachusetts Aggression Reduction Center, Bridgewater State College*. Retrieved from http://webhost.bridgew.edu/marc/that%27s%20confidential.pdf.

Englander, E. (2010a). *Cyberbullying*. Paper presented at the American Academy of Child and Adolescent Psychiatry Annual Conference, New York.

Englander, E. (2010b). *Cyberbullying: Recent research*. Paper presented at the Family Online Safety Institute Annual Conference, Washington, DC.

Hinduja, S., & Patchin, J. W. (2008). Personal information of adolescents on the Internet: A quantitative content analysis of MySpace. *Journal of Adolescence, 31*(1), 125–146.

Hinduja, S., & Patchin, J. W. (2009a). *Bullying beyond the schoolyard: Preventing and responding to cyberbullying*. Thousand Oaks, CA: Sage Publications (Corwin Press).

Hinduja, S., & Patchin, J. W. (2009b). Safe and responsible social networking: Strategies for keeping yourself safe online. *Cyberbullying Research Center*. Retrieved from www.cyberbullying.us/safe_responsible_social_networking.pdf.

Patchin, J. W., & Hinduja, S. (2010a). Changes in adolescent online social networking behaviors from 2006 to 2009. *Computers and Human Behavior, 26*, 1818–1821.

Patchin, J. W., & Hinduja, S. (2010b). Trends in online social networking: Adolescent use of MySpace over time. *New Media & Society, 12*(2), 197–216.

Shariff, S. (2008). *Cyber-bullying: Issues and solutions for the school, the classroom and the home*. New York: Routledge.

Snell, P. A., & Englander, E. K. (2010). Cyberbullying victimization and behaviors among girls: Applying research findings in the field. *Journal of Social Science, 6*, 510–514.

Willard, N. E. (2007a). *Cyber-safe kids, cyber-savvy teens, helping young people use the Internet safely and responsibly*. San Francisco, CA: Jossey-Bass.

Willard, N. E. (2007b). *Cyberbullying and cyberthreats: Responding to the challenge of online social aggression, threats, and distress*. Champaign, IL: Research Press.

10

SCHOOL LAW ENFORCEMENT AND CYBERBULLYING

Sameer Hinduja and Justin W. Patchin

> I believe that cyberbullying is a serious issue occurring nationwide. In order to stay ahead of the curve we as law enforcement must continue to train and develop strategies that equip us to deal with the ever-changing times.
>
> *School Resource Officer from Missouri*

Adolescent aggression and school violence have long concerned parents, educators, and law enforcement officers. The school shootings of the late 1990s forced Americans to closely examine the safety and security of its educational settings. Interestingly, an in-depth analysis of these shootings conducted by the US Secret Service identified that experience with bullying and peer aggression was one of the only common factors among the shooters involved in the various incidents (Vossekuil, Fein, Reddy, Borum, & Modzeleski, 2002). Indeed, interviews with survivors (victims, shooters, and witnesses) revealed that being tormented by classmates was one of the primary elements that contributed to the violent outbursts. That said, it is important to remember that schools continue to be among the safest of environments for adolescents (Dinkes, Kemp, & Baum, 2009). Far fewer youth are harmed inside the walls of a school than outside. Nevertheless, it is clear that reducing the frequency and seriousness of all forms of violence committed at school is a critical objective.

A number of studies have demonstrated that a significant proportion of adolescents experience bullying at school. For example, a study by the National Institute of Child Health and Human Development found that 17% of students report being bullied and 19% report bullying others "sometimes" or "weekly" (Ericson, 2001). The Bureau of Justice Statistics' *Indicators of School Crime and Safety Report* noted that approximately 32% of students between 12 and 18 years of age were bullied at school during the 2007–2008 school year (Dinkes et al., 2009). Of those, 21% experienced it once or twice a month, 10% once or twice a week, and 7% almost daily (Dinkes et al., 2009). However, research has also found that bullying incidents can be reduced following the introduction of law enforcement officers at school. For example, in one study bullying victimization among students decreased 67% with a School Resource Officer (SRO) on campus (Humphrey & Huey, 2001). Students who reported bullying others also declined 53% after the SRO arrived. Moreover, of those students who reported feeling unsafe in their school prior to the introduction of an SRO, 66% reported feeling safe afterward. These findings underscore the important position that school police occupy, and that the difference they can make on campus is not only substantiated, but also substantial.

While bullying historically has occurred within or in close proximity to the school, advances in communication technologies have allowed bullies to extend their reach. Cyberbullying, defined as "willful and repeated harm inflicted through the use of computers, cell phones, and other electronic devices" (Hinduja & Patchin, 2009:5), has become an even greater concern among adolescents and adults alike. Estimates of the number of youth who experience cyberbullying vary widely (5–40% or more – see Chapter 2), depending on the age of the group studied and how cyberbullying is defined (Hinduja & Patchin, 2009; Kowalski & Limber, 2007; Patchin & Hinduja, 2006; Williams & Guerra, 2007; Ybarra & Mitchell, 2004).

While it is clear that cyberbullying is a significant problem facing teens and schools, the question remains: What role does school law enforcement play in preventing and responding to these issues? Based on the consistency of current research findings (Hinduja & Patchin, 2009), it is probable that cyberbullying behaviors and other forms of online aggression will continue to affect a meaningful proportion of adolescents. As a result, school-based law enforcement officers will increasingly be called upon to intervene.

This chapter will discuss the role of school police in preventing and responding to cyberbullying incidents. Most SROs are now keenly aware of the new challenges created by the intersection of teens, technology, and the school, while many traditional law enforcement officers are just now confronting these new issues. In a recent survey of SROs, 83% told us that they needed additional training on preventing and responding to cyberbullying. While some have training and experience with the threat of sexual predators in chatrooms, research suggests that many more youth will encounter a cyberbully as compared to those who might be groomed, abducted, and assaulted by a stranger on the Internet (Palfrey, boyd, & Sacco, 2009).

The following text is intended to serve as a primer for school police, who play a crucial role in responding to and preventing cyberbullying among students. Specific actions on their part should also improve a number of other issues on campus, such as related misbehavior and rule-breaking, peer conflict, and more serious forms of school violence. Making progress in improving social relations among students by addressing cyberbullying can also contribute to a safer and more positive school climate, which tends to improve academic achievement, attendance, extracurricular participation, and social and emotional growth (Fraser, 1998; Freiberg, 1999; Stover, 2005). To be sure, harassment among students via computers and cell phones is often a component and symptom of a larger issue. Dealing with it should pay valuable dividends across the entire landscape of student–student interaction, student–teacher interaction, scholastic performance, and general conduct.

Below, we first discuss our findings on SRO needs in this area. After a brief review of the current state of cyberbullying laws – with which school law enforcement would do well to familiarize themselves – we summarize the ways in which school police can enlist the student body and the administration in confronting the reality and consequences of this problem. Prevention, though, is a duty as equally as important as their investigative response. We therefore subsequently clarify exactly how SROs should get involved to deal with cyberbullying incidents when they arise. Here, a number of strategies and plans of action are covered for the purpose of providing pragmatic advice and stimulating other creative implementations to address cyberbullying.

Outside of this guidance, the chapter focuses on some of the major legal implications that affect the way SROs can act – especially as it relates to the search and seizure of digital evidence from students. What does the law say with regard to the standard of proof that frees officers to dig deep into the contents of electronic devices to search for evidence of a violation of school policy or law? Are there any differences in investigative abilities between school police and school administration, and if so, how does this play out in terms of what can or cannot be done? Are there any pitfalls of which SROs should be aware, and any best approaches when working with staff and students in a coordinated response? These and other key issues are parsed out with the hope of truly informing officers – and other school personnel with whom they interact – of the ideal way to counter and preempt harm of adolescents by their peers in cyberspace and the real world.

Law Enforcement Views of Cyberbullying

An SRO walking through the halls of the school today will observe many behaviors, see many devices, and hear many words that would be foreign to his or her contemporaries from even just five years ago. It is remarkable how much has changed with the explosion of cell phones and Internet usage among youth, and how these technologies have altered the landscape upon which social and conduct norms must be enforced (with transgressions addressed informally or formally). Cyberbullying is one of the most significant new issues with which current and future SROs will have to wrestle, and anecdotal and research-based accounts from school districts across the nation depict a lack of clear guidance, training, and support received by law enforcement in schools. This is unfortunate when considering that bullying is an age-old problem, that bullying in recent times frequently implicates technological devices and mediums, and that research has shown a strong link between online and offline bullying (Hinduja & Patchin, 2007, 2008a, 2009; Patchin & Hinduja, 2011). Without a doubt, SROs need explicit and comprehensive assistance in dealing with these issues in order to ensure the safety and security of kids at school. Moreover, they must work to protect the integrity of a (hopefully) positive climate and supportive atmosphere among students, teachers, staff, and administrators.

BOX 10.1 "IN THEIR OWN WORDS"

SROs told us about what's promising, what doesn't work, and what is needed to prevent and respond to cyberbullying.

What's Promising

"Getting parents on board right away."
"Mediation and counseling."
"Having a clear policy and following it consistently."
"The most effective means of ending cyberbullying is education and sound policy."
"Sitting down with all the parties and working out a solution and talking about potential consequences."

What Doesn't Work

"Lecturing kids doesn't seem to be too effective."
"There is no proven action that will work on all kids. Some have no fear of consequences."
"...advised of criminal harassment law and given report # for court. Did not stop the bullying."
"None have worked well, kids do not care about laws yet, parents are the same."

What's Needed

"We need more training – this is predominately an SRO role."
"More education needs to be presented to students and parents to address the problem."
"We need to do a better job of getting the message out, and getting legislation to stop these pain-in-the-ass crimes."
"The laws need to catch up to this technology so a girl sending a pic of herself to her boyfriend isn't prosecuted and charged as a sex offender."

In a recent survey, we queried over 300 SROs about their experiences dealing with cyberbullying. Officers were invited to participate in the study if they were members of the National Association of School Resource Officers during the summer of 2010. We first learned that the vast majority of SROs (95%) view cyberbullying as a serious problem warranting the response of law enforcement. In addition, over 70% of officers reported investigating an average of 13 cyberbullying cases during the previous school year. This is a non-trivial number that illuminates the pervasiveness of the problem.

We also asked officers to rate the extent to which law enforcement should play a significant role in several different cyberbullying scenarios. Respondents reported the greatest law enforcement role in examples which involved a threat of physical harm. For example, when officers were asked to rank on a scale of 0–10 (with 0 meaning "no law enforcement role" and 10 meaning "a significant law enforcement role") the following situation: "A male student receives an email from an unknown person threatening to kill him at school tomorrow," the average score was 9.1. Alternatively, respondents suggested that a formal law enforcement response was not necessary in situations which simply involved potential rule breaking of student codes of conduct. For example, when given the following scenario: "A teacher confiscates a cell phone from a student in class and wants to determine if it contains any information that is in violation of school policy," the average score was 2.4. To be sure, law enforcement officers understand their role more clearly when the behavior is an obvious violation of state or local law, and less so if there is no immediate safety concern to another person. While this makes sense on the surface, the latter scenario should warrant at least some of the same response steps that the SRO would take with the former. Collectively, this points to a need for greater awareness, education, and training for these professionals in a variety of areas. One of these involves the current legal climate related to online aggression, and it is this topic to which we now turn our attention.

Cyberbullying Laws

It is imperative that law enforcement officers stay up-to-date on the ever-evolving state and local laws concerning online behaviors, and equip themselves with the skills and knowledge to intervene as necessary. In our previously discussed survey of SROs, we found that almost one-quarter of respondents did not know if their state had a cyberbullying law. This is surprising since their most visible responsibility involves addressing actions that are in violation of law (e.g., harassment, threats, stalking). At last count, 45 states had laws (or policies that have the effect of law) regarding bullying, and 31 of those included some mention of electronic forms of harassment. Almost all of these laws simply direct school districts to have a bullying and harassment policy, though few delineate

TABLE 10.1 SRO Perceptions of their Role in Responding to Examples of Cyberbullying (N = 339)

Scenario	Score
A male student receives an email from an unknown person threatening to kill him at school tomorrow.	9.1
A female student, Jenny, covertly takes a picture of another female student, Margaret, in her underwear in the girls' locker room, and posts it on "HotOrNot.com" without permission. This site allows the rest of the student body to rate or judge Margaret's physical appearance.	8.9
A parent calls to report that her son has a naked image of a female student from his school on his cell phone.	8.4
A parent calls the police department to report that her son is being cyberbullied by another youth in their neighborhood.	7.8
A student creates a Facebook Fan Page called "Give Mary a Wedgie Day." Mary is a student at a school in your jurisdiction.	5.7
A male student reveals another student's sexual orientation (without permission) via Twitter to the rest of the student body.	5.7
A female student receives a text message from another student saying that she is a slut.	4.2
A student creates a webpage making fun of the school principal.	4.1
A teacher confiscates a cell phone from a student in class and wants to determine if it contains any information that is in violation of school policy.	2.4

Note
Scale ranges from 0 to 10. How much of a role law enforcement should play in investigating or responding to the incident with 0 = no law enforcement role/responsibility and 10 = very important/significant law enforcement role/responsibility.

the actual content of such policies. See Appendix B for a list of states that have bullying and cyberbullying laws as of March 1, 2011.

Some states, like Wisconsin, have both a bullying law (which recently passed) and separate statutes regulating telephones and other forms of electronic communication. Specifically, in Wisconsin it is a misdemeanor crime to threaten to "inflict injury or personal harm" through the use of email or another computerized communication system. It is also illegal to harass, annoy, or otherwise offend another person electronically. In most states, electronic bullying is not a crime, but is still prohibited in schools, and requires districts to set up notification, reporting, investigation, training, and assessment procedures. For example, New Hampshire's new law defines bullying as "actions motivated by an imbalance of power based on a pupil's actual or perceived personal characteristics, behaviors, or beliefs, or motivated by the pupil's association with another person and based on the other person's characteristics, behaviors, or beliefs" and states that cyberbullying is the same conduct except utilizing electronic devices. Each state is different with respect to the extent that they specifically address electronic forms of harassment. All law enforcement officers, but especially school-based officers, need to be sure to carefully review and understand the statutes in their own state to understand the formal legal implications of engaging in cyberbullying.

Even if no criminal statute currently exists which explicitly refers to cyberbullying, it does not mean SROs should ignore the behavior. Law enforcement officers should help school administrators understand their legal obligations and authority with respect to when and how they should respond. Current case law clearly allows school officials to discipline students for their behavior, assuming they have a clear policy prohibiting it, even in situations where the student is away from campus, if it can be demonstrated that their behaviors *substantially disrupted* the learning environment at school (or has a significant likelihood of doing so; see Chapter 3 for more information).

Finally, some forms of online harassment may fall under traditional statutes. For example, we have heard about many instances of officers charging students with disorderly conduct in incidents which clearly interrupt the main educational purpose of schools (e.g., making embarrassing videos at school and distributing them online). Law enforcement officers should consult with their local district attorney to determine what existing criminal statutes might apply. Ideally, cyberbullying incidents that do occur should be addressed early so that they do not rise to the level of a substantial disruption or criminal violation. To that end, SROs have a responsibility to use their discretion to develop an appropriate response protocol that seeks to prevent inappropriate behaviors from occurring or escalating to the point where it becomes a crime.

Most youth-serving adults who work on the front lines of the cyberbullying problem know that law enforcement can and should get involved in the rare event that it rises to the level of a criminal offense. As explained earlier, the primary factor in these cases is a threat to the physical safety or personal property of oneself or one's family. Threats are often made by youth involved in interpersonal squabbles and adolescent melodramas, and most have limited potential to escalate into serious real-world violence. Still, some merit deeper inquiry and demand a formal response. Discerning which threats are viable is difficult, to say the least. The matter is complicated when considering Internet-based content, as it is largely devoid of socioemotional cues (such as tone of voice or body language) that can reveal the seriousness of seemingly threatening words. Criminal law may also be implicated when the behavior involves stalking or coercion, can be characterized as a hate or bias crime (against protected populations of race, religion, or sexual orientation), or involves sexually explicit images or the sexual exploitation of youth. In situations where a student is threatening another student or a staff member and an attempt at informal resolution does not immediately end the problem, law enforcement should (and must) get involved. In our post-Columbine era, no threat – regardless of how trivial it might seem – should be taken lightly or rationalized away.

Preventing Cyberbullying

> I think educating kids about these dangers is the first step to stopping this behavior.
>
> *SRO from California*

We tend to think of law enforcement – both at schools and outside of schools – as individuals we contact for help when something bad happens to us. Of course, they are there for that purpose – and generally come through in valuable ways. However, much of what they do is "behind the scenes" and preventive in its goal and intent. These actions can go a long way in reducing the number of incidents that require their formal response, and increasing the general social, emotional, and physical health of those they police. As such, there are a number of strategies school-based law enforcement officers can employ to prevent cyberbullying from getting out of control in the first place.

First, SROs can speak with students about responsible Internet use in classroom discussions and school-wide assemblies. Students need to realize that inappropriate online conduct may result in serious legal consequences offline. In addition, most students (and younger students in particular) still largely respect (and in some cases admire) police officers, and therefore may be more receptive to their guidance and suggestions if their message is presented in a relevant and accessible manner. It bears mentioning that attempting to scare students with severe criminal sanction or the possibility of abduction and assault (sexual or otherwise) by strangers due to online participation is not the best approach. First, most teens are not usually deterred by these messages because they don't think it could happen to them. Second, it generally *does not* happen to them. Despite what the media would have us believe, the chances of any one American child being kidnapped and killed by a stranger is 0.00007% (Skenazy, 2009).

A better strategy would be to provide basic information about what the law says about certain types of behaviors in a way that is non-threatening but informative. Students need to know that threatening someone online could be a violation of the law – even if they didn't intend to carry out the threat. They also need to realize that just about everything done online has a traceable record. It is even more likely that they will be held accountable for their actions and interactions in cyberspace as compared to what they do offline, due to the comparatively permanent nature of digital content and the ease with which it can be investigated or accessed in the future (Hinduja & Patchin, 2008b; Patchin & Hinduja, 2010).

Furthermore, SROs must take the time to discuss cyberbullying in front of students whenever the opportunity presents itself, and proactively engage students in conversations about a variety of negative online experiences and possible solutions. To do this effectively, they need to be someone whom students feel comfortable approaching for help. They should also be able to convey to the student body that they understand the technology, can speak to them on their level, and alleviate any fears they might have of the situation getting worse if they turn to an adult for assistance. Partnering with teachers, tech-education instructors, and media specialists can be a valuable way to ensure students receive regular and consistent messages about online safety and responsibility.

> Some kids say they'd rather be a victim than show weakness, than be seen as a snitch [but] you can't address a problem you don't know about.
> *Officer from New Hampshire*

Stemming from a historically disproportionate focus on online sexual predators, and the current-day glut of attention to sexting and its link to child pornography, law enforcement arguably has lacked balance, comprehensiveness, and rationality in its approach to cyberbullying. Due to this, most students will not feel comfortable going to SROs about any form of online victimization for fear of a draconian (or completely dismissive) response. SROs would do well to discuss this perception with students and attempt to address their concerns and foster an open line of communication with them for any future incidents. They should own up to their position's history of largely failing to be someone that youth are motivated to approach, and they should emphasize that times have changed, and that teens should give them a shot to come through for them, and that they will not make their situation worse.

Real-world cyberbullying scenarios also might be presented to foster dialogue on the topic in relatable ways; many examples are provided for free online (see, e.g., the Cyberbullying Research Center at www.cyberbullying.us). Officers also can consider using a recent media example of a cyberbullying incident that occurred at another school to help explore the issues associated with such behavior. They could inform students about how that type of incident would be handled in their own school, and encourage students to discuss what they can do to prevent similar situations from happening to them. We recommend SROs set up "Google Alerts" (www.google.com/alerts), where news articles that include certain keywords a user specifies (such as "Facebook privacy" or "sexting" or "bullying law" or "digital evidence") are sent to that person's email inbox on a daily basis. Indeed, this is one way we ourselves stay abreast of the latest developments and stories in the areas of technology misuse by youth.

To share helpful information and relatable stories, SROs can organize regular assemblies or presentations that provide information for the school community about safe and responsible Internet use and "netiquette" (Internet or online etiquette). Vivid and true-to-life video clips also can be used (search for "cyberbullying" on YouTube.com) which powerfully portray the real-world harm that online aggression can inflict. Repeatedly piquing the consciences of youth about questionable or deviant behavior seems to make them more sensitive to the issues at hand and more apt to "think twice" before making an unwise decision.

> We have to increase their awareness – if we continue to do that we'll have more kids saying, "This is not okay."
>
> *Safe and Drug Free Schools Coordinator from Florida*

In general, most of the potential hazards that are naturally present when interacting in cyberspace can be minimized with proper guidance and supervision, where SROs clearly explain to youth why it is unwise to mouth-off online, or text inappropriate pictures, or unwittingly render themselves vulnerable to victimization by posting personally identifying or embarrassing information in public online venues. In fact, many teens (and adults!) who interact online who set their social networking profile to "private" may have a false sense of security because they feel the information they include on their profiles is only accessible by those they include in their "friend" network. As a result, they may include more detailed information about themselves than they would if it were completely open to the public. Since youth are more likely to be victimized by friends and acquaintances rather than strangers (Finkelhor, Turner, Ormrod, & Hamby, 2005; Magid & Collier, 2007), and because they may include as friends individuals they do not necessarily know all that well, they may still open themselves to potential harm by what they include on their private profiles.

Additionally, SROs will often have the opportunity to appear in front of parents. Hopefully this occurs in a preventive capacity, and not following a major incident of interpersonal or self-inflicted violence. Whether at an evening community program or during a one-on-one meeting, they must realize that parents are sometimes completely freaked out about the problem of cyberbullying (or technology in general) due to messages from the popular media – and must consequently do their best to bring about a rational and calm perspective. Officers in uniform with a sidearm strapped to their belt tend to be naturally imposing and intimidating, and so the tips and strategies they aim to convey should be covered in a manner to invite interaction in the future, should the parents or their children need help.

Law enforcement officers, and especially SROs or other officers who are specifically assigned to a school setting, can also work to educate and inform school staff about their responsibilities with regard to intervening in incidents of cyberbullying (perhaps with the help of a school district attorney familiar with the legal responsibilities of adults on campus). This can be accomplished by encouraging the district to sponsor or provide workshops, opportunities to earn continuing education units, memorandums, and curriculum enhancements that require and help teachers and administrators to get "up to speed" on these issues. By preempting confusion as to how to respond, and proactively discussing what will be done (and how best to do it) *prior* to the onset of a major cyberbullying incident, SROs will be better able to coordinate efforts with other staff on campus. Consequently, this will enhance their ability to improve the situation and will lead to tighter and more productive working relationships across the school to meet its goals of safety.

As a final suggestion, SROs should work with a team of administrators at the school(s) to which they are assigned to help create comprehensive policies that can constrain student behavior and that can be enforced. First, schools must have a clearly defined and up-to-date policy regarding all portable electronic devices (e.g., smartphones, portable gaming consoles with WiFi connectivity, netbooks, iPads, etc.). Some schools have simply elected to ban all such devices from campus. These actions have led to criticism by some parents, who say they need to be able to contact their kids in the case of an emergency. It can also be very difficult to enforce a complete ban without searching all students as they enter the school each day. A better approach would be to have clearly specified guidelines for when and where the devices will be allowed and what will happen if students are caught using them at a prohibited time or place. We also recommend policies that focus on particular *behavior* rather than particular *technologies*. The problem isn't the cell phone. The problem is when the cell phone is used to cheat, or to take pictures of students or staff without their permission, or when it becomes a distraction to learning in general. Policies should identify and prohibit these and other problematic uses of these devices rather than the devices themselves.

Furthermore, all schools should have policies on the books that explicitly prohibit bullying and cyberbullying incidents, and outline their disciplinary consequences along a continuum. This policy should be disseminated at the beginning of the school year so that parents and students understand what behaviors are within the disciplinary reach of the school. It may also be instructive to highlight particular situations that have resulted in disciplinary actions (examples from within the district or elsewhere). The type of response should be proportionate to the weight of the offense and convey the extent of its gravity and severity (and go no further). The measure of an effective response is that the offender comes away knowing that the behavior is clearly inappropriate and will not be tolerated, and that subsequent refusal to follow the rules will result in future disciplinary action.

> [What is most important is] having a clear policy in the student handbook and consistently following the policy. We have worked on climate change for six years. That is probably the most effective means of ending cyberbullying – education and sound policy. There will be a slow decrease over time. But all efforts must be consistent and constant, starting in the elementary schools and progressing upward. Parent education is included in

this as well. LEOs need to understand that it is a culture change with students and they must be patient. The administration must be willing to consistently enforce the policy and both must make a stand together.

School Resource Officer Lieutenant with 17 years of experience working in schools

Responding to Cyberbullying

Law enforcement officers who are assigned to schools will undoubtedly need to become involved in cyberbullying at some point during their time on the job, but will be most frequently called upon to act *after* incidents occur within the student body. While most instances of cyberbullying do not warrant the formal intervention and response of law enforcement, some cases do (those that are "criminal" are summarized earlier in this chapter). Even if the cyberbullying behavior doesn't immediately appear to rise to the level of a crime, officers should use their discretion to handle the situation in a way that is appropriate for the circumstances. For example, a simple discussion of the legal issues involved in cyberbullying may be enough to deter some first-time bullies from future misbehavior. Officers might also talk to parents about their child's conduct and express to them the seriousness of online harassment. The law enforcement response typically varies based on how the case is discovered, how much harm has occurred, how evidence is collected, who is involved, and how well trained the officer may be.

> With texting, Facebook, blogs, and other avenues for kids to do this stuff, we're fortunate that we have a school resource officer in each school and we work closely with [school officials].... We've had incidents ... that have been brought to the attention of school officials. Many times the [resource officer] can intercede, maybe call a parent and it will put an end to it.
>
> *Officer from Massachusetts*

SROs also need to vigilantly remind adolescents of the importance of documenting all cyberbullying instances so they can be used as evidence to guide disciplinary actions against the bullies. Victims must be encouraged to save all evidence without internalizing or becoming otherwise consumed by the experience. This can be done by printing out logs of instant messages, chats, email, or webpages. Youth must know and be repeatedly reminded to not delete them even if they seem minor – they may be highly useful in building a case against a stubborn bully. Indeed, automatic logging and archiving can be set up through many programs so that every computer-based communication with others is tracked and stored on the device's hard drive or a portable flash drive.

To be sure, teens should also know that they can (and should) control their online experience. They can consider installing filters on their email, instant messaging, and chat programs to block or regulate the content they receive. They do not have to respond to messages from jerks. They do not have to participate in comment threads that are harassing or mean towards them in an attempt to defend their name or reputation. Facebook and other social networking websites also have tools to moderate and delete questionable or objectionable content that is posted or sent. It does take time to read "help files" and "frequently asked questions" documents within the software and sites they use to learn how to apply the proper settings to delete, block, filter, and log certain messages, but this should be strongly encouraged. Officers should convince youth to take advantage of these "in-house" protections to give themselves a more pleasant and productive experience in cyberspace.

> Many times the answer to a minor problem lies within the social network's help files. The Facebook Safety Center covers most common problems and the solution. This is probably an underutilized resource. I use these with students/parents with great success. Of course the more serious problems need more of an effort than the help files, such as parent assistance or the school resource officer.
>
> *Detective from Connecticut*

Screenshots of cyberbullying examples and other offending content can also made. A screenshot, screen dump, or screen capture is an image taken by the computer to record the visible items displayed on the monitor (Casey, 2000). It is like a "photograph" taken of the contents of your screen – and is most often done using the *print screen* (PrtScn) button on one's keyboard, and then the paste function within a word processing program (such as Microsoft Word) or graphics-editing program (like Adobe Photoshop) to "insert" the image into a digital file that can be saved and archived.

Additionally, victims should note specific incidents with as much detail as possible, including who was involved, where and when it happened, how they responded, who witnessed the incident, and what was done to prevent its reoccurrence (perhaps in a log or diary of sorts). This will become powerful evidence if disciplinary action is to be taken against the bully. Moreover, writing the experiences down may help youth reconcile and then expel the experiences from their mind, much like sitting down with a close friend and sharing a difficult time.

Investigating Cyberbullying Incidents

When an SRO is initially informed that a student has been cyberbullied, there are a number of steps to take. First and foremost, he or she should determine if the target is at-risk for self-harm, or harm to, or by, others. If so, immediate intervention with the help of other school and community professionals can occur. If not, move to the next step – which involves assessment of the details of the case. This includes the venue(s) and environments in which the harassment occurred, the device(s) used to perpetrate the harm and also how others might access it, all individuals directly or indirectly involved (including bystanders and second-hand cyberbullies – those who continue or escalate the bullying), and the extent of victimization that has taken place (which, of course, has subjective and objective components). Additionally, investigation into the psychology behind the mistreatment, as well as the social context in which it took place, can greatly help inform the extent of the response. Working with the school psychologist, social worker, or guidance counselor can be very helpful in this regard.

During these first stages, digital evidence should be obtained. This process may be easy if, for example, the victim or the bully or a bystander provides it to the officer. It may be hard, though, if no one is coming forward with content or screenshots on their devices to serve as evidence, nor bringing hardcopy printouts to examine. Interviews with those who witnessed the cyberbullying, or who were a third-party to it, may reveal text, pictures, or video that represent the harm inflicted and point to individuals who were responsible. SROs may also need to work with the relevant Internet service provider, cell phone service provider, or content provider to obtain content, logs, or identifying information (if a criminal law was transgressed), or to get the problematic material removed, deleted, or otherwise taken down (see below for further details on this procedure).

If the incident is non-criminal but compromised the ability of the victim to feel safe and secure at school, or otherwise undermined the sanctity of the learning environment, officers should allow school administrators to formulate a response and assist as necessary. If the incident may implicate criminal law and involves physical threats to one's personal safety or property, coercion or extortion, a hate crime, or the sexual exploitation of a minor, officers must inform the offender and his/her parents, as well as the victim and his/her parents. They can also work with school administrators to assess whether it is appropriate to take the case to the school attorney, who can then consult with the local prosecutor as necessary. Finally, school police must make sure all of these incident details, as well as all investigative efforts, are tracked – we suggest using the Cyberbullying Incident Tracking Form we have created and make available for free at www.cyberbullying.us. It contains form fields that will help law enforcement record all of the information needed to document what happened for record-keeping and formal disciplinary actions.

Digital Evidence

It almost goes without saying that all officers must have a basic level of knowledge regarding how to investigate high-tech deviance, including collecting and preserving digital evidence. SROs who are uncomfortable or lacking in this regard should obtain training and/or partnerships with other officers who do possess these skills. Everything that is done online leaves a "digital footprint" which can be traced back to the account from which the content was posted or sent. When individuals are online, they are assigned an Internet protocol (IP) address by their Internet service provider (e.g., Earthlink, Bellsouth, Qwest, Comcast, their school) or cell phone service provider (e.g., Sprint, AT&T, Verizon,). This IP address is unique and is bound to a person's current online session – whether it is via a computer, a cell phone, or another piece of hardware capable of connectivity. It is continually associated with the data transactions (sending [uploading] and receiving [downloading], interacting, communicating) that are made between one's device and the rest of the World Wide Web, and between one's social networking page, email, instant message, and chat software and the existing population of Internet users. All data transactions are stamped with one's IP address and the exact date and time (to the millisecond) that it occurred, and are kept in log files on computers owned by service providers and content providers (Facebook, Google, Hotmail, Yahoo, etc.).

> Each time the Internet is accessed, an IP [Internet protocol] address is established. [This is an] electronic fingerprint that can be accessed by the authorities to trace all electronic communications between computers and/or mobile phones. No computer or mobile phone – or its user – is really anonymous in cyberspace.
>
> *Dean of Students in a Philadelphia charter school*

When attempting to discover the offender behind the keyboard or textpad, it is vital to know the IP address bound to the malicious message or piece of content. Once that is discovered, the relevant provider can assist school police in identifying the online session in question, which points to the Internet service provider or cell phone service provider through whom the online connection was made, and then to the person connected to that specific account (by way of the billing information), and finally to the family member who was logged in at the time the cyberbullying took place.

There is generally a specific process to follow in order to obtain subscriber records from service providers, and so officers should make sure they know what to do, or at least know where to obtain guidance. Some SROs and the local police departments in which they are assigned do not have the expertise to deal with cases involving digital evidence. As such, it is often a good idea to contact state- or county-level agencies, as they usually do have the personnel and experience to help. These external agencies can assist with digital forensic analyses, individual search warrant creation and execution, and by advising local officers in the investigative process.

Generally speaking, though, SROs should be very comfortable contacting and interacting with Internet service providers, cell phone service providers, and content service providers to deal with cyberbullying incidents. Typically, online harassment or threats violate the Terms of Service Agreements and policies of each company, and allow for the offending material to be taken down (ideally within 24 hours), while also often shutting down the user account tied to the misbehavior.

According to Facebook's Terms of Service – known as their "Statement of Rights and Responsibilities" (www.facebook.com/terms.php) – a number of commitments must be made by individuals who use their site and network resources. Those conditions related to cyberbullying include:

- You will not bully, intimidate, or harass any user.
- You will not post content that: is hateful, threatening, or pornographic; incites violence; or contains nudity or graphic or gratuitous violence.
- You will not use Facebook to do anything unlawful, misleading, malicious, or discriminatory.
- You will not provide any false personal information on Facebook, or create an account for anyone other than yourself without permission.
- You will not create more than one personal profile.
- If we disable your account, you will not create another one without our permission.
- You will not post content or take any action on Facebook that infringes or violates someone else's rights or otherwise violates the law.
- You will not post anyone's identification documents or sensitive financial information on Facebook.

A subpoena is generally required to obtain the identity (i.e., whatever was provided during sign-up, such as an email address, cell phone number, etc.) behind a Facebook profile page. They advise SROs to email them at subpoena@facebook.com to preserve suspicious accounts and to initiate collection of IP logs. Officers must make clear that they want Facebook to hold off on restricting access to the user's account, or deleting it altogether if that will compromise an ongoing investigation.

Facebook also allows for any user (SROs, educators, parents, teens – anyone who is logged onto the site) to "report" problematic content. Any individual can report an inbox message, status update, wall post, note, picture, video, comment, group, event, profile – anything! This granular level of control allows the entire population of Facebook account holders the ability to help keep the site clean and free of inappropriate and objectionable content. They also allow those who report to classify the content into specific categories (e.g., scam, hate speech, violence, sexually explicit content) to help speed the response of site administrators, provide a copy-and-paste functionality of the questionable text into the report, and even specify the exact time at which the abuse occurs in a video. Facebook's new "social reporting" feature allows targets of cyberbullying to report the objectionable content to Facebook and to a trusted friend (such as a parent, teacher, counselor, or SRO). A copy of the problematic information is then sent to whomever the target specifies, which may allow for a quicker response. SROs can help students and families by reminding them to take advantage of this functionality.

Internet service providers and cell phone service providers also have similar protocols in place – usually they can be contacted at "abuse@domain.com" (for example, abuse@comcast.net, abuse@verizon.com, or abuse@sprint.com). Otherwise, phone numbers are easily retrievable by visiting the "Contact Us" section of the company's website. It is critical to remember that these companies receive hundreds of complaints per day. As such, do your best to keep your initial communication short, informative, and courteous. Try to figure out what it will take to induce the administrator who receives your call or email to take immediate action – and then do that.

> Website administrators can track IP addresses which can be used to locate the computer used to post [a cyberbullying] message. Keep log files of their offenses as evidence, report it to someone (parent, teacher, police), nobody will just stand by and allow this to happen and these people can be found and will be dealt with seriously.
>
> *17-year-old boy from Canada*

Investigation Steps

With regard to investigations of cyberbullying incidents, school police can easily access the logs, records, and digital evidence of district email account use and lab computer use. This means they can (with the help of the technology staff) identify and track the behaviors of students as they access any part of the Web from a computer on campus that is using the wired or wireless network of the school, and even laptops owned by the school but distributed to students to take home. This can prove to be helpful, but only to a degree. We know that students will likely use their personal computers, Web-enabled cell phones, and other handheld devices (and their family's or personal Internet or cellular service account) to cyberbully others, and likely much more so than school-owned computers. In these situations, an SRO cannot easily obtain access to the information held on the privately owned devices or from the privately subscribed Internet or cell phone service provider. However, there are informed steps to take that will allow officers to make progress in a cyberbullying investigation, and do so without overstepping their legal authority.

First, it is essential to point out that students have privacy rights that must be acknowledged and protected. To be sure, all Americans do because of the Fourth Amendment of the US Constitution, which states:

> the right of the people to be secure in their persons, houses, papers and

effects, against unreasonable searches and seizures, shall not be violated, and no warrants shall issue, but upon probable cause, supported by oath or affirmation, and particularly describing the place to be searched and the people or things to be seized.

A key word that jumps out when reading the content of the Fourth Amendment is "unreasonable." Searches and seizures – which are a routine part of all law enforcement investigations – cannot be unreasonable in nature. Considering this, though, it also means that searches and seizures by law enforcement can take place *if they are reasonable.* Law enforcement officers can search and seize a student's property if there is *probable cause* that the student has committed a crime (if a search warrant is issued by a judge, or if circumstances are "exigent" and necessitate an immediate search prior to acquisition of a warrant). Again, with criminal law, the search must be based on probable cause *that a crime has occurred.*

However, under education law, a search can be conducted in certain circumstances without probable cause, or even a warrant, by school administrators and possibly also by SROs. According to the US Supreme Court: "The accommodation of ... the substantial need of teachers and administrators for freedom to maintain order in the schools does not require strict adherence to the requirement that searches be based on probable cause" (*New Jersey* v. *T. L. O.*, 1985). In such cases school officials can generally conduct a search of student property, including lockers (*Isiah B.* v. *State*, 1993; *State* v. *Jones*, 2003; *Zamora* v. *Pomeroy*, 1981), backpacks (*DesRoches* v. *Caprio*, 1998; *In re F.B.*, 1999; *In re Murray*, 2000), purses (*New Jersey* v. *T. L. O.,* 1985), clothing (*In re William V.*, 2003; *Thompson* v. *Carthage School District*, 1996), and cars (*Anders ex rel. Anders* v. *Fort Wayne Community Schools*, 2000; *Covington County* v. *G. W.*, 2000; *F.S.E.* v. *State*, 1999) when they have *reasonable suspicion* (*Phaneuf* v. *Cipriano*, 2004) that a violation of school policy will be found.

It is also important to point out that this "reasonable suspicion" standard should not be equated to the "preponderance of the evidence" civil standard we may know. It is often still reasonable even if there is much less than a 50% chance that the suspicion is correct. However, it does have to be based on more than "mere curiosity, rumor, or hunch" (*People* v. *William G.*, 1985). It has also been shown that

> reasonable suspicion is a less demanding standard than probable cause not only in the sense that reasonable suspicion can be established with information that is different in quantity or content than that required to establish probable cause, but also in the sense that reasonable suspicion can arise from information that is less reliable than that required to show probable cause.
>
> Alabama *v.* White, 1990

The standard of reasonable suspicion generally involves a logical belief based on observations, reports, and facts available. It bears mentioning that the *scope* of the search has to be reasonable as well – which means that it cannot overstep certain bounds and "fit" the needs of the administration in investigating an issue. To be sure, a search's "fit" must take into account the characteristics of the person being searched – for example, his/her maturity, age, and gender. Searches must also be *individualized* and not sweeping in nature, and a specific student or group of students must be identified with certain articulable reasons. Finally, the search must be *justified at its onset* – which means that reasonable and individualized suspicion existed to prompt or warrant the search.

If a student has violated a school rule or policy concerning *possession* of a portable device, such as a cell phone for instance (and, of course, the rule or policy has been made known to students and their families through a discipline manual or memorandum), the law is clear in demonstrating that administration or other staff can *seize* the device. When it comes to *search*, however, standards for administrators and sworn law enforcement may differ, based on various legal rulings over the years. While the Supreme Court acknowledges that they did not provide clarity on the differential authority given to school officials versus law enforcement officials in *New Jersey* v. *T. L. O.*, the decisions of lower courts have gone in both directions. Some have ruled that SROs only need reasonable suspicion to perform searches (*Commonwealth* v. *J.B.*, 1998; *In re Angelia D.B.*, 1997; *In re William V.*, 2003; *People* v. *Dilworth*, 1996; *Russell* v. *State*; *S.A.* v. *State*, 1995). Others indicate that SROs, because they are sworn law enforcement officers, must have probable cause rather than mere reasonable suspicion to perform searches (*A. J. M.* v. *State*, 1993; *State* v. *Scott*, 2006).

Overall, it seems that the legal standard varies across different states depending on whether SROs are considered *agents of the school* or *agents of the state*. For example, school administrators and law enforcement officers in South Carolina (where they are considered agents of the school) may conduct reasonable searches of school property (lockers, desks, cars, etc.) and personal property (purses, backpacks, wallets, etc.) with or without probable cause, and do not need a search warrant to do so at school (South Carolina Code of Laws, 2009). In Georgia, a police officer assigned to work at a school is considered law enforcement and not a school official, and therefore requires probable cause for a search and seizure (*Ortiz* v. *State*, No. 10-1200 (Ga. App. Oct. 27, 2010)). Lower courts have also considered a myriad of other factors – such as whether the SRO was acting in conjunction with a school administrator (and not conducting their own independent investigation) and doing so to maintain a safe environment at school (*In re D.D.*, 2001). Other factors include whether the SRO was in uniform, had an office on campus, how the duties of the SRO were delineated in the school handbook, whether the SRO was employed by the school system or an independent law enforcement agency, and how long each day the officer is at school. Generally speaking, though, courts have categorized SROs as agents of the school, and have allowed them to partake in school searches as long as they have "reasonable suspicion" and have not required that they meet the ordinary probable cause standard which all other law enforcement officers must meet.

Ludwig, 2010:6

To be sure, it may also depend on the purpose of the investigation. The question is whether a search, for example, is being conducted for the purposes of a criminal investigation or to determine if there is a violation of school policy. This can be a tricky determination, but ultimately a judge will determine the purpose of the search and whether it was reasonable, given all of the circumstances.

In short, student cell phones can be seized in schools where these devices are prohibited from being possessed, shown, or used. Whether they can be searched depends on whether administrators or SROs reasonably believe that a search will turn up evidence of a violation of school policy or the law. This cannot be a fishing expedition: authorities must have clear articulable evidence upon which to base this additional level of intrusion. According to T. L. O., the search has to be *reasonably related* to the circumstances which justified the intrusive action in the first place.

> Under ordinary circumstances, a search of a student by a teacher or other school official will be justified at its inception when there are reasonable grounds for suspecting that the search will turn up evidence that the student has violated or is violating either the law or the rules of the school. Such a search will be permissible in its scope when the measures adopted are reasonably related to the objectives of the search and not excessively intrusive in light of the age and sex of the student and the nature of the infraction.
>
> New Jersey *v.* T. L. O., 1985

At this point, it is instructive to learn from the cases that have been previously decided, and act in accordance with their finding. In one example, where phones were completely banned from campus in written policy, the seizure and subsequent search of those devices from some students was not challenged (*Miller* v. *Skumanick*, 2009). This may illustrate a need to have a clear policy in place at school which allows for SROs to act similarly. In another case, the search of the number directory and call log in a phone that was seized was completely acceptable (because they are not "communications" under the Federal Stored Communications Act of 1986 (18 U.S.C. § 2701). However, calling other students and impersonating the owner of the seized phone was not acceptable; it exceeded the scope of the investigation and was done as a fishing expedition for further violations (by the defendant and other students) (*Klump* v. *Nazareth Area School District*, 2006).

Court rulings, though, are not consistent due to the nuances and vagaries associated with each individual case and situation. But in a November 2010 ruling (*J. W.* v. *Desoto County School District*, 2010), a Mississippi federal court identified no Fourth Amendment violation when a coach seized and administrators reviewed photos and texts in a cell phone confiscated from a boy who used it in violation of a school-wide ban. Of course, the seizure was unproblematic due to the school policy deeming student cell phones as contraband; the issue at large was the legitimacy of the search of its content. With this in mind, the court stated:

> Upon witnessing a student improperly using a cell phone at school it strikes this court as being reasonable for a school official to seek to determine to what end the student was improperly using that phone. For example, it may well be the case that the student was engaged in some form of cheating, such as by viewing information improperly stored in the cell phone. It is also true that a student using his cell phone at school may reasonably be suspected of communicating with another student who would also be subject to disciplinary action for improper cell phone usage.
> J. W. *v.* Desoto County School District, *2010*

The *J.W.* ruling is at odds with the weight of the evidence regarding the extent to which school officials or SROs can search student devices possessed at school. Searching the student's phone will not yield any additional evidence that he is in violation of the school's policy prohibiting possession of the phone at school. Seeing the phone in school already sufficiently established that point. Any additional search seems unreasonable when applying the standard set in *T.L.O.*

At both ends of the continuum of circumstances, the law is fairly clear. For example, if a reputable student advises a staff member that another student has the answers to the math exam on his mobile device, this would almost certainly allow for a search by an administrator. At the other extreme, conducting a search of a cell phone that was confiscated because it was ringing in a student's backpack would likely not be allowed. Of course, there is quite a bit of gray ground in between to cover. With all of this said, schools would be wise to include a specific statement in their policies that regulate student-owned devices brought to school. The policy should advise everyone that students who bring their own devices to school are subject to a <u>reasonable</u> search if suspicion arises that the device contains evidence of a violation of school policy or the law. Students, staff, parents, and law enforcement officers working in the schools need to be aware of this policy so that no one is surprised if/when certain actions are taken.

SROs must also determine whether they are considered agents of the school or agents of the state. If the latter, then their search and seizure of a student cell phone will be protected only if executed with probable cause that a law violation has occurred. If the former, they are able to seize student cell phones with reasonable suspicion that a law or a school policy has been transgressed, and so they can search that phone as long as the search is intended to determine the extent of the violation, and does not go further than that. It is difficult to wrap parameters around how far is "too far," but it should become clear as more cases involving students and the school search of their personal devices are brought to court. If a student is cyberbullying a male classmate via text messages, it seems logical that only those text messages are viewed. Text messages and photos to/from others (other students or adults) are not privy to the search because they would not contain the evidence being sought. We are currently only able to base our suggestions for future actions by SROs on some clarity provided to us by past actions supported or rejected by the courts (and as noted above, there is disagreement in the courts). This should not be construed as legal advice; we are not attorneys and the laws – as well as the practices that stem from them – are constantly and rapidly shifting.

Conclusion

Law enforcement officers are increasingly finding themselves confronting high-tech wrongdoing committed by adolescents. While their responsibilities are straightforward when there has been a clear violation of the law, most incidents of cyberbullying fall short of this standard. So, how should they respond? As this chapter has pointed out, there are many activities law enforcement officers can engage in to not only respond to cyberbullying when it occurs, but to help prevent cyberbullying from occurring in the first place or escalating out of control. Officers need to educate themselves about what cyberbullying is and fully understand the psychological, emotional, and behavioral consequences associated with experiencing cyberbullying. It goes without saying that all law enforcement officers need to be knowledgeable about how their state and local laws can be marshaled to discipline individuals who engage in extreme forms of cyberbullying (those which involve threats to physical safety or frequent and repeated harassment), but they also need to be aware of informal strategies to address inappropriate online behaviors. Law enforcement officers need to work closely with school administrators and other school staff, as well as parents and others in the community to establish a clear and consistent understanding that all forms of harassment will be potentially subject to discipline.

Acknowledgment

The authors would like to thank Detective Frank Dannahey of the Rocky Hill (Connecticut) Police Department for useful feedback on an earlier draft of this chapter. This research was also partially supported through the Federal Bureau of Investigation's Futurist in Residence program.

References

Alabama v. *White* (496 U.S. 325, 330 (1990)).

Anders ex rel. Anders v. *Fort Wayne Community Schools* (124 F.Supp. 2d 618 (N.D. Ind. 2000)).

Casey, E. (2000). *Digital evidence and computer crime.* San Diego, CA: Academic Press.

Commonwealth v. *J. B.* (719 A.2d 1058 (Pa.Super. 1998)).

Covington County v. *G. W.* (767 So.2d 187 (Miss. 2000)).

DesRoches v. Caprio (156 F.3d 571 (4th Cir. 1998)).

Dinkes, R., Kemp, J., & Baum, K. (2009). *Indicators of school crime and safety* (Vol. NCES 2010-012). Washington, DC.: National Center for Education Statistics, Institute of Education Sciences, US Department of Education, and Bureau of Justice Statistics, Office of Justice Programs, US Department of Justice.

Ericson, N. (2001). Addressing the problem of juvenile bullying. *OJJDP Fact Sheet, 27.* US Department of Justice, Office of Justice Programs, Office of Juvenile Justice and Delinquency Prevention. Washington, DC: US Government Printing Office.

Federal Stored Communications Act (1986). Retrieved March 20, 2011, from www.justice.gov/criminal/cybercrime/ECPA2701_2712.htm.

F. S. E. v. *State* (993 P.2d 771 (Okla. Ct. Crim. App. 1999)).

Finkelhor, D., Turner, H. A., Ormrod, R. K., & Hamby, S. L. (2005). The victimization of children & youth: A comprehensive, national survey. *Child Maltreatment, 10*(1), 5–25.

Fraser, B. J. (1998). Classroom environment instruments: Development, validity, and applications. *Learning Environments Research, 1,* 7–33.

Freiberg, H. J. (Ed.). (1999). *School climate: Measuring, improving, and sustaining healthy learning environments.* London: Falmer Press.

Hinduja, S., & Patchin, J. W. (2007). Offline consequences of online victimization: School violence and delinquency. *Journal of School Violence, 6*(3), 89–112.

Hinduja, S., & Patchin, J. W. (2008a). Cyberbullying: An exploratory analysis of factors related to offending and victimization. *Deviant Behavior, 29*(2), 1–29.

Hinduja, S., & Patchin, J. W. (2008b). Personal information of adolescents on the Internet: A quantitative content analysis of MySpace. *Journal of Adolescence, 31*(1), 125–146.

Hinduja, S., & Patchin, J. W. (2009). *Bullying beyond the schoolyard: Preventing and responding to cyberbullying.* Thousand Oaks, CA: Sage Publications (Corwin Press).

Humphrey, J. A., & Huey, M. P. (2001). *School resource officer effectiveness in New Hampshire: A longitudinal analysis.* Justiceworks, University of New Hampshire. New Hampshire Department of Justice.

In re Angelia D. B. (564 N.W.2d 682 (Wis. 1997)).

In re D.D. (146 N.C. App. 309, 554 S.E.2d 346 (2001)).

In re F. B. (726 A.2d 361 (Pa.1999)).

In re Murray (525 S.E.2d 496 (N.C.Ct.App. 2000)).

In re William V. (4 Cal. Rptr. 3d 695 (Cal. App. 1 Dist. 2003)).

Isiah B. v. *State* (176 Wis. 2d 639, 646, 500 N.W.2d 637, cert. denied, 114 S. Ct. 231 (1993)).

A. J. M. v. *State* (617 So.2d 1137 (Fla. 1st DCA 1993)).

J. W. v. *Desoto County School District* (09-cv-00155-MPM-DAS (N.D. Miss.; Nov. 1, 2010).

Klump v. *Nazareth Area School District* (425 F. Supp. 2d 622 (E.D. Pa. 2006)).

Kowalski, R. M., & Limber, S. P. (2007). Electronic bullying among middle school students. *Journal of Adolescent Health, 41,* S22–S30.

Ludwig, M. K. (2010). School resource officers, the special needs doctrine, and in *loco parentis*: the three main attacks on students' Fourth Amendment rights within the schoolhouse gate. *Child Law and Education Institute Forum*, 1–13. Retrieved from www.luc.edu/law/academics/special/center/child/childed_forum/pdfs/2010_student_papers/Mary_Ludwig.pdf.

Magid, L., & Collier, A. (2007). *MySpace unraveled: A parent's guide to teen social networking*. Berkeley, CA: Peachpit Press.

Miller v. *Skumanick* (605 F.Supp. 2d 634, 643 (M.D.P.A. 2009)).

New Jersey v. *T. L. O.* (469 U.S. 325 (1985)).

Ortiz v. *State*, No. 10-1200 (Ga. App. Oct. 27, 2010).

Palfrey, J. G., boyd, d., & Sacco, D. (2009). *Enhancing child safety and online technologies: Final report of the Internet Safety Technical Task Force*. Durham, NC: Carolina Academic Press.

Patchin, J. W., & Hinduja, S. (2006). Bullies move beyond the schoolyard: A preliminary look at cyberbullying. *Youth Violence and Juvenile Justice, 4*(2), 148–169.

Patchin, J. W., & Hinduja, S. (2010). Trends in online social networking: Adolescent use of MySpace over time. *New Media & Society, 12*(2), 197–216.

Patchin, J. W., & Hinduja, S. (2011). Traditional and nontraditional bullying among youth: A test of general strain theory. *Youth and Society*.

People v. *Dilworth* (661 N.E.2d 310 (Ill. 1996)).

People v. *William G.* (40 Cal.3d 550, 563 (CA. Supreme Court, 1985)).

Phaneuf v. *Cipriano* (330 F.Supp. 2d 74 (Dist. Conn. 2004)).

Russell v. *State* (74 S.W.3d 887 (Tex. Ct. App. 2002)).

S. A. v. *State* (654 N.E.2d 791, 795–96 (Ind. Ct. App. 1995)).

Skenazy, L. (2009). *Free-range kids: Giving our children the freedom we had without going nuts with worry at 16*. San Francisco, CA: Jossey-Bass.

Search of persons and effects on school property. Searches by school administrators or officials with or without probable cause., 59-63-1120 Cong. Rec. (2009).

State v. *Jones* (666 N.W.2d 142 (Iowa 2003)).

State v. *Scott* (279 Ga.App. 52, 55(1), 630 S.E.2d 563 (2006)).

Stover, D. (2005). Climate and culture: Why your board should pay attention to the attitudes of students and staff. *American School Board Journal, 192*(12), 30–33.

Thompson v. *Carthage School District* (87 F.3d 979 (8th Cir. 1996)).

Vossekuil, B., Fein, R. A., Reddy, M., Borum, R., & Modzeleski, W. (2002). *The final report and findings of the Safe School Initiative: Implications for the prevention of school attacks in the United States*. Retrieved August 29, 2003, from www.secretservice.gov/ntac/ssi_final_report.pdf.

Williams, K., & Guerra, N. G. (2007). Prevalence and predictors of Internet bullying. *Journal of Adolescent Health, 41*, S14–S21.

Ybarra, M. L., & Mitchell, J. K. (2004). Online aggressor/targets, aggressors and targets: A comparison of associated youth characteristics. *Journal of Child Psychology and Psychiatry, 45*, 1308–1316.

Zamora v. *Pomeroy* (639 F.2d 662 (10th Cir. 1981)).

APPENDIX A

Select Cyberbullying Curricula, Lesson Plans, and Materials

The following is a summary of available and comprehensive curriculum or lesson plans for helping children with knowledge, skills, and attitudes about cyberbullying and technology safety. Resources where chosen if they included a set of coherent and comprehensive curriculum. Compiled by R. Sabella. For updates visit: www.guardingkids.com

APPENDIX A

Source	Levels	Cost
ADL Curriculum Connections The purpose of this lesson is to encourage safe and kind Internet communication among young children, and to provide students with basic skills for responding productively to online bullying and social aggression. Students use literature, fictional scenarios and creative expression to explore the ways in which Internet communication can amplify hurtful words and to practice responses to hurtful online messages. Students also focus on ways that they can use the Internet to make others feel good and implement online kindness projects in class. www.adl.org/education/curriculum_connections/cyberbullying/cyberbullying_lesson_1.asp?cc_section=lesson_1	2–5	Free
Cyber Bullying Curriculum for Grades 3–5 A prevention curriculum; facilitators manual with CD-ROM. www.hazelden.org/web/go/cyberbullying	3–5	$99
Cyber Bullying Curriculum for Grades 6–12 A prevention curriculum; facilitators manual with CD-ROM. www.hazelden.org/web/go/cyberbullying	6–12	$99
CyberSmart Non-sequential, the free CyberSmart! Student Curriculum is easily integrated, in part or in full, into your current curriculum. Each lesson stands on its own. A consistent lesson model, including free reproducible student activity sheets, makes planning easy for thousands of educators worldwide. http://cybersmartcurriculum.org	K–12	Free
Digital Citizenship and Creative Content program Students interact with music, movies, software, and other digital content every day. Do they understand the rules that dictate the ethical use of these digital files, and do they understand why these issues are relevant? The Digital Citizenship and Creative Content program is a free, turnkey instructional program. The goal is to create an awareness of the rights connected with creative content. Because only through education can students gain an understanding of the relevance of and a personal respect for creative rights and grow to become good digital citizens. www.digitalcitizenshiped.com	8–10	Free

Resource	Grade	Cost
FBI-SOS (Safe Online Surfing) Internet Challenge A free, educational, online program that teaches elementary- and middle-school students how to recognize and react to online dangers. Students take web-based quizzes and review specific websites aimed at promoting online safety. Developed in cooperation with the FBI Crimes Against Children Unit at the Miami FBI Office, the program is administered by the Common Knowledge Scholarship Foundation, part of the Fischler School of Education and Human Services at Nova Southeastern University in Fort Lauderdale, Florida. www.fbi-sos.org	K–8	Free
Internet Smarts from Power to Learn Explore important topics in Internet use at school or at home. These guided, multimedia activities allow you to examine issues affecting schoolwork, class papers, entertainment activities, and online safety. www.powertolearn.com/internet_smarts/index.shtml	4–8	Free
Internet Keep Safe Coalition A broad partnership of governors and/or first spouses, attorneys general, public health and educational professional, law enforcement, and industry leaders working together for the health and safety of youth online. iKeepSafe® use these unique partnerships to disseminate safety resources to families worldwide. www.ikeepsafe.org/iksc_educators	K–12	Free
Media Awareness Network To help educators address this issue in their classrooms, Media Awareness Network has developed a series of lessons, in English and in French, to give students a better understanding of the ethical and legal implications of cyberbullying and to promote positive Internet use. www.media-awareness.ca/english/resources/educational/lessons/cyberbullying.cfm	5–12	Free
Michigan Cyber Safety Initiative The state of Michigan has developed programs to discuss social networking with elementary-school children. www.michigan.gov/ag/0,1607,7-164-17334_17364-170948-,00.html	K–8	Free

continued

Source	Levels	Cost
Netsmartz.org The NetSmartz Workshop is an interactive, educational safety resource that teaches kids and teens how to stay safer on the Internet. NetSmartz combines the newest technologies available and the most current information to create high-impact educational activities that are well-received by even the most tech-savvy kids. Parents, guardians, educators, and law enforcement also have access to additional resources for learning and teaching about the dangers children may face online. NetSmartz was created by the National Center for Missing & Exploited Children® (NCMEC) and Boys & Girls Clubs of America (BGCA). www.netsmartz.org/educators.htm	K–12	Free
Seattle Public Schools Middle School Cyberbullying Curriculum Seattle Public Schools and a grant from Qwest Foundation Mike Donlin, Senior Program Consultant, SPS Curriculum Writers: Linda Bakken, SPS, Chris Gentes, counseling consultant, and Neilia Solberg, writing consultant Prevention webmaster: Susan Hall, Office for Community Learning, SPS www.seattleschools.org/area/prevention/cbms.html	6–8	Free
Understanding Cyber Bullying – Virtual vs. Physical Worlds In this three-hour lesson, students explore the concept of cyberbullying and learn how the attributes associated with online communication may fuel inappropriate or bullying behavior. Connections between other contributing factors to bullying – online and offline – are also reinforced as students develop an understanding of the role played by bystanders and the ways in which our own responses may fuel or stop this kind of behavior. As a class, students will establish a class "code of (N)ethics" for online conduct. www.media-awareness.ca/english/resources/educational/lessons/secondary/cyberbullying/cyberbullying_virtual.cfm	7–8	Free

APPENDIX B

List of States with Bullying and Cyberbullying Laws

Compiled by Justin W. Patchin and Sameer Hinduja. Updated as of March 1, 2011. For subsequent updates or corrections, visit www.cyberbullying.us/laws.

APPENDIX B

	Bullying law	Update or law proposed	Include "cyber-bullying"[1]	Include electronic harassment	Criminal sanction	School sanction	Requires school policy
AL	Yes	No	No	Yes	No	No	Yes
AK	Yes	Proposed	No	No	No	Yes	Yes
AZ	Yes	No	No	No	No	No	Yes
AR	Yes	No	Yes	Yes	No	Yes	Yes
CA	Yes	No	No	Yes	No	Yes	Yes
CO	Yes[2]	No	No	No	Proposed	Yes	Yes
CT	Yes	No	No	No	No	Yes	Yes
DE	Yes	No	No	No	No	Yes	Yes
DC	Yes	No	No	No	No	No	Yes
FL	Yes	No	No	Yes	No	Yes	Yes
GA	Yes	No	No	Yes	No	Yes	Yes
HI	No	Proposed	No	No	Proposed	No	No
ID	Yes	No	No	Yes	Yes	Yes	Yes
IL	Yes	No	No	Yes	No	Yes	Yes
IN	Yes	Proposed	No	Proposed	No	Yes	Yes
IA	Yes	No	No	Yes	No	Yes	Yes
KS	Yes	No	Yes	Yes	No	Yes	Yes
KY	Yes	No	No	Yes	Yes	Yes	Yes
LA	Yes	Proposed	No	No	No	Yes	Yes
ME	Yes	Proposed	No	No	No	Yes	Yes
MD	Yes	No	No	Yes	No	Yes	No
MA	Yes	No	Yes	No	No	Yes	Yes
MI	Proposed	Proposed	Proposed	Proposed	Proposed	Proposed	Proposed
MN	Yes	Proposed	No	Yes	No	Yes	Yes
MS	Yes	No	No	Yes	No	Yes	Yes
MO	Yes	No	No	Yes	Yes	Yes	Yes
MT	No	No	No	No	No	No	No

State							
NE	Yes	No	No	Yes	No	Yes	Yes
NV	Yes	Yes	Yes	Yes	Yes	No	Yes
NH	Yes	Proposed	Proposed	Yes	No	No	Yes
NJ	Yes	No	No	Yes	No	Yes	Yes
NM	Yes	Proposed	No	No	No	Yes	Yes
NY	Yes	No	Proposed	Yes	No	Yes	Yes
NC	Yes	No	No	No	No	Yes	Yes
ND	No	No	No	No	No	Yes	No
OH	Yes	Proposed	Yes	Yes	No	Yes	Yes
OK	Yes	No	No	Yes	No	No	Yes
OR	Yes	No	No	Yes	Yes	Yes	Yes
PA	Yes	No	Yes	Yes	No	Yes	Yes
RI	Yes	No	No	Yes	No	Yes	Yes
SC	Yes	No	No	Yes	No	Yes	Yes
SD	No	No	No	No	No	No	No
TN	Yes	No	Yes	Yes	Yes	Yes	Yes
TX	Yes	Proposed	Proposed	No	No	No	No
UT	Yes	No	No	Yes	No	Yes	Yes
VT	Yes	No	No	No	No	Yes	Yes
VA	Yes	No	No	Yes	No	Yes	Yes
WA	Yes	No	No	Yes	No	Yes	Yes
WV	Yes	No	No	No	No	Yes	Yes
WI	Yes	No	No	No	Yes	Yes	Yes
WY	Yes	No	No	Yes	No	Yes	Yes
State totals	45	11	6	31	7	39	43
DC	Yes	No	No	No	No	No	Yes
Federal	No	Proposed	Proposed	Proposed	Proposed	No	No

Note

1. Indicates laws that actually include the terms "cyberbullying" or "cyber-bullying." This is compared to states that simply refer to electronic harassment or bullying using electronic means. See actual law for more details.

2. Colorado has a "legislative declaration" that is not an official law, but directs school districts to adopt a written discipline code concerning bullying.

BIOGRAPHIES

Editors

Justin W. Patchin, Ph.D., is an Associate Professor of Criminal Justice in the Department of Political Science at the University of Wisconsin-Eau Claire. He is also Co-Director of the Cyberbullying Research Center. He received his Ph.D. in Criminal Justice from Michigan State University. He has presented on various topics relating to juvenile justice, school violence, policy and program evaluation, and adolescent Internet use and misuse at academic conferences and training seminars across the United States. His first book, *The Family Context of Childhood Delinquency*, explores the role of parenting in the prevention and intervention of serious delinquent behaviors of children. Since 2002, his research has focused on adolescent behavior online. His recent book, *Bullying Beyond the Schoolyard: Preventing and Responding to Cyberbullying* (co-authored with Sameer Hinduja), was named Education Book of the Year by ForeWord Reviews. He has appeared on CNN, NPR, in the *New York Times*, and in other respected print media as an expert on cyberbullying and the intersection of teens and technology.

Sameer Hinduja, Ph.D., is an Associate Professor in the School of Criminology and Criminal Justice at Florida Atlantic University. He is also Co-Director of the Cyberbullying Research Center. He works nationally and internationally with the public and private sector to reduce online victimization and its real-world consequences. His research has been featured in hundreds of print and online articles around the world, as well as on radio and television. Dr. Hinduja has written two books, his latest entitled *Bullying Beyond the Schoolyard: Preventing and Responding to Cyberbullying* (co-authored with Justin W. Patchin), and his interdisciplinary research is widely published in a number of peer-reviewed academic journals. He is a member of the Research Advisory Board for Harvard University's Internet Safety Task Force, and has given presentations for a range of audiences, including Fortune 500 companies, federal law enforcement, school districts, and community organizations. He received his Ph.D. in Criminal Justice from Michigan State University (focus area: computer crime). At FAU, he has won both Researcher of the Year and Teacher of the Year, the two highest honors across the university.

Together, Dr. Patchin and Dr. Hinduja have published numerous works and have presented nationally and internationally on the topic of cyberbullying. Their research has involved data from approximately 12,000 youth regarding their experiences with cyberbullying offending and victimization, and their work has been featured in many national and international news programs and outlets. They are currently partnering with school administrators at a number of different school districts to explore the nature of traditional and online victimization among their student bodies. In addition, they have given presentations to thousands of educators, counselors, law enforcement, parents, and youth on how to prevent and address the school-based consequences of cyberbullying. Finally, they have served expert witnesses and consulted with attorneys on cases involving cyberbullying.

Contributors

Patricia Agatston, Ph.D., is co-author of the book, *Cyber Bullying: Bullying in the Digital Age*, with Robin Kowalski, Ph.D. and Susan Limber, Ph.D., recently published by Wiley–Blackwell Publishers. She is also co-author of the *Cyber Bullying Curriculum for Grades 6–12* and the *Cyber Bullying Prevention Curriculum for Grades 3–5*. Dr. Agatston is a nationally certified trainer and Technical Assistance Consultant for the Olweus Bullying Prevention Program. She has been quoted in articles on cyberbullying in the *Washington Post*, *Time Magazine*, and *Good Housekeeping Magazine*, and has appeared on local and national radio and television to discuss cyberbullying and other youth online high-risk behavior. She was a participant in the CDC's Expert Panel on Electronic Media and Youth Violence, and has presented nationally and internationally on cyberbullying. Dr. Agatston is a Licensed Professional Counselor with the Cobb County School District's Prevention/Intervention Center in Marietta, Georgia. A founding board member for SafePath Children's Advocacy Center in Marietta, Georgia, Dr. Agatston received the Coalition for Child Abuse Prevention's VIP Award in 2005.

Anne Collier is founder and Executive Director of the 11-year-old non-profit organization, Net Family News, Inc., editor of NetFamilyNews.org, and co-director of ConnectSafely.org. She has just completed her year's work as co-chairperson of the Washington-based national task force, the Online Safety & Technology Working Group, which sent its 150-page report – "Youth Safety on a Living Internet" – to Congress on June 4, 2010. A writer and journalist who has worked in the news media since 1980, she co-authored with SafeKids.com's Larry Magid *A Parents' Guide to Facebook* (http://fbparents.org) and the first parents' guide to teen social networking, *MySpace Unraveled* (Peachpit Press, 2006). She served on the Harvard Berkman Center's Internet Safety Technical Task Force in 2008 and currently serves on the advisory boards of several national and international non-profit child advocacy organizations. Anne holds B.A. and M.A. degrees from Principia College and the University of Chicago, respectively. She blogs at NetFamilyNews.org and lives and skis with her husband and two teenage sons in the Wasatch Mountains of Utah.

Stan Davis has worked for human rights in many different ways. In the 1960s he worked in the civil rights movement. As a social worker and child and family therapist in the 1970s and 1980s, he worked with abused, traumatized, and grieving children and trained child protective workers. He designed and implemented training for a network of rape crisis centers and collaborated with police to develop effective interventions for domestic abuse. In 1985 he became a school counselor. After working at high-school and middle-school level, he moved to the James H. Bean elementary school in Sidney, Maine, where he continues to work three days a week. Since the mid-1990s he has put his energies toward helping schools prevent bullying. Stan's work has been featured in national newspapers and radio articles, and on a special 20/20 report on bullying with John Stossel. He is the author of the 2004 book, *Schools Where Everyone Belongs: Practical Strategies to Reduce Bullying* (2nd edition, 2007) and the 2007 book, *Empowering Bystanders in Bullying Prevention*. With Dr. Charisse Nixon, Stan is co-leading the Youth Voice Research Project, which has collected information from more than 11,000 young people in the United States about what works and what doesn't work in bullying prevention. His training integrates research, practical experience, specific techniques, storytelling, and audience participation.

Mike Donlin has a degree in English Education and a graduate degree in Linguistics. He has taught at all grade levels, provided teacher in-service training and taught a variety of university-level courses. With Seattle Public Schools from 1980 through 2010, Mike taught for years and was a central administrator, supervising programs throughout the district. As an administrator, he wrote and managed several federal, state, and privately funded grant programs. Mike's administrator position was the only district position split between Learning and Teaching and Operations. In that capacity, Mike managed technology grants, including a Federal TICG grant and EETT programs, and worked in Prevention–Intervention bullying prevention programs, with an emphasis on Internet safety and cyberbullying. Currently a consultant, Mike received the 2008 Spirit of Online Safety Leadership Award, presented by Qwest Communications and NCMEC, is also an alumnus of the FBI Citizens' Academy training, participates on the National Cyber Security Alliance K–12 Working Group and the WA Attorney General's K–12 Internet Safety Task Force.

Elizabeth Kandel Englander, Ph.D., is a Professor of Psychology and the founder and Director of the Massachusetts Aggression Reduction Center at Bridgewater State University, a center that delivers anti-violence and anti-bullying programs, resources, and research for the state of Massachusetts. She is the author of three editions of *Understanding Violence*, has written for the *New York Times* and has published dozens of journal articles. She was the Guest Editor of the 2010 *Special Edition: Cyberbullying* of the *Journal of Social Sciences*. She is a nationally recognized expert in the area of bullying and cyberbullying, childhood causes of violence and aggression, child development, and characteristics of juvenile and adult violent offenders.

Robin Kowalski, Ph.D., is a Professor of Psychology at Clemson University. She obtained her Ph.D. in social psychology from the University of North Carolina at Greensboro. Her research interests focus primarily on aversive interpersonal behaviors, most notably complaining, teasing, and bullying, with a particular focus on cyberbullying. She is the author or co-author of several books, including *Complaining, Teasing, and Other Annoying Behaviors*, *Social Anxiety*, *Aversive Interpersonal Behaviors*, *Behaving Badly*, *The Social Psychology of Emotional and Behavioral Problems*, *Cyber Bullying: Bullying in the Digital Age*, and two curriculum guides related to cyberbullying. Her research on complaining brought her international attention, including an appearance on NBC's *Today Show*. Dr. Kowalski has received several awards, including Clemson University's Award of Distinction, Clemson University's College of Business and Behavioral Science Award for Excellence in Undergraduate Teaching, the Phil Prince Award for Excellence and Innovation in the Classroom, Clemson University's College of Business and Behavioral Science Senior Research Award, Clemson University's Bradbury Award for contributions to the honor's college, and the Clemson Board of Trustees Award for Faculty Excellence.

Susan Limber, Ph.D., is Director of the Center on Youth Participation and Human Rights at the Institute on Family and Neighborhood Life and Professor of Psychology at Clemson University. She is a developmental psychologist who received her masters and doctoral degrees in psychology at the University of Nebraska-Lincoln, where she also received a Masters of Legal Studies. Dr. Limber's research and writing have focused on legal and psychological issues related to youth violence (particularly bullying among children). She directed the first wide-scale implementation and evaluation of the Olweus Bullying Prevention Program in the United States and co-authored *Cyber Bullying: Bullying in the Digital Age* with Dr. Robin Kowalski and Dr. Patricia Agatston.

Charisse Nixon, Ph.D., received her Ph.D. from West Virginia University and is currently an Associate Professor of Psychology at Penn State Erie. Her primary research interest focuses on covert aggression (e.g., relational aggression), including both prevention and intervention efforts. She is the co-author of *Girl Wars: 12 Strategies That Will End Female Bullying* (Fireside, 2003), as well as several scholarly articles. She is currently conducting a large-scale national study with Stan Davis to examine the effectiveness of bullying strategies from the students' perspectives. Their study samples over 13,000 students in grades 5–12 from all over the United States. Dr. Nixon trains educators throughout the United States; her workshops and consultations provide a unique integration of empirical research and practical strategies to help educators create learning environments that optimize student development.

Russell Sabella, Ph.D., is a Professor of Counseling in the College of Education, Florida Gulf Coast University and President of Sabella & Associates. Russ is author of numerous articles published in journals, magazines, and newsletters. He is co-author of two books entitled *Confronting Sexual Harassment: Learning Activities for Teens* (Educational Media, 1995) and *Counseling in the 21st Century: Using Technology to Improve Practice* (American Counseling Association, 2004). He is also author of the popular *SchoolCounselor.com: A Friendly and Practical Guide to the World Wide Web* (2nd edition, Educational Media, 2003), *GuardingKids.com: A Practical Guide to Keeping Kids Out of High-Tech Trouble* (Educational Media Corporation, 2008), and well-known for his Technology Boot Camp for Counselor workshops and technology safety training conducted throughout the country. Dr. Sabella is past president (2003–2004) of the American School Counselor Association.

Jenny Walker, Ph.D., is President of Cyberbullying Consulting Ltd. Her website (www.cyberbullyingnews.com) summarizes rapidly changing cyberbullying and online safety/digital citizenship information to help busy researchers, professionals, and educators stay up-to-date. She holds a Ph.D. in Educational Psychology, an M.A. in Literature from Arizona State University, and a B.A. in Business Administration from Humberside University in the United Kingdom. In the United States she has taught at high-school level, and served at a residential group home for teens experiencing emotional and behavioral challenges. Born in England, she held key positions in business and finance institutions for over 25 years in London, Hong Kong, and the United States, with business dealings in various European countries. Her travels to Europe, Australia, Indonesia, the Philippines, and Mexico have added to her global perspective regarding online safety and digital citizenship. She is currently working with professors at Arizona State University, University of Arizona, and Auburn University on articles regarding cyberbullying and online safety/ digital citizenship. She offers presentations, training seminars, and workshops on the topic of cyberbullying.

Nancy Willard, M.S., J.D., is the Director of the Center for Safe and Responsible Internet Use. She has degrees in special education and law. She taught at risk" children, practiced computer law, and was an educational technology consultant before focusing her professional attention, since 1995, on issues of youth risk online and effective management of student Internet use. Nancy's focus is on applying research insight into youth risk and effective research-based risk prevention approaches to these new concerns. Nancy is author of two books: *Cyberbullying and Cyberthreats: Responding to the Challenge of Online Social Cruelty, Threats, and Distress* (Research Press, 2007) and *Cyber-Safe Kids, Cyber-Savvy Teens, Helping Young People Use the Internet Safely and Responsibly* (Jossey-Bass, 2007). She has just self-published a book entitled *Cyber Secure Schools in a Web 2.0 World*. Her book on teaching Internet safety is under development.

INDEX

Page numbers in *italics* denote tables, those in **bold** denote figures.